ANTIRACIST JOURNALISM

ANDREA WENZEL

ANTIRACIST
JOURNALISM

The Challenge of Creating

Equitable Local News

Columbia University Press / *New York*

Columbia University Press
Publishers Since 1893
New York   Chichester, West Sussex
cup.columbia.edu
Copyright © 2023 Columbia University Press
All rights reserved

Library of Congress Cataloging-in-Publication Data
Names: Wenzel, Andrea, 1977– author.
Title: Antiracist journalism : the challenge of creating equitable
local news / Andrea Wenzel.
Description: New York : Columbia University Press, 2023. |
Includes bibliographical references and index.
Identifiers: LCCN 2023024343 (print) | LCCN 2023024344 (ebook) |
ISBN 9780231209687 (hardback) | ISBN 9780231209694 (trade paperback) |
ISBN 9780231558068 (ebook)
Subjects: LCSH: Journalism—Objectivity. | Press—Pennsylvania—
Philadelphia. | Racism in the press—Pennsylvania—Philadelphia. |
Anti-racism—Pennsylvania—Philadelphia. | American newspapers—
Pennsylvania—Philadelphia. | Local mass media—Pennsylvania—Philadelphia.
Classification: LCC PN4784.O24 W46 2023 (print) | LCC PN4784.O24
(ebook) | DDC 070.4/33—dc23/eng/20230710
LC record available at https://lccn.loc.gov/2023024343
LC ebook record available at https://lccn.loc.gov/2023024344

Cover design: Noah Arlow

For my late colleague Bryan Monroe and
all journalists who identify as Black, Indigenous, and
people of color who have pushed journalism
in the direction of greater equity.

CONTENTS

ACKNOWLEDGMENTS

L ocal journalists and others working to make journalism more equitable are a fierce but overworked group. Asking them to do yet one more thing upon the many, many things they have already been asked to juggle is not something to be taken for granted. I am incredibly grateful for the numerous journalists who spoke with me as part of the research for this book, especially those at *Kensington Voice*, the *Philadelphia Inquirer*, Resolve Philly, and WHYY.

In addition, many of the people I write about in the pages of this book are people I have called and continue to call collaborators and friends. When I began this project, I attempted to steer clear of writing about the work they have been doing in Philadelphia media. While I did not feel beholden to a fiction of "objectivity," it still felt too fraught. But in the end, I decided it would be insincere not to include their stories and the important work many of them are doing—and decided further to try to be as open as possible about how my positionality intersects. I am grateful to all of them, including Sandra Clark, Letrell Crittenden, and Jean Friedman Rudovsky—as well as others in Philly and beyond I cannot name but who were kind enough to share anonymized insights.

ACKNOWLEDGMENTS

Temple University's Klein College of Media and Communication has been incredibly supportive of my work, especially our dean, David Boardman, a strong advocate for local journalism. Our audit of the *Philadelphia Inquirer* would never have been initiated without his leadership. Critically, the audit was only possible thanks to the coleadership of my incredible late colleague Bryan Monroe, a long-time champion of diversity, equity, and inclusion in journalism, to whose legacy I do not have adequate words to do justice. The audit was truly a team effort, drawing on the hard work and insights of colleagues from Temple as well as staffers of the *Inquirer* and the Lenfest Local Lab. In addition, many of my Klein colleagues helped me with research and offered feedback on various sections of this book, especially Jillian Bauer-Reese, David Brown, Brian Creech, Marc Lamont Hill, and Christopher Malo. And I am grateful for the support, generosity, and mentorship of my amazing journalism department colleagues, from whom I am constantly learning on multiple levels.

This book has benefited greatly from feedback and input from its anonymous reviewers as well as feedback and conversations with Sue Robinson, Jacob Nelson, Fiona Morgan, and many of those mentioned above. I am grateful for the thoughtful guidance of my editor, Philip Leventhal, and the Columbia University Press team. Financial support for this research came from institutions including the Lenfest Institute for Journalism, Temple University, and the Tow Center for Digital Journalism.

Finally, I wrote much of this book as a solo-pandemic-parent of a toddler. I have huge gratitude to my community of neighbors, family, and friends (near and far) who have allowed me to emerge with at least a small shred of sanity—and of course to my amazing daughter, Ruby.

ANTIRACIST JOURNALISM

INTRODUCTION

The Case for Reimagining

You talk about us like we're one big glob of people. And like we don't have nuance, we don't have interests beyond crime and voting rights. Like, there are Black people who care about the environment, right?

—BLACK RESIDENT OF WEST PHILADELPHIA NEIGHBORHOOD

I'm raising my children here. We've gone to plenty of events where we've seen people from all different walks of life, all different economic backgrounds, all living in Germantown, all striving for the same goal, but you don't ever see that reported on TV. You see somebody's momma in a bonnet or a rag crying or fighting, or something happened to somebody because they got shot.

—BLACK RESIDENT OF PHILADELPHIA'S GERMANTOWN NEIGHBORHOOD

Normally, I never hear of anything going on around here. Which is nice, you know. There's nothing negative.

—WHITE RESIDENT OF THE PHILADELPHIA SUBURB OF COLLEGEVILLE

Paper plates bearing slices of rapidly cooling pizza jostled for space on a table crowded with Post-It notes, easel paper, and name tags. We were midway through a focus group discussion in Germantown, a majority Black, socioeconomically diverse neighborhood in Philadelphia. It was a community replete with historic buildings, vibrant arts and cultural spaces, and well-known Black-owned businesses—but also a community with a troubled history of redlining and disinvestment and a present abuzz with gentrification concerns.

Turning their attention to a screen on the wall, residents sat together watching images of how their neighborhood was portrayed by local news media. After viewing a video of television coverage of a shooting, they reflected on whom they thought the story was being told for.[1]

> *Participant 1:* The white people in Philly who live in segregated parts.
> *Participant 2:* So, they can sit there and say, "See, told you. Can't live up there."
> *Participant 3:* I agree with everything that they've said so far, but just the way it made me feel is kind of why I don't watch the news.[2]

After watching the same clip, a resident in another group summed up the narrative that they thought it was shaping about their community: "People who are looking and says, 'Oh, I'm not surprised that that happened in Germantown. That kind of thing is always happening with Black folks in Germantown.'"[3]

There's nothing particularly surprising about a finding that mainstream local journalism is perceived as offering less than nuanced coverage of Black and Brown communities. Numerous scholars and activists have documented how news media has stigmatized neighborhoods; neglected or distorted issues of concern to Black, Indigenous, and people of color communities; reproduced racist stereotypes; and affirmed state violence and repression.[4] The *Philadelphia Inquirer*, whose public confrontation with racist coverage I explore in chapters 2 and 3, has chronicled how racism has been intertwined with the history of journalism in Philadelphia from its own beginnings to the rise of crime-centric television "action news."[5] But the experiences of the residents I spoke with underline some points to consider for anyone hoping to make local journalism less racist and more equitable. First, they show that assessing coverage of BIPOC communities requires more than looking at numbers.[6] A quantitative audit of the television package that residents viewed would have shown both Black sources and a Black reporter. While quantitative snapshots of coverage can offer valuable insights, they do not reveal how a story was framed or the narrative with which audiences walk away. They also do not reveal how the meanings that audiences make from coverage are shaped by what is not included in an overall body of coverage, whether positive or banal narratives of Black life or analysis of how the experiences of white suburbs are intertwined with the disinvestment of majority-Black Philadelphia neighborhoods. Similarly, while quantitative snapshots of newsroom personnel can offer important context, they do not reveal an understanding of the news logics and norms either followed or challenged by BIPOC or white reporters and editors.

The reflections of these residents and the gap they identified between how they experience their neighborhoods and how media depicts them also point to another key challenge. Improving the quality of local news requires a critical look at how whiteness operates within and distorts media narratives. As I discuss later, I follow Eduardo Bonilla-Silva's conceptualization of whiteness as "embodied racial power" that gives systemic privileges to those socially regarded as "white" but that often operates through covert discourses that make mechanisms reproducing racial inequity less visible.[7] Local journalism can be complicit in reinforcing these discourses, even if unintentionally. For example, the gap between the complex and heterogeneous ways that residents experienced their neighborhood and the flattened image of their neighborhood reflected by coverage illustrates how local journalism can reinforce what the sociologist and whiteness studies scholar George Lipsitz has called the "white spatial imaginary" that can "racialize space and spatialize race."[8] The structured advantages that benefit white people and impose unjust obstacles on the life chances of Black people are layered onto the largely segregated places people live and learn because of a long history of discriminatory regulations and practices of surveillance.

These sites, Lipsitz argues, "produce and sustain racial meanings" and enact "a public pedagogy about who belongs where."[9] The resulting white spatial imaginary offers race-neutral narratives to explain how it is "natural" that privileged white geographies thrive and to mask how structural racism operates in Black communities—for example, the "why" behind stories about gun violence in neighborhoods such as Germantown.

At the same time, for many, the white spatial imaginary conceals from view the "Black spatial imaginary," which can offer more generative and democratic spaces of resistance—for all BIPOC and white people. As Lipsitz argues, "Black negotiations with the constraints and confinements of racialized space often produce ways of envisioning and enacting more decent, dignified, humane, and egalitarian social relations for everyone."[10] While some Germantown residents may participate actively in the Black spatial imaginary, including via cultural, intellectual, and social spaces within their own neighborhood, the continued pull of the white spatial imaginary means that distorted perceptions of the neighborhood continue to circulate. Stigmatizing the neighborhood has potentially damaging material consequences, and it leaves both BIPOC and white Philadelphians with an incomplete understanding of their city and region.

These residents of course are not alone in grappling with the influence of the white spatial imaginary within media narratives in the United States. As a 2020 Center for Media Engagement study outlined, many Black Americans do not trust journalists to cover their communities with context and nuance. Study participants shared examples of coverage that offered distorted slivers of a news event, like allowing a single act of vandalism to overshadow coverage of largely peaceful protests. Among other recommendations, the study called on journalists to "diversify Blackness" by including a greater range of perspectives and to "report on variations within Black thinking about solutions to problems." While the study did not use the term "white spatial imaginary," participants' observations evoked it. Participants noted the failure of media to include a range of Black voices and how this distorted audiences' understanding of issues and acted as a barrier to possible solidarity. As one participant explained, "Rural, poor people and Black people actually have a lot in common, but the media likes to act like they just have completely separate problems that aren't related."[11]

This sentiment that media was missing opportunities to help audiences develop shared analyses of social issues, combined with a feeling that media contributed to harming Black and Brown communities, has been a familiar refrain in conversations I have had with residents of U.S. communities since 2015. In the Philadelphia region in particular, from 2017 to 2022, my colleagues and I have had many conversations with residents about how they use local journalism and how they imagine a better relationship with local media.[12] Some of these conversations informed my book *Community-Centered Journalism*, which focused on local interventions that used engaged journalism and solutions-journalism practices. But the more conversations I've had, the more I believe efforts to address both the quality and sustainability of local news and information cannot be separated from the problem of dismantling the whiteness of news media in the United States. The issue is not only that BIPOC and other marginalized communities cannot see themselves or trust what they see in local news but also that cishet, able-bodied white residents also have a distorted understanding of their communities based on the news they see. That includes the white suburban resident quoted earlier, who spoke of news as something connected to negative things happening "down in Philadelphia." The fact that her area received almost no news coverage was a sign that all was well in her "peaceful" community.[13] For the resident, the news offered no insights into the systemic links that connected issues in the region; if anything, it reinforced a white spatial imaginary that "seeks to hide social problems rather than solve them."[14] In this way, local news was failing to meet a basic function of helping readers understand the place they live. It was not helping residents understand their own geographic or identity-based communities and the larger region and communities around them—let alone how their community fits within larger communities and systems.

In this book, I offer a critical examination of these residents' local news and information system as news organizations within it grapple with how they have contributed to the persistence of colorblind ideology and a white spatial imaginary that masks racial inequity. Drawing on empirical case studies, I explore the current realities of the system as well as multiple and competing visions for what a local news system might look like if it were representative of and responsive to the intersectional identities of the communities in the areas it covers.[15] I follow attempts to shift the system in this direction and examine the obstacles to making such a system a reality. In doing this, I tie together conversations taking place in industry and activist circles about making journalism more "antiracist" with conversations about making it more connected to communities. I follow two established newsrooms, WHYY public media and the daily legacy newspaper the *Philadelphia Inquirer*, as they undertake diversity, equity, inclusion, and belonging (DEIB) initiatives in their news organizations.[16] The cases illustrate how journalists within these local news organizations are taking steps to challenge racist norms and practices but also how this work is unlikely to be meaningful without *accountability infrastructure* that supports both repairing news organizations and strengthening collaborative ties between these organizations and community stakeholders. I define *accountability infrastructure* as systems, structures, or programs that facilitate a process of holding stakeholders with more power (e.g., news organizations, editors, CEOs) responsible for listening to and addressing the needs and concerns of those with less (e.g., BIPOC journalists and community members). In the context of local journalism this can include everything from setting performance-review goals based on DEIB and engagement aims to establishing community-led boards.

The book then shifts to follow two start-up journalism organizations, Resolve Philly and *Kensington Voice*, and their efforts to develop both collaborative and accountability infrastructure. I'll look at how their initiatives bridge the circulation of information and stories at the community level and metro level and at what the visions they are pursuing reveal about both opportunities and challenges to pushing for greater equity and accountability infrastructure within the region's news and information built environment.[17] Finally, I look at the influence of metaorganizations offering external support for journalism and civic information on local news systems, including DEIB workers and philanthropic supporters attempting to build accountability infrastructure in Philadelphia and beyond, and examine the extent to which this work does or does not challenge norms and practices in the industry that overrepresent white sources, center white audiences and white journalists, and cumulatively reinforce white power structures. I conclude by exploring what the cases in this book suggest for the possibilities of building more equitable local storytelling networks, offering practical recommendations for newsrooms and supporters of local journalism. I argue that meaningful structural transformation in local journalism or civic media (as with many other fields) will require tackling complicated and often uncomfortable work.[18] This includes challenging race-neutral policies, looking beyond quantitative measures of representation, and grappling with difficult questions of power sharing within and between institutions. For local news and information built environments to become more equitable and antiracist, local journalism organizations and their supporters must develop internal and external infrastructure that openly acknowledges racial inequities and incentivizes collaboration and accountability to communities.

"ANTIRACIST" LOCAL JOURNALISM INITIATIVES IN CONTEXT

Journalism has been implicated in racism and harm to BIPOC communities, especially Black and Brown communities, since its earliest days. As the Media 2070 initiative argues, "Anti-Black racism has always been part of our media system's DNA." In their essay, they document how over the years, U.S. news outlets have profited from the slave trade by selling slave ads, provided sympathetic coverage of racist violence, and offered distorted coverage of BIPOC communities.[19] Such critiques sit within a long tradition of critically assessing how majority white news media outlets in the United States cover anti-Black violence, uprisings, and BIPOC communities more broadly.

Historically, many of these critical examinations have focused on the news landscapes of major U.S. metro areas, such as Los Angeles and

Chicago. As early as 1922, the Chicago Commission on Race Relations issued a report exploring the causes of riots and critiquing white newspapers for distorted coverage of Black Chicagoans. This included disproportionately representing Black residents as criminals and failing to seriously cover crimes committed against them (for example, racist bombings to discourage Black families from moving into white neighborhoods). The commission noted that "throughout the country it is pointed out by both whites and Negroes that the policies of newspapers on racial matters have made relations more difficult, at times fostering new antagonism and enmities and even precipitating riots by inflaming the public against Negroes."[20] Decades later in 1965, the McCone Commission, assessing the aftermath of the Watts Rebellion in Southern California, would echo similar themes, including recommendations that continue to resonate: "The press, television, and radio can play their part. Good reporting of constructive efforts in the field of race relations will be a major service to the community. We urge all media to report equally the good and the bad."[21] Of course just three years later the landmark Kerner Commission Report would offer similar recommendations and critiques: "By and large, news organizations have failed to communicate to both their black and white audiences a sense of the problems America faces and the sources of potential solutions. The media report and write from the standpoint of a white man's world."[22]

Following the 2020 Black Lives Matter protests, Media 2020 and numerous others have argued that variations of these critiques remain salient and that transformation of the system will require reconciliation and repair and "media reparations," or what the scholar Meredith Clark calls "reparative journalism."[23] In this book I extend this tradition of critique by connecting it with conversations about the future of local journalism and community engagement. I'll explore what efforts at transformation look like in Philadelphia, a large metro region where BIPOC journalists have been working within a long tradition of mobilizing antiracist activism in journalism. But before I offer more background on Philadelphia as a site of research or on individual media organizations, I outline some of the interdisciplinary race scholarship concepts I will draw on to analyze diversity, equity, inclusion, and belonging (DEIB) initiatives within news organizations.

WHITENESS AND NEWSROOM NORMS

Inequitable coverage in journalism has persisted up to the present through the infusion of structural racism—"a system in which public policies, institutional practices, cultural representations, and other norms work in various, often reinforcing ways to perpetuate racial group inequity"—into the industry's day to day operations.[24] As scholars have documented, it influences who gets to frame and tell stories (mostly white journalists) and whose stories and voices are represented (mostly white people).[25] As Nikki Usher argued in *News for the Rich, White, and Blue*, "Newsrooms are white places of power, which affects the way journalists approach their work and the coverage we ultimately see. . . . White majority newsrooms lose out from being able to cover their cities, states, and regions, and journalists stand to miss important stories that they may not even know to ask about."[26]

Structural racism does not depend on individual journalists consciously holding overtly racist beliefs or prejudices. Rather, structural racism can be infused into practices and norms that produce racist outcomes. Researchers have devoted particular attention to how the journalistic norm of "objectivity" has been interpreted in a way that reinforces structures of patriarchy and whiteness.[27] As already noted, whiteness as "embodied racial power" plays a social role that makes "an oft-hidden claim to the social and cultural 'center.'"[28] This socially constructed "unacknowledged norm" acts as a "system of privilege" and must be analyzed in connection with "material structure and the operation of power."[29] Critical race and whiteness studies scholars have flagged how whiteness is bolstered by media's use of colorblind racism—a versatile ideology that suggests that given our universal humanity, race no longer matters and should play no role in legal, social, or cultural decision making.[30] The rhetoric of colorblindness, which often circulates through "code words," can be used to minimize racism or racist microaggressions and to reinforce a "colorblind public consensus."[31] Scholars such as Michael Omi and Howard Winant have pointed to the "cojoint rise" of colorblind and neoliberal ideologies, noting that these ideologies have worked in combination to co-opt racial justice movements, offering an "antiracism 'lite'" or "an aspirational post-racism."[32] By failing to recognize difference and racial power hierarchies, narratives of colorblind universalism function to obscure structural racism. As such, whiteness can be particularly pernicious in journalism because it is often operationalized through absences—the stories not told, the perspectives not centered.

Journalism scholars have expressed particular concern about the complicity of a distanced interpretation of objectivity in contributing to whiteness and colorblind racism. Objectivity has had multiple interpretations within journalism's history, particularly in the U.S. context. Notably, in *Elements of Journalism*, Kovach and Rosenstiel argued that objectivity was never intended to suggest that journalists could be free of bias but rather that they could deploy objective methods in their craft.[33] However, since the 1910s and 1920s, a dominant interpretation of objectivity in the United States positioned reporters as operating outside of the structures of communities and societies and expected to be capable of presenting all sides of any given story in a neutral way, free from bias.[34] Historians of objectivity have noted how the operationalization of this interpretation of objectivity has been intertwined with anti-Black racism since the times of Ida B. Wells, where it was used to discredit her investigative reporting on lynching.[35] Looking at more contemporary cases, Callison and Young argue that claims to objectivity are premised on centering whiteness as neutral: "Journalism authority has been about a view from somewhere all along, specifically the performance of white masculinity as the default identity."[36] The norm of objectivity, they argued, has been operationalized in majority-white newsrooms in a way that bolsters a social order that privileges whiteness. Likewise, Robinson and Culver trace how journalistic practices associated with objectivity, for example, maintaining distance from communities or only using sources willing to be named, similarly reinforced the overrepresentation of white perspectives.[37] Indeed, recent reckonings over racial justice in U.S. newsrooms have critiqued how objectivity norms have perpetuated whiteness in coverage—such as barring Black journalists from covering

Black Lives Matters protests—thereby marginalizing journalists of color.[38] Attempting to offer alternatives to the dominant interpretation of objectivity, scholars have offered frameworks such as "pragmatic objectivity" or "strong objectivity"—where journalists are called to acknowledge the interpretative nature of their work and their social locations.[39] Likewise, advocates seeking to center racial justice within both academia and industry have offered alternative approaches such as movement journalism, solidarity journalism, or Clark's framework for a reparative journalism that centers Black women as it challenges norms and practices.[40] Robinson's forthcoming work on a journalism that centers an "identity-aware caring practice" likewise offers a potentially promising alternative framework for trust building.[41] However, to date, among journalists working at established mainstream news organizations such as the ones profiled in this book, there has not been a popular consensus on preferred terms or concepts to replace "objectivity."

"ANTIRACISMS" AND JOURNALISM PROJECTS

One term that has been adopted by some within the journalism industry in recent years is "antiracism" and the pursuit of an "antiracist journalism" that opposes racism and racist policies.[42] It is important to note that the concept of "antiracism," while popularized in recent years by Ibram Kendi's 2019 book, has a long and contested history.[43] Scholarship on antiracism has attempted to delineate types of antiracism—including individual/interpersonal and institutional/structural, as well as critical antiracism that prioritizes a focus on power relationships.[44] Some scholars, such as Adolph Reed Jr., have critiqued contemporary discourse on antiracism for being "focused much more on taxonomy than politics," becoming detached from critiques of capitalism, and failing to focus on specific inequalities and specific goals.[45]

Others have suggested a more grounded analysis may be found by situating any understanding of antiracism and contemporary social movements such as Black Lives Matter within an intersectional analysis informed by Black feminism.[46] As the authors of the Combahee River Collective

Statement outlined in 1977, "Major systems of oppression are interlocking"; that is, their understanding of antiracism was intertwined with opposition to sexism, heterosexism, and class oppression. By working against the oppression of Black women, they would in turn ensure the freedom of all: "If Black women were free, it would mean that everyone else would have to be free since our freedom would necessitate the destruction of all the systems of oppression."[47]

How "antiracism" is understood in connection with contemporary efforts to address racism within the field of journalism is highly variable. While this allows a wide range of actors to connect to the term, it also makes it a somewhat slippery concept, particularly when many of the news organizations who state they aspire to antiracism operate within neoliberal capitalist frameworks that others see as presenting inherent barriers to racial equity.[48] This presents the potential for internal tensions within organizations attempting antiracist projects. These projects may seek to challenge the status quo of existing power relationships within news organizations that have investments in the maintenance of such power hierarchies.

Scholars following antiracist journalistic projects have documented some of the challenges and limitations that can arise in such cases. Drew examined journalistic projects that attempted to more critically cover race, including through "audits" tracking the sources and subjects featured in content (not unlike the work undertaken by the news organizations profiled in this book). She found that participation in these projects in itself could raise the consciousness of journalists about how racial power structures operate in their work. However, she also noted where these interventions tended to fall short—particularly when they were not institutionalized and stayed at the level of the individual: "The greatest value for reflexivity as an intervention strategy is when it does not stop with the news consciousness and actions of a few, but, rather, when it begins to challenge the methods of knowledge production and the values undergirding this process."[49]

Other scholars have similarly offered valuable insights into where antiracism efforts within journalism can go awry, such as Mellinger's exploration of the ASNE (American Society of News Editors) Goal 2000 plan, which sought to increase the diversity of newsroom staffing. Mellinger noted the importance of tracing "contradictions between words and deeds, as well as omissions—inactions and silences," focusing on key moments of an institution's racial history.[50] The limitations of ASNE seem to have followed it into its new incarnation as the News Leaders Association. The scholar Meredith Clark attempted to encourage greater participation in its annual diversity survey only to conclude that news executives lacked political will and that the survey could not be a mechanism of transparency unless there were stronger imperatives to encourage participation.[51] The News Leaders Association was taking some steps to incentivize participation, such as making it a requirement for awards, but this experience illustrates the limitations of moral appeals and the need for infrastructure to support DEIB work.

These examples, then, raise critical questions: How can journalists support meaningful institutional shifts in organizations that may be implicated in the power hierarchies antiracist efforts seek to change? How could underlying changes be made and supported by accountability infrastructure in a way that would allow them to push beyond antiracist projects toward more equitable and antiracist institutions and local journalism systems?

STORYTELLING NETWORKS AND PHILADELPHIA'S NEWS AND INFORMATION BUILT ENVIRONMENT

This book explores the messy work of challenging racial inequities not only within news organizations but also within a larger system of metro area news and information. Because of this, I focus on several organizations and initiatives taking place within one region, the metro area of Philadelphia. As I will explore, the Philadelphia region is home to a particularly complex media system and has a history of racial justice and media justice movements, as well as a tradition of place-based research. To undertake this study, I draw on a theory that takes a place-based approach and centers the communicative health of communities rather than focusing narrowly on the health of particular news organizations.

Because I explore the connective tissue and relationships between news organizations and community stakeholders, I adapt a communication infrastructure theory (CIT) framework to conceptualize how the system is linked together and how narratives circulate within it.[52] CIT offers a place-based framework that centers the concept of local "storytelling networks." These networks refer to the discursive micro- and meso-level links between different storytelling actors—including local media but also residents and community organizations (see figure 0.1). When these links are strong, researchers have found that storytelling networks tend to have higher levels of civic engagement and community belonging.[53] But researchers have also found that these networks can be weakened by the circulation of exclusively negative narratives and can be bounded by ethnicity and language.

I first encountered CIT in graduate school at the University of Southern California while working with Dr. Sandra Ball-Rokeach's

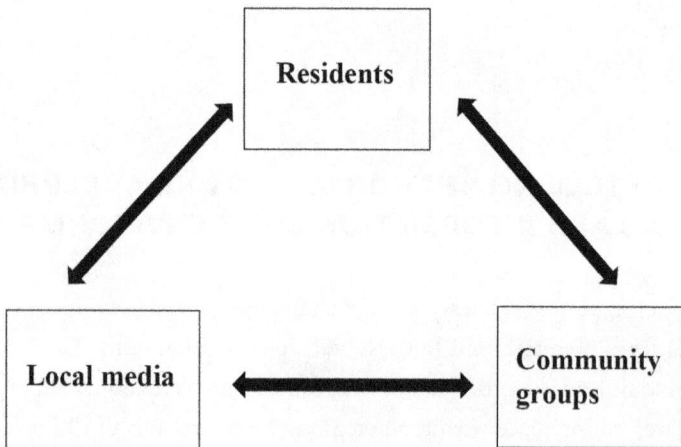

FIGURE 0.1. Communication infrastructure theory's "storytelling network."

Metamorphosis Project research group, which had developed the theory before my arrival. Ball-Rokeach's work on CIT had been inspired in part in response to witnessing the 1994 Los Angeles civil unrest and wanting to understand how communication might contribute to greater social cohesion and community belonging. I was struck by how researchers used CIT as a framework both to diagnose the state of local storytelling networks and to guide interventions seeking to strengthen them.[54] While the theory always grappled with divisions along lines of race and ethnicity, in this book I have tried to more directly infuse CIT with interdisciplinary race studies concepts, particularly focusing on how colorblind ideology can circulate within the storytelling network and by doing so obscure structured advantages bestowed on those socially regarded as "white"— contributing to a white spatial imaginary.[55] Using this framework, I will explore what infrastructure is needed to support more antiracist storytelling networks, ones where narratives skewed by whiteness are challenged and access to networks is more equitable. Drawing on CIT will also allow me to reflect on the overall local news and information built environment and interventions that aim to build connections between metro-level news organizations and hyperlocal info hubs, including Resolve Philly's community newswire service, detailed in chapter 4.

When I talk about the interconnected web of news organizations and resources in the Philadelphia region, I generally refer to them as the "built environment." While a great deal of excellent scholarship and industry studies deploy the more common "ecosystem" metaphor, I generally avoid this unless quoting others. Here I am following Nadler's critique, which argues that "ecosystem" implies that news will flourish naturally through an apolitical "invisible hand" rather than because of actual policies.[56] While the "built environment" metaphor may not be as elegant, it helpfully acknowledges how power operates and suggests the possibility of deliberate change via systems and policy.[57]

As noted, Philadelphia's news and information built environment is a dynamic one. It is home to more than fifty commercial, nonprofit, community, activist, Black-owned, and immigrant-serving news outlets and is the fourth-largest television market in the United States.[58] It is also home to a number of journalism-supporting organizations (such as Resolve Philly), foundations who support local journalism and media (including Independence Public Media Foundation and the Lenfest Institute for Journalism), and multiple universities where journalism is taught and researched.[59] Perhaps unsurprisingly then, it is also relatively well-trodden ground for exploring how local journalism systems function and adapt to change.

Over the past two decades, several foundations have embraced the "ecosystem" terminology and have funded research studies attempting to map and assess Philadelphia's news and media landscape and information needs. In 2010, the William Penn Foundation commissioned a J-Lab study that suggested a "robust media ecosystem" had emerged in the city, noting the city's "community of creative technologists," in particular. The report noted a decline in public affairs news and made the case for the creation of a "networked journalism collaborative."[60] Some of the recommendations around collaboration sit in conversation with the more recent experiences of the Resolve Philly collaborative journalism project discussed in more detail in chapter 4. But reaction to the J-Lab study and who was noted (mainstream and majority white digital first outlets) and not noted in it (community media and BIPOC-owned/serving media) underscored a long-present rift between mainstream majority white media and BIPOC-serving and activist media.[61] Joshua Breitbart, then with the New America Foundation, wrote a scathing critique that feels timely even though more than ten years have elapsed since it was written:

> The challenge of addressing these historic inequities in the media is not a secondary issue in current debates about the future of journalism. It is the fundamental question. Are we content to preserve an institution that, while venerable, has served different communities unevenly and fragmented audiences along economic and ethnic lines? Or do we take the opportunity of current technological, demographic and financial upheavals to realize more fully journalism's democratic potential? Frustratingly, in discussions of journalism, we often hear

claims of inclusiveness while paradoxically seeing a proposal to preserve it as an exclusive domain.[62]

More recent foundation-commissioned studies have more directly acknowledged issues of exclusion. A 2018 Lenfest Institute study used demographically segmented focus groups to explore residents' information needs and in so doing revealed inequities. The study on the whole suggested Philadelphia was more "news jungle" than "news desert," but Black and Latinx/e participants noted a lack of information on issues they felt connected to.[63] The study also recommended diversifying newsrooms and increasing audience engagement as strategies to build trust.[64] Similarly, a 2020 study commissioned by the Democracy Fund, Google News Initiative, and the Knight Foundation concluded that while "Philadelphia's ecosystem is stronger than many," it had "relatively few BIPOC serving media outlets in Philadelphia for the size of its diverse communities."[65] A 2022 academic study supported by Independence Public Media Foundation, whose findings were published in the *Journal of Communication*, analyzed content produced by Philadelphia local media and found that younger and less wealthy residents were less likely to have their critical info needs met.[66] Foundations continue to invest resources in research exploring both information needs and the diversity of media providers. This includes a survey by the Center for Media Engagement supported by the Lenfest Institute that explored how residents felt represented by local news and how they assessed coverage of issues they prioritized.[67]

While attempts to map the overall system of Philadelphia offer valuable context, more granular exploration is needed to understand the relationships and power dynamics among news organizations, let alone how they fit within local storytelling networks that include relationships with community organizations and networks of residents. Fortunately, the Philadelphia metro region has also been the geographic site of a number of valuable scholarly studies, going back to Phyllis Kaniss's 1991 work on the role of metro news media on the formation and maintenance of regional identity.[68] Roughly two decades later, Chris W. Anderson's *Rebuilding the News* followed how local legacy, digital-first, and activist news organizations adapted to the shift to digital journalism—and how they attempted a series of largely failed cross-institutional collaborations.[69] Collaborations between some of these same players have since been followed by other research, including Magda Konieczna's case study of the Re-entry Project, a solutions-journalism collaboration among multiple newsrooms that would later become Resolve Philly.[70] These previous studies raised a number of issues that continue to dog collaboration efforts in local journalism, such as the challenges of navigating power dynamics between smaller and larger (more resourced) news actors, as well as "local journalism's vision of itself" and its "unreflexive commitment to a particular and historically contingent version of this self-image."[71] While Anderson made this latter statement referring to a failure to adapt to new digital realities at the start of the 2010s, much of this language could be transposed onto local journalism's struggle to better serve BIPOC communities at the start of the 2020s.

Like Anderson, I am interested in the interplay between established "mainstream" institutions like the *Inquirer* and WHYY and more community-centered and activist media efforts that have not always been included in studies mapping journalistic outlets in the region. I am interested in how these interactions take place both via formalized collaborations as well as through the informal ways that these actors influence one another. Philadelphia has a history of vibrant (and well-documented) community and activist media initiatives. Anderson demonstrated the significant role that groups like Philadelphia Independent Media Center (PhillyIMC) played in contributing to Philadelphia's news landscape. While PhillyIMC is no longer active, its ethos of radical and grassroots media lives on in organizations such as the Movement Alliance Project (previously known as the Media Mobilizing Project, which originally was a project of PhillyIMC) and Philadelphia Community Access Media (PhillyCAM). Since 2005, the Movement Alliance Project has contributed to the larger communication infrastructure of Philadelphia with a radical "movement media model."[72] The project has worked with community organizations to produce participatory media and strategic campaigns in the service of "building the power of poor and working people."[73]

PhillyCAM was initiated somewhat later in 2009 as a public, educational, or government (PEG) access media organization. PhillyCAM sits within the tradition of citizen journalism where "news content [is] created by ordinary people in a coordinated, professionally-supervised way that addresses local issues not covered by legacy news organizations."[74] Philly-CAM identifies as a "full-service community media organization" with a television channel, low-power FM radio station, youth programs, and community news programs in English and Spanish. In addition to having a member base of some eight hundred people, PhillyCAM also has "staff-led creative projects that amplify the voices of over 100 Philadelphia-based nonprofits and community groups."[75]

In addition to these participatory media initiatives, Philadelphia is home to an array of hyperlocal online sources, community newspapers, Black-owned media, and immigrant-serving media producing content in multiple languages. There is a long history of outlets serving Philadelphia's Black community such as the *Philadelphia Tribune*, *Philadelphia Sunday Sun*, *Scoop USA*, WURD, and others. There are also numerous outlets serving immigrant and diaspora communities including *Al Día*, *El Sol*, Dos Puntos Radio, *FunTimes* magazine, *Metro Chinese Weekly*, *Metro Viet News*, *Korean Phila Times*, and others. Other outlets attempt to serve information needs at the level of neighborhood or region, including established community newspapers and radio stations as well as newer hyperlocal initiatives serving majority-BIPOC communities. These include nonprofits like *Kensington Voice* (the focus of chapter 5) or the Germantown Info Hub (discussed more in chapter 4), which use engaged journalism and solutions journalism strategies (and benefited from being incubated with support from faculty at Temple University's Klein College), and advertising-supported community newspapers such as the *Uptown Standard*. In addition to media outlets that serve communities segmented by geography, ethnicity, or language, there are also outlets serving other identity-based communities, such as the *Philadelphia Gay News*. The journalism community is also served by active chapters of national professional associations (which will be discussed more in chapter 6). The Philadelphia Association of Black Journalists is the oldest professional association of Black journalists; it is the founding chapter of the National Association of Black Journalists. Philadelphia also has chapters of the National Association of Hispanic Journalists, Asian American Journalists Association, and the Association of LGBTQ Journalists.

I list these different news outlets and organizations not to offer a comprehensive overview but to contextualize the case studies that I explore in this book. There are many players in Philadelphia's news and information built environment. News organizations such as the *Philadelphia Inquirer* and WHYY are not islands—they are both competitors and collaborators with many of these various groups and with each other. Likewise, as will be discussed in chapter 4, many of these different outlets are involved in collaborative projects through Resolve Philly. I want to underline the important contributions many of these outlets make, alongside communication resources outside the traditional boundaries of "journalism"—such as those used by the 30 percent of residents who reported either "sometimes" or "often" getting local news direct from local organizations in a 2019 Pew Research Center survey.[76] Efforts to push local news and information built environments toward antiracism must grapple with how the different parts of a system brush up against one another, how finite resources might be distributed in ways that are more equitable, and what synergies may be created in the spaces between these different actors to nudge the system as a whole toward structural change.

While there are limits to any single-sited study, Philadelphia in many ways offers an ideal site to explore efforts to both repair and reimagine local journalism. While the city has the unfortunate distinction of having the most people living in poverty of the ten largest cities in the United States, it is also one of the most well-resourced cities in terms of philanthropic investment in media (at over fifty dollars per capita).[77] This means that although the metropolitan area reflects many of the challenges and realities facing other metro areas in the United States, a lot has been and is being tried to address the challenges facing local journalism—including efforts to push local journalism in the direction of antiracism. For this reason, there are opportunities within this site both to learn from failure and to try to understand what may hold more promise in terms of accountability infrastructure to support transformation within both organizations and systems.

ON BEING PART OF THE PROBLEM
(AND TRYING NOT TO MAKE IT WORSE)

As someone who identifies as a cisgender non-Hispanic white former journalist, there are limitations to my ability to identify and assess how white power and privilege operate within the news organizations and systems that I explore in this book. And while I can listen to and attempt to respectfully represent the perspectives of BIPOC journalists and residents, I cannot speak on their behalf. Indeed, I am asking myself many of the questions I ask of journalists and journalisms more broadly. I have tried to be reflexive about my own positionality and blind spots, but there are inevitably nuances and layers I will miss. Despite these limitations, I do think it is necessary for white people to attempt, albeit imperfectly and often messily, to contribute to efforts to grapple with structural racism and efforts to dismantle it. Given that white people such as I have and continue to benefit from inequitable and racist systems, we must take responsibility for confronting them. At the same time, we must also take our cues from and be accountable to BIPOC colleagues who have been (and continue to be) most harmed by these systems, preferably without creating additional labor for them. I have attempted to avoid unintentionally recentering whiteness in my research and writing, but I have not always gotten it right. I will try to be as transparent as possible in sharing such moments throughout.[78]

I also am not writing this book as an outside observer. In the cases I document in depth, I have been involved as a participant-observer in the process of codesigning audits to assess newsroom content and culture (as in the cases of the *Inquirer* and WHYY)[79] or of co-creating projects that have evolved to become part of the initiatives studied (as in the case of the Germantown Info Hub, a pilot bureau in Resolve's community newswire service) or as a collaborator (when Germantown Info Hub collaborated with *Kensington Voice*). Because I live and work within the Philadelphia news and information built environment, a number of the people I talk with are also people I have called collaborators, colleagues, funders, and friends. I have approached engaged research efforts as a dialogue where I share aggregated findings at various intervals in the process with the organizations I am following. I also take the normative stance that journalism that is more antiracist and connected to diverse communities is a goal that can and should be pursued through both academic scholarship and practice. I also grapple with my own role within academia, which like journalism is a field shaped by structural racism and where I must continually be mindful of my positionality as I attempt to work with students and colleagues to nudge journalism education in the direction of antiracism. As such I am doing this research not from a comfortable distance but rather from an often uncomfortably close proximity from which I hope I too can learn to contribute to this work more effectively.

OVERVIEW

By looking at multiple cases within the Philadelphia region, this book explores some of the many questions that emerge from attempts to transform newsrooms and the larger metro system toward greater equity and antiracism. The pages that follow explore efforts to repair established majority-white outlets and the ways they are and are not shifting norms and power. I also examine how work to challenge the dominance of white power structures in local newsrooms connects with efforts to encourage more community-centered local news systems and new start-ups that have been instrumental to these efforts. I argue that transformative change will require the creation of accountability infrastructures that shift how we talk about advancing diversity and equity in local journalism and the policies and practices that we implement. Meaningful change will require an embrace of uncomfortable conversations around not only culture change but also power sharing.

I have approached each of the qualitative case studies guided by Burawoy's extended case method of ethnography—where the researcher is involved as a participant in activities under study and engaging in dialogue both with key actors and theoretical concepts. I offer more detail on the methods I used in the appendix, but in general my research involved a combination of participant observation, semistructured interviews, and focus-group discussions. The methods used in each chapter vary somewhat because of the nature of the cases (in some cases I participated by working with outlets to design audits; in other cases I was involved as a collaborator on applied projects), and in some instances I have included perspectives from community members as well as from within journalism organizations.

The book begins with three chapters examining cases of two established majority-white newsrooms that function as key news organizations in what communication infrastructure theory calls the local "storytelling network." I explore how these organizations are attempting to create accountability infrastructure to repair their relationships with BIPOC communities in local storytelling networks as well as with BIPOC journalists internally. Chapter 1 explores an attempt by WHYY public media, beginning in 2017, to take stock of its own "cultural competency" and create internal infrastructure to push toward antiracism. Their experience offers insights into obstacles and opportunities for newsrooms that seek to challenge public radio's association with a rarified white elite. I draw on participant observation and interviews from my experience assisting with their setting up of a source diversity audit and then following their efforts, which included a series of trainings and initiatives to strengthen their coverage of and engagement with BIPOC communities. In chapter 1, I focus particularly on WHYY's efforts to introduce DEIB interventions and accountability measures into day-to-day newsroom operations, from implementing a process for reporters to self-track the diversity of their sources to weaving representation and engagement goals into performance reviews.

Chapter 2 shifts to the region's metro daily, the *Philadelphia Inquirer*, and its high-profile public reckoning on racial justice. While the *Inquirer* has a long history of fraught relationships with communities of color, tensions reached a boiling point in June 2020 following its publication of the headline "Buildings Matter, Too" in the wake of Black Lives Matter protests. Here too I draw on participant observation and interviews from my experience coleading a "diversity and inclusion audit" of the *Inquirer*'s content, processes, and practices. I then follow their efforts to push their newsroom and its coverage toward antiracism through a massive newsroom-wide DEIB initiative, sparked by a movement led by BIPOC staff. I examine how whiteness is layered into journalism norms and practices that overrepresent white sources and center white audiences and how journalists either reproduce or seek to transform them. I reflect on both the shortcomings of reactive repair efforts, as well as openings in which journalists have agency to push for the implementation of accountability infrastructure.

In chapter 3, I synthesize what these two news organizations' efforts suggest regarding the challenges of shifting from DEIB "projects" to sustainable antiracism accountability infrastructure. I compare how each organization has approached questions of institutional transformation and their orientation toward other community and information stakeholders. Through this I note the challenge both organizations face in navigating disconnects between their newsrooms' goals and their organizational business and institutional governance models. I also note that while WHYY to date has made a greater investment in community engagement and collaboration, the *Inquirer* has established more internal infrastructure for DEIB work.

The next two chapters follow two community-centered start-up journalism organizations with visions for a more equitable and collaborative news and information built environment in Philadelphia. In chapter 4, I look at an effort to stitch together connective ties between metro-level news organizations and community-centered journalism resources. Using a combination of participant observation and interviews, I follow the initial development of Resolve Philly's Community Newswire Service (CNS) project, "a network of hyperlocal bureaus meeting neighborhood information needs and serving as a mechanism for more authentic and accurate community-level coverage."[80] I also draw on nearly four years of participant observation of the Germantown Info Hub, a neighborhood-level community journalism project I cofounded following an engaged research initiative. The chapter follows the Info Hub as it evolves to become the first pilot hyperlocal bureau site of Resolve's CNS project. The CNS project seeks to work with nontraditional community journalists and "info captains" to tell stories about their own communities and then circulate these through a wire service that Resolve's more than twenty partner news organizations (including the *Philadelphia Inquirer* and WHYY) may draw from. Using a communication infrastructure theory framework, I examine how the CNS network is attempting to create infrastructure that connects local storytelling networks and what this intervention may mean for residents' sense of multicommunity belonging. I also explore how this work is supported by Resolve's institutional culture and what the CNS efforts suggest about the growth of collaborative practices in the Philadelphia region. While the CNS is too new to be able to offer conclusive findings about the circulation of narratives at the metro level, I reflect on both the potential of its work to affect how historically marginalized communities are represented as well as obstacles it may face.

Chapter 5 explores the case of the community journalism project *Kensington Voice*, a hyperlocal initiative that has partnered with Resolve in the past and could act as a partner bureau in the CNS in the future. The chapter follows how *Kensington Voice* has developed and shifted to "direct service journalism" and how their approach offers an alternative vision for how local journalism can sustainably meet a community's needs. I focus on their approach to accountability infrastructure—which unlike any of the other cases in this book centers a community-led board with governance powers. I look at how their work to reimagine what local journalism might look like for one neighborhood offers more radical models for pursuing equity but also reveals challenges of establishing a counterinfrastructure that is largely oppositional to dominant funding practices and editorial norms within journalism. I also explore how their experiences with collaboration as a hyperlocal start-up reveal persistent inequities in how power (and funding) is distributed within the local news and information built environment.

Chapter 6 looks at the larger context that these four journalism organizations are situated in and how they are and are not supported by external metaorganizations, including some with stated commitments to push local journalism systems toward greater equity and antiracism. It examines the role of philanthropy in incentivizing repair or reimagining and how funds get allocated between efforts to repair majority-white newsrooms and efforts to build and grow organizations focused on BIPOC audiences and run by BIPOC managers. I also look at the role played by DEIB workers attempting to build accountability infrastructure in Philadelphia and beyond. I explore attempts to create external accountability bodies locally and nationally—from efforts to hold media like the *Philadelphia Inquirer* to its antiracism commitments to efforts by national actors like City Bureau's Documenters to create alternative community-centered infrastructure and how these may both support and compete with local efforts. I also examine how a lack of infrastructure to hold leadership accountable can interrupt progress on DEIB and engagement work.

The book concludes by synthesizing what the experiences of these different actors and initiatives in the Philadelphia news and information built environment suggest for the possibility of a more equitable and antiracist local storytelling network. I discuss how I attempt to advance communication infrastructure theory by noting how colorblind ideology acts as a barrier to strengthening ties *between* storytelling actors (local media, community organizations, and residents) and *within* storytelling network nodes (in particular, local media outlets). I review how colorblind ideology has affected not only who connects to storytelling networks (making it less likely for BIPOC residents and organizations to do so) but also what narratives circulate within the storytelling network (e.g., narratives that obscure racial inequity and offer a distorted understanding for all). I then discuss the extent to which the interventions I explore are challenging colorblind ideology and how they may affect the local storytelling network. I argue that antiracist interventions that challenge colorblind ideology have the potential to strengthen storytelling networks and contribute to more accurate narratives and equitable journalism. However, for these to be effective, they need to focus on shifting processes and establishing internal and external accountability infrastructure at both the organizational and system level. These cases demonstrate that antiracist transformation in local journalism and communication infrastructure is less about the personal intentions of journalistic actors than about the infrastructure they implement both at the granular level of reporting and editing processes and at the levels of institutional leadership, funding, and systemic collaboration and power sharing. I also analyze the place-based dynamics that have allowed these cases to unfold as they have in the city of Philadelphia and explore what lessons may be learned for journalists and those interested in supporting journalism beyond this region. Although I argue that any intervention must be responsive to place and power dynamics, I offer practical recommendations for journalists, newsroom management, journalism support organizations, funders, and journalism educators. These include recommendations for incentivizing concrete goals around reporting and editing practices, community engagement, collaborative partnerships, and organizational governance reforms (including suggestions for reforming norms around executive leadership and investing community boards with governance powers). I also outline areas that would benefit from additional research and exploration. Ultimately, I hope to offer takeaways that tie together visions for more equitable and antiracist newsrooms with visions for broader local news and information systems that can foster multicommunity understanding and belonging.

1

REPAIRING AND REIMAGINING
A MORE PUBLIC MEDIA

I n a training seminar focused on increasing the diversity of sources, a reporter at WHYY, Philadelphia's public media station, shared a challenge they saw with the goal of including more BIPOC perspectives in their stories.[1] They had just had an overview of an internal "source audit" that found that roughly 80 percent of their sources and 80 percent of newsroom staff were white. This reporter, who was also white, expressed an agreement that increasing the diversity of sources to better represent the roughly 66 percent of the city that did not identify as non-Hispanic white was a valid goal.[2] But implementing this goal across various beats was the tricky part—what to do if, say, they were working on a story about bike riders in Philadelphia? Was it not inevitable that they'd mostly feature young white guys?

Keith Woods, National Public Radio's (NPR) chief diversity officer, who at the time was NPR's vice president of newsroom training and diversity, was leading the training. "Everything is about range, not one story," Woods responded to the reporter. "It adds up to something for the audience." Woods suggested that even if some stories had more white people, they could think of such stories as akin to "trees" and focus on the overall "forest" of their beat's contribution. But the reporter countered, "Which forest?" They noted statistics about which demographic groups were using which forms of transportation in the city. They suggested if they used this as a guide, their stories would inevitably skew white. Woods, who identifies as Black, responded: "My experience of Philadelphia is not the data. It's my world. My world is Blacker than yours might be."

Woods built upon this interchange by highlighting the importance of considering representation beyond goals for parity in reflecting populations. While he acknowledged that certain fields such as politics did tend to have more white and male people in roles of traditional "expertise," there were other ways to approach coverage. Furthermore, he noted, if journalists only aimed for demographic parity, the perspectives of groups such as Native Americans would never be heard.

As I sat observing this training back in 2018, this was one of several moments that illustrated the challenges of operationalizing intentions to represent the diversity of a region, and particularly marginalized BIPOC communities, within daily reporting practices. Between positive intentions and stated objectives lay a moat of routines and norms that reinforced whiteness and colorblind ideology, a moat some seemed to be swimming in like fish who cannot see the water.[3] We were all sitting in that room because key newsroom leaders at WHYY were acutely aware of the need to critically reappraise how the work of reporting and editing had always been done. To move in this direction, they had undertaken a grant-funded "cultural competency" initiative.[4] I had gotten involved when they were seeking input on their "source audit" for this project, and I continued to follow their diversity, equity, inclusion, and belonging (DEIB) and community engagement efforts over the course of the five years that followed. In this chapter I share what I learned from their initial efforts to create a newsroom that more fully represented the city it sought to report on and from how they attempted to implement internal accountability infrastructure that challenged race-blind reporting practices and objectivity norms that bolstered whiteness.[5] As I do this, I'll draw on a communication infrastructure theory framework,[6] noting how colorblind ideology and efforts to counter it were affecting WHYY as a node in the storytelling network and the narratives circulating in it.

PUBLIC RADIO'S WHITENESS PROBLEM

By the time the wave of public reckonings over race in newsrooms began in the summer of 2020, public radio had long been grappling with its association with whiteness and socioeconomic privilege. Public media, which was launched in the United States following the 1967 Public Broadcasting Act, has been the subject of studies on diversity almost since its inception. As early as 1978, the Task Force on Minorities in Public Broadcasting produced a detailed report, "A Formula for Change," which criticized public media for failing both BIPOC audiences and media makers:

> An appropriate analogy as regards minorities in public broadcasting is that they are still being sent to the back of the bus. They are still drinking from the segregated water fountains. They are still nonentities. The findings in this report would suggest that any serious Asian, Latino, Native American, or Black actors, managers, producers, directors, and writers interested in making a career in public broadcasting would be well advised to keep their rent low![7]

The lengthy report levied some seventy recommendations in areas that seem eerily contemporary, including programming, hiring, training, audience research, and funding for BIPOC-led stations and initiatives. Other reports on public media's relationship with diversity followed, as did a number of initiatives and action plans.[8] The NPR network itself eventually undertook DEI/B work through the leadership of Woods and others to address the disproportionate whiteness of its programming and media workers. They offered public disclosures and reflections on the diversity of their staff and their sources even when the numbers were not favorable, such as when they acknowledged some 83 percent of voices on their news magazines were white.[9] Through leaders like Woods, they also offered trainings and consultations with local member stations across the United States.

This is not to say public radio was not touched by public reckonings over race in 2020. Public radio workers, especially BIPOC journalists, spoke out about their experiences within member stations and programs across the system via social media and public-facing letters, as well as in numerous trade press reflections and in demands by NPR union staffers.[10] Many complaints about racist encounters and assumptions made in the journalistic process about a white audience resonate with concerns raised by BIPOC journalists in other mediums. However, the auditory nature of the medium meant that BIPOC journalists also were forced to grapple with the sonic centering of whiteness by the standardizing practices of NPR and public radio more broadly.[11] As the sociologist Laura Garbes documented through a series of interviews with seventy-five nonwhite public radio workers from January through October of 2020, the medium's production process also includes practices of "racialized voice evaluation." Through this, when "voices evaluated for broadcast are coded as nonwhite, their clarity and expertise are more likely to be questioned."[12] Garbes argues that this creates an additional layer of labor for nonwhite journalists who seek to challenge institutional norms around "the sonic color line."[13]

The outpouring of concern around racial inequities in public radio led to the formation of multiple collective initiatives organized by public radio workers across the system. This included Public Media for All, a group that identifies as a "diverse coalition of public media workers, led by people of color," with the objectives of "raising awareness of the negative effects of a lack of diversity, equity and inclusion in public media, and sharing solutions for individuals and organizations."[14] Public Media for All's co-founder, Oregon Public Media's Sachi Kobayashi, mentioned taking inspiration from the "sick out" protest organized by the *Philadelphia Inquirer*'s BIPOC journalists (discussed more in chapter 2). Kobayashi adapted this idea to organize colleagues from across the United States for a "Day of Action."[15] For the day, they offered a range of suggested actions, which included inviting BIPOC workers to call out sick, but Kobayashi explained that most participated in other ways, such as taking the day to do relevant reading or participating in webinars. More than a thousand people attended the public webinar offered by Public Media for All.[16] Following the day, the group continued its work through several areas—offering supportive resources like closed Facebook groups for BIPOC public media workers, offering educational resources open to white public media workers, and offering support and accountability for public media organizations who commit to pursuing DEI action items. Kobayashi noted that over forty public media organizations had joined to date (notably, not WHYY).[17] Their annual report for 2020–2021 noted that they have connected with "over a thousand public media workers."[18]

A few months after Public Media for All began, a letter was circulated by Celeste Headlee on behalf of the Public Radio Antiracist Partnership, a group of more than two hundred current and former public radio station workers who had joined her for a series of Zoom discussions about their experiences.[19] The open letter called for public media to shift toward antiracist journalism and outlined recommendations organized under themes of (1) amends; (2) hiring, promotions, and pay structures; (3) training; (4) transforming coverage; and (5) accountability. For each area, it listed its vision/demands, rationale, and notes on implementation and on accountability. But while the letter circulated widely and had influential signatories from across the U.S. public radio system, Headlee reflected back a year later that despite her call for follow-up and her continued work convening discussions with public media workers, she had been contacted by fewer than ten public radio stations: "The most common reaction has been stasis."[20] There was a challenge, Headlee explained, in that every radio station "is its own little fiefdom." I will return to the work of these national-level public media accountability initiatives in chapter 6, but first I will look more closely at the work some were taking in one such fiefdom, one of the larger public media stations in the United States, Philadelphia's WHYY.

AUDITING "CULTURAL COMPETENCY"

The first time I met Sandra Clark for a one-on-one meeting in 2017, I remember leaving the meeting energized and contemplating whether I would have stayed in public radio had I had a manager like her. Clark was WHYY's vice president for news and civic dialogue. She had joined WHYY's executive team in 2016, after spending two decades at the *Philadelphia*

Inquirer. Clark, who herself identifies as a cisgender Black and Japanese woman, came to the position with a commitment to increasing WHYY's connections to communities of color by addressing who was represented in the newsroom, in coverage, and in outreach to both existing and potential listeners.

As we sat in a café around the corner from the station, some of what Clark described of WHYY sounded familiar. The station was a white space across multiple dimensions. Not only were both the newsroom staff and their sources 80 percent white, but nearly 80 percent of the station's listeners were as well.[21] None of the regular local on-air hosts identified as people of color, and when they conducted an online survey, only 5 percent of participants who identified as African American expressed any awareness of the radio station or its website (more were familiar with WHYY as a public television station).[22] The station management had expressed a desire to change this status quo, and Clark had ambitious goals to increase both the diversity of staff and WHYY's programming.

I had connected with WHYY because of my research on community engagement in local journalism, having recently moved to Philadelphia. I had worked for more than a decade in public radio in Chicago and Washington, DC, and so had some familiarity with the challenges of majority-white newsrooms attempting to cover and engage with diverse regions. I was particularly interested to learn about their newly launched "Creating Culturally Competent Newsrooms" project. With funding from the Lenfest Institute for Journalism, Clark was managing this project along with a team including a coordinating producer/editor of community media and a project manager. Clark defined "cultural competency" as "understanding the nuances of the communities we cover, building relationships that further our knowledge and ability to accurately cover these communities, and recognizing and doing something about our own skewed lenses and how they impact the narratives we present."[23] She suggested this concept informed their practices of news production, their strategies of engaging with the region's many diverse communities, as well as their strategies for recruiting, hiring, and retaining staff from a range of backgrounds in their newsroom. As a result, the project was multifaceted—including the audit of the demographic backgrounds of sources in WHYY's local programming and the follow-up staff trainings on sourcing strategies referenced earlier. It also included trainings for both WHYY editors and journalists from other news outlets in Philadelphia on a broader curriculum on implicit bias. In addition, the project description referred to building "two-way collaboration whereby WHYY and other Philadelphia-based reporters will train community members in storytelling and community partners will train reporters about their communities."[24] To this end, the project supported a series of workshops for external journalists of color interested in developing audio skills and a series of community events aimed at encouraging residents to develop their storytelling skills.

I was intrigued to learn about the project's holistic approach to DEIB and community engagement work. If executed to plan, it represented an intervention in what communication infrastructure theory calls the local storytelling network—it not only would address the narratives WHYY was producing as a local media node in the network but also potentially strengthen ties between storytelling network actors by reaching out to community stakeholders. After initial discussions, I offered some pro bono consultation on their efforts to adapt a plan for auditing the diversity of their sources from the system used by NPR, and I connected them with graduate students to work with them on the coding of sources. From there I followed their work as a participant observer, sitting in on an array of staff meetings, staff DEI/B trainings, and outreach events and workshops that aimed to increase the participation of community storytellers and freelance journalists of color in WHYY programming. I also conducted interviews and focus groups with staff and community members and stayed in conversation with Clark and others about what I was learning throughout their initial grant-funded project and into additional phases of DEI/B and community engagement work.[25] While I return to what I learned from their efforts more in chapter 3, in this chapter I will focus on how different actors at WHYY began tackling a vision for a more "culturally competent" public media newsroom. In the sections that follow, I'll chronicle their efforts to grapple with norms and practices that reinforce a social order privileging whiteness. I'll explore how WHYY responded by developing accountability infrastructure aimed at shifting reporting and editing processes, workplace culture, and community engagement.

SOURCING "DIVERSITY"

To make diversity count, keep a count.

—FROM CULTURAL COMPETENCY TRAINING AT WHYY, MAY 2018

In the training workshop referenced in the previous section, Keith Woods attempted to establish a shared understanding of the baseline WHYY was working with after its source audit of three randomly constructed weeks of local programming. As we adapted the framework used by NPR, WHYY decided the initial audit would note not only race, gender, and geographic location but also the role the source played in the story, with options including doer/subject, explainer/analyst/expert, reactor/opinion/comment, affected, reporter, and host. They also recorded the themes of the stories and the organizational and political affiliation of the person, if known. The audit put some difficult home truths about the whiteness of whose voices were heard in local programming onto paper—or, in this case, a Power-Point slide. WHYY managers correctly sensed that some staff might react defensively to the findings, so Woods focused the discussion on efforts to increase the diversity of sources that had been attempted in other public radio newsrooms where white voices were overrepresented, including at NPR.

Woods explained how various programs at NPR had undertaken "experiments" aimed at adjusting their habits to get more sources of color and women and investing in building contacts when journalists were not under deadline pressure. He shared examples, such as how NPR staffers had sought to build up lists of sources by calling up people they had already talked to and asking them, "Whom do you know and respect on this topic who is also a woman or a person of color?" Some WHYY staffers participating in the training expressed concern that explicitly asking people to refer them to BIPOC sources required them to talk about race in ways that made them uncomfortable. Some raised concerns that people would feel tokenized. Woods responded with suggestions for how to explain that they were contacting people because of their qualifications but also so they could include a fuller representation in their programming. Critically, Woods encouraged staffers to approach their work more reflexively and to question some practices connected with traditional objectivity norms and sourcing that masqueraded as race-neutral. For example, when it came to sourcing choices, he pointed out: "You may think you haven't made a racial or gender decision by talking to a professor, but you have." Echoing Bonilla-Silva's argument that "colorblind" narratives can obscure racism,[26] Woods outlined how what some thought of as race-neutral decisions allowed for white to remain the unquestioned default, such as when reaching out to an overwhelmingly white male academic institution. He stressed the importance of being aware of how journalists set their criteria for what counted as expertise and of how failing to question traditional habits could lead to the overrepresentation of white men.

While the conversation around sourcing strategies was dynamic, I noted that the most contested conversation came when the discussion shifted to how to talk to people about race when it came up during reporting. The group had listened to a series of radio stories that had taken different approaches. Analyzing these stories, Woods pointed to the value of asking questions like "what do you mean" when someone made a potentially racist statement during an interview. He also talked about norms around identifying the race of sources—and the value of saying a source was white when it was relevant to the story. However, some staff members, all white, challenged Woods's interpretation of the approach of the journalists in the sample stories. Signaling their allegiance to objectivity norms, they suggested the reporter in one of the examples would be perceived to be biased against conservatives. One person said, "This is why people don't trust us." While the training module was intended to focus on racism and a lack of representation of BIPOC communities, the discussion of trust raised by staff in the workshop focused entirely on trust among white conservatives. By shifting the focus of the conversation to the political sensitivities of potential conservative white listeners, the WHYY staffers, whether intentionally or not, ensured that whiteness remained centered.

When I asked Wood about the training later, he reflected that the way the conversation went revealed a lot of areas that would benefit from follow-up. He noted an example of a reporter who asked a question about choosing whom to talk to. "'I can go back to the Black guy on the bus, or I can talk to the well-educated.' You know, it's when people don't hear that sort of parsing of humans that happened in that sentence." Woods explained that if he were doing a week-long seminar, as he often did, he would have spent time just talking about that sentence. There was a limit to the ground he could cover and the critical self-reflection he could encourage in a half-day workshop.

Recognizing the need for follow-up, Sandra Clark and the team managing the cultural competency initiative convened all programming staff and assigned everyone to work with the teams of their respective desks or shows to set goals for making their sourcing more representative of the region's communities and to come up with an experiment to meet their goals. Many of the proposed projects used a colorblind framing of seeking "diverse" people and perspectives rather than denoting specific goals in terms of race or ethnicity. Some outlined more granular actions for particular roles, such as for news reporters:

> Each reporter will:
> a) Identify one diverse person or organization on their beat that they have not used before and arrange an in-person conversation. This is to get into the community more and get ideas for future stories or sources.
> b) Identify two regular sources on their beat and find a diverse alternative.[27]

Notably, while these goals had the intention of moving reporters away from habits and practices that disproportionately represented white people, the language they used to state their goals still referenced a colorblind framework ("diverse person") and implied a transactional/extractive relationship (sources were "used"). Other projects stated goals that were even more nebulous and did not reference racial or ethnic diversity at all, such as "develop sources who are women scientists."

Four months later we gathered back in the station's large event space, where all the teams were to present their progress. NPR's Keith Woods returned to offer input and guidance on next steps.[28] While the projects had varied in their specificity, as they stood in front of the room, team leaders did indeed have progress to report and examples of how their intervention was altering some of the narratives they were circulating in the local storytelling network. There was some talk of meeting or not meeting quantitative benchmarks for the diversity of sources, and some teams had struggled more than others. But the most substantive discussions explored how staff had adjusted their journalistic practices. For example, news editors shared how they were attempting to be more mindful of adjusting deadlines when needed to make it more likely to include voices from BIPOC communities. One editor spoke of trying to give reporters the time and space to go to meetings even when they weren't sure they would generate a story. Another editor shared how they had held off running a story until they could get voices from key BIPOC stakeholders, in this case parents in a story about police in schools. The editor also shared how they were thinking about upcoming local election coverage and how they planned to talk to voters of color particularly if the candidates running were not "diverse."

At the same time, the discussion of the challenges that staffers faced attempting to implement their sourcing projects revealed limitations both in terms of who was included in the process of making journalism and whose voices got heard (e.g., white radio hosts doing "two-way" interviews with white reporters) and how logics of colorblind ideology continued to shape the decision making of staffers. For example, one staffer said they had felt awkward asking people how they identified. Referencing a logic of colorblindness and objectivity, they explained, "One of the things I've been taught is it's not what you are, it's who you are." Woods responded to this by suggesting that a request to sources should begin with a clear statement of intent about how WHYY is trying to represent the whole of Philadelphia, what they need to do to do that, and how they'll use that information. He noted how other stations in the system had recently begun taking similar approaches and shared strategies that they had found helpful.

ACCOUNTABILITY INFRASTRUCTURE: SOURCE TRACKING

When WHYY first planned its source audit in 2017, they didn't have a lot of models to reference when it came to the newsroom-led tracking and monitoring of who was represented in their programming. At the time, NPR's approach to conducting periodic studies of source diversity was one of the few prominent examples. But others were emerging, and the project manager for the "Cultural Competency" initiative began asking around, reaching out to other stations that had started to try to follow the demographics of who was included in coverage over time. They spoke to KUT public media in Austin, which shared a system they were using, where reporters entered the demographic data of their sources directly into a Google form and could follow graphs visualizing their source demographics. The project manager adapted this, tailoring it to fit the needs of WHYY's various news and programming units. Under Clark's leadership, they rolled out an ongoing system for reporters and editors to self-track the diversity of their sources. Reporters began verbally asking the people they interviewed to self-identify and then logged the information in a tracking sheet that documented progress by show or desk over time. Participation was mandatory and noted in performance reviews. Clark and her team would organize periodic meetings with each unit to talk through their strengths and weaknesses and identify goals for follow-up and improvement.

In the early days of WHYY's work on source tracking, they were noted nationally as an early adopter of this practice. Clark and her team fielded calls from other news organizations interested in trying similar initiatives, and she was frequently invited to speak publicly at events around the United States about this work. As interest in source diversity tracking grew, so too did the range of models attempted by newsrooms. Systems varied in the type and amount of data they collected, the way they collected it, and how they used it. Key differences included whether reporters were directly involved in asking people how they identified. Some news organizations took steps to develop succinct verbal scripts for reporters, hoping to address the concern that it would take too much time and to aid those who feared the conversation would be prohibitively awkward. But others, like Wisconsin Public Radio, took the gathering of data off the reporter's plate, instead using follow-up surveys asking interviewees to volunteer demographic data.[29] Other approaches were even more removed from the journalists producing stories; for example, the American Press Institute offered "an easy automated tool" that used automation to extract and track source information.[30]

The education reporting organization Chalkbeat worked with the Reynolds Journalism Institute to reach out to journalists around the United States doing source diversity auditing and noted trends, including concerns newsrooms had around the sustainability of reporters manually entering information and security concerns about where that information would be stored.[31] They also noted how some newsrooms were using source auditing to build source databases, as well as how many struggled to determine meaningful benchmarks to aim for with their data (e.g., parity with census demographics or something different?) and to design systems of accountability (Would journalists be accountable for their coverage internally? Would the news organization share their findings publicly?). Their overview of practices revealed a considerable range and raised questions about the limitations of data when it was connected to larger accountability plans. Indeed, as I learned from my conversations with the *Philadelphia Inquirer* about their work on source auditing in chapter 2, determining the best approach raised a number of strategic and logistical considerations that could cumulatively prove to be almost paralyzing for news organizations working to get a system started.

Over time, WHYY's own source tracking process evolved. Staffers shared with me both strengths and weaknesses of the system. On the one hand, involving reporters and editors in the process of determining how sources were identified was an intervention in itself, encouraging them to be reflexive about their choices of whose perspectives to include in a story. At the same time, reliance on reporters and editors also left an opening for inefficiencies, primarily when the project manager had to remind people to catch up on a backlog of data or when staffers made errors in entering the data. Clark and her team worked to incentivize participation by connecting it to internal accountability infrastructure, namely, the performance reviews. But they noted that compliance could be difficult—and not always in the ways they had expected. They noted, for example, that one of their teams that consistently included better-than-average percentages of BIPOC sources was also one that struggled to report their data.

Nevertheless, staffers did note progress as they tracked sources over time. By their third year of tracking, the percentage of local sources who were white had dropped from the original 80 percent to 63 percent. Sources identified as Black jumped from 7 percent in 2018 to 27 percent in 2019.[32] This was still well short of parity with the demographics of Philadelphia, where only 34 percent of the population was non-Hispanic white, but they were considerably closer to parity with their regional coverage area (which includes surrounding suburbs), which they estimate was 67 percent white.

RECRUITING BIPOC JOURNALISTS

Clark and others on her team recognized that tracking people as "sources" alone would not make WHYY or its coverage "culturally competent." Journalists would need to question norms and change their practices in order to fundamentally shift whom they included in their reporting. Beyond this, when it came to the narratives they were contributing to the local storytelling network, there was a question of not only who was represented but *how* they were represented and for whom. For Clark, providing more meaningful representation of the region's BIPOC communities also meant there needed to be more BIPOC journalists telling these stories and more outreach to strengthen relationships with these communities.

Clark acknowledged that the composition of the newsroom and who directed the editorial processes affected how communities of color were represented. When the cultural competency initiative first started, the newsroom overall was 80 percent white, and all the editors who vetted story ideas and managed the pitching process were white. And while Clark identified as Black and Japanese, her supervisors were white. Identifying as BIPOC does not necessarily mean a journalist will challenge interpretations of norms and practices that bolster whiteness, like the idea that objectivity requires reporters to maintain a distance from communities. Nevertheless, when newsroom staff represented a broader range of demographic backgrounds (ideally accounting for a range of variables including race, gender, class, disability, age, etc.), they were more likely to bring a range of lived experiences to their production and assessment of stories. As NPR's Keith Woods pointed out while conducting a cultural competency training, when they tracked sources included in news stories, they repeatedly found that journalists tended to use sources who shared their background. For example, Latinx/e sources were much more likely to be interviewed by a Latinx/e journalist.

Recognizing this, Clark and WHYY sought to change the way they recruited and screened potential hires and take other measures to develop pipelines into the station. Over her career, Clark had witnessed firsthand how even with stated intentions to recruit and hire more diverse candidates, the way the process was implemented could determine whether implicit bias was allowed to creep into the vetting process and derail the chances of BIPOC candidates. Because of this, Clark implemented changes to the recruitment and interviewing process, explicitly asking all candidates questions related to cultural competency. She explained that this not only created a more equitable space for BIPOC candidates; it also helped ensure that the white candidates they were considering had thought about cultural competency and valued it as an essential part of their job. This was combined with a recruitment process that deliberately sought to advertise through channels and networks that had the potential to reach a greater range of candidates, a process that sometimes took longer.

The initial cultural competency project period also included an outreach and training component that aimed "to send a message that our doors are open at WHYY."[33] This included a series of workshops on radio storytelling skills primarily for journalists of color who were freelancers or working for other outlets and were interested in gaining audio skills. While the experiences of participants I spoke with were mixed, for at least two participants, both of whom identified as Black, the workshop did function as a pathway to career opportunities. One participant was able to leverage their experience to find a job that involved audio in another state. Another was able to use the workshop experience "to get in the building": "It just seemed like a good opportunity for me to go in there and continue to show my face and let them know that I'm here and I can do good work and I could be a value to their publication."[34] Their efforts worked, and they were eventually hired by WHYY first as a freelancer and then as staff.

During Sandra Clark's time promoting WHYY as a newsroom committed to cultural competency, the composition of the newsroom staff did change. From 2018 to 2021, WHYY's newsroom went from 80 percent non-Hispanic white to 59 percent non-Hispanic white. This was not to say they had reached parity. While the city of Philadelphia reported roughly 41 percent of the population as Black, only 21 percent of the newsroom identified as Black (up from 7 percent in 2018).[35] Still, Clark's work illustrates that implementing infrastructure to encourage more equitable and antiracist practices around interviewing, outreach, and recruitment can have an impact.

CHALLENGING WHITENESS IN THE NEWSROOM

At the same time, getting people into the building was only a first step, and one that demanded follow-up regarding how the workplace could be one that would encourage BIPOC journalists to stay. The retention of BIPOC journalists has been challenging for many news organizations, and WHYY was no exception.[36] As will be discussed more in chapter 3, there has been considerable turnover at WHYY in recent years, including among BIPOC journalists. Over the time I followed WHYY's work, I spoke with a number of BIPOC journalists who would later leave, some newer staffers who came and left within the five years I was observing, others who were station veterans. These journalists left for a wide range of personal and professional reasons, but some did share with me frustrations and doubts that their work to center more BIPOC stories was not valued at every level of the organization. As one staffer explained, "Sometimes I feel like I'm pushing, I'm trying to sell a product that they do not want." While WHYY had established infrastructure to encourage the station to bring BIPOC journalists in, transforming the organization to become a sustaining workplace environment where people felt their perspectives and stories were valued was a more nebulous challenge.

In the early phases of WHYY's "cultural competency" efforts, nearly all of the staff and freelancers of color I spoke with expressed frustration with the labor of cultural translation required to navigate an editorial structure where whiteness was the default. As one BIPOC journalist explained, "When your entire editorial staff happened to be straight white people . . . trying to explain to them why certain things are important is difficult."[37] Journalists of color at WHYY shared a number of examples of pitching stories and running up against "colorblind" editorial practices that centered whiteness. These included editors failing to initially recognize the value of stories that were critical to Philadelphia's Black community and BIPOC journalists having to take the initiative to pursue such stories outside their official assignments. Others spoke of either being ignored or being pigeonholed into covering "Black stories." One journalist called it "the Black person's burden in public media." Another said she sometimes would talk with her Black colleagues and decide, "Yeah, that's a Black story. I'm going to have to do it, or it will not get done."[38] However, for some, there was also a sense that they had a positive opportunity to represent the Black community fairly: "Most of my stories put me in front of Black folks. So, on behalf of WHYY I think I do a pretty good job of making sure that you know, the Black community out here is properly represented in the press."[39]

In addition, a number of WHYY reporters and editors expressed concerns that they were creating narratives *about* communities of color that were not *for* those communities. As one BIPOC journalist explained, they felt that this resulted in telling communities "stuff they already know." They told me how uncomfortable they felt about a story and event they did that basically focused on well-known deficiencies: "That's what happens when a story is written by someone who is on the outside looking in."[40] While some, including white editors, expressed reflexivity about wanting to do better to serve communities, objectivity norms where the unstated default perspective and audience were assumed to be white and middle or upper class seemed to win out. This potentially skewed the narratives circulating in the storytelling network and made it less likely that residents who were not white and middle or upper class would connect to them. As one staffer explained, there was an "unintentional elitism": "I think that a lot of the news, what they feel is news, is really about politics and is really stories told at a level that . . . is more of interest to someone who isn't a stakeholder in that issue. So, they're talking about gentrification perhaps in an economic way as opposed to talking about what it really means to not be able to pay your taxes."[41]

As a white former public radio journalist myself, I connected with many of these critiques and cringed thinking about some of my own past work telling stories more *about* BIPOC communities than *for* them. In my conversations with white WHYY staffers, I had several moments where I could relate to their genuine concern about issues in a community, but I could also see that the stories they produced would be unlikely to be seen or heard by members of said community and that the framing of the stories seemed to have other audiences in mind. These conversations illustrated how supporting antiracism or cultural competency goals required accountability infrastructure beyond quantitatively tracking the demographics of sources or increasing the number of BIPOC reporters. Meaningful shifts would require changes to the editorial process (some possibilities attempted by the *Philadelphia Inquirer* are discussed in chapter 2). But they would also require rethinking assumptions about a default white audience and deepening relationships with BIPOC communities.

CONNECTING WITH COMMUNITIES

Some of WHYY's most notable work challenging objectivity norms that reinforced colorblind ideology and whiteness came in its initiatives around community engagement. This work took varied forms over the time I observed it, but cumulatively it attempted to strengthen the local storytelling network by building relationships between WHYY as local media and historically marginalized BIPOC communities that had not traditionally been prioritized by public radio marketing.

Efforts to rethink how community members could be involved in sharing their own stories began during WHYY's initial grant-funded "cultural competency" initiative. This ranged from public events featuring community storytellers sharing experiences with issues such as immigration and gun violence to hands-on workshops for residents from historically marginalized neighborhoods to learn storytelling skills. The producer/editor of community media followed up with some participants to see if they would be interested in working with them to share their stories with WHYY. But overall, the emphasis was less on content generation for WHYY than on extending agency to residents to craft their own narratives.

While these community storytelling efforts primarily involved Clark and the producer/editor of community media working with external community members, during this initial project period they also worked to supplement the training they did with newsroom staff on source diversity and implicit bias. In particular, they created opportunities for staffers to interact with and get perspectives on their coverage directly from community members, with the hope that community engagement could contribute to a new approach to ongoing reporting built on more nuanced relationships with communities. Activities included a visit to a majority Black neighborhood, Germantown, where WHYY reporters and editors met with community organization representatives and advocates. This was the same neighborhood where I had been working with other researchers and residents to understand what lay behind their distrust of local news coverage and to collaborate on interventions to serve their hyperlocal information needs (this would grow into the Germantown Info Hub discussed more in chapter 4). When WHYY staffers met this group of community leaders and residents, much of the discussion centered around questions of sourcing and representation. Community members expressed frustration with reporters speaking repeatedly with the same limited number of community representatives and suggested they could do more to build relationships by showing up and earning trust.

Following this discussion, some reporters did return to the neighborhood and attempt to follow up with residents, but the experiences they shared illustrated the challenges of building trust and divergent perspectives on journalistic practices that were standard to many reporters but alienating to some community members. For example, one community member complained to me about his interaction with a reporter who had interviewed him: "Journalists come in with assumptions even after having a conversation about the assumptions."[42] The reporter later expressed frustration that "the story" the resident had originally suggested had turned out to be a dead-end in their assessment. Other reporters and editors had more productive interactions with residents, which led to stories that were broadcast. Some even participated in follow-up discussions with residents.[43]

These early efforts to involve newsroom staff in outreach efforts highlighted a spectrum of attitudes among WHYY journalists toward community engagement. Some staffers shared observations of how some reporters seemed to disengage during trainings or meetings related to community engagement or cultural competency. Others noted a tension between the investment of time and resources need to build relationships with community stakeholders and the productivity pressures of the news cycle. As one staffer suggested, for some reporters, success was measured by page views rather than building sustainable relationships. For some, "engagement" was still associated more with social media management, and face-to-face engagement skills were seen as peripheral to the core work of journalism and at odds with assumed norms of distanced objectivity. At the same time, Clark and some key members of her team were committed to more relational approaches to engagement that sought, at least in some respects, to share power with communities. This commitment would continue to evolve beyond the period of their original "cultural competency" grant as they turned their attention beyond the newsroom to the larger local news and information built environment and the many nontraditional actors influencing it.

A MUTUAL-AID MODEL TO EXPAND LOCAL JOURNALISM

"Big mad, little mad?"

"It makes me real mad."

"I'm gonna say 'or nah.'"

"I'm pissed to the max."

"Oh yeah, it makes me very angry."

Listening to WHYY in my car during an afternoon rush hour, I was surprised one day to hear this series of person-on-the-street reactions layered over ambient sound and beats and followed by the introduction by the host of the series *Mad or Nah?*: "Yep yep to the yep yep. You already know what time it is. It's your girl P.O.C. and I'm back for another edition of *Mad or Nah?*"

Tamara Russell, the program's host, goes by P.O.C., standing for "Proof of Consciousness." On the WHYY website, her series *Mad or Nah?* is described as "an original woman-on-the-street interview series from Revive Radio that asks Philadelphians about issues impacting their everyday life." Segments come out roughly once a month and invite residents to share their views on issues ranging from voting rights to COVID vaccination requirements, using an extended adaptation of the "vox pop" format, where the reporter asks one question of multiple people on the street and then edits them into a montage. But what makes the series stand apart is less its content than its style—and its challenge to "the sonic color line."[44] It strays from the norms of "public radio sound" by integrating sound effects and music and overlaying P.O.C., speaking in a high-energy emcee style, referring back to the "Are you mad or nah?" question with catchphrases like "Keep your radios locked."

In addition to being the founder and host of the online broadcaster Revive Radio, P.O.C., who identifies as a Black Millennial, is also a member of the inaugural cohort of WHYY's News and Information Community Exchange, better known as the NICE project.[45] Following WHYY's initial work on cultural competency and community engagement, Sandra Clark sought to continue to build relationships with communities WHYY historically had not connected with and to use community organizing strategies to do so. She hired a new editor and a community organizer who both had ties to Philadelphia's Black communities and backgrounds that extended beyond the parameters of mainstream journalism. With a new foundation-funded grant,[46] in January 2021 they launched NICE, a "mutual aid journalism collaborative" with the goal of organizing, supporting, and developing "grassroots news and information content creators who serve their communities and who, in turn, share content, sources, wisdom, and audiences with WHYY and each other."[47] In addition to P.O.C., the first NICE cohort included a mix of community and ethnic media journalists, podcasters, bloggers, and social media influencers, most of whom had a mission of serving BIPOC communities. Many were themselves members of BIPOC communities. Partners received a stipend and participated in regular meetings that included skills training as well as discussions about potential collaborations with one another and WHYY, though only a few partners, like P.O.C., produced content regularly broadcast on WHYY.

WHYY staff organizing NICE framed the project as mutual aid but emphasized a nonpolitical interpretation of "people working cooperatively to meet the needs of everyone in the community." WHYY's understanding diverges from more radical traditions that combine service provision with efforts to change political conditions and disrupt harmful systems by connecting people with shared needs or concerns and working to build shared analysis of problems and shared practices.[48] WHYY staff did not want their interpretation of mutual aid to be labeled as political, but their reading of the concept did align with a call by City Bureau's Darryl

Holliday to apply mutual aid to journalism: "Mutual aid efforts suggest a way forward, a new type of newsroom that serves as the nerve center for local information hubs by reflecting and connecting the people it serves, prioritizing lived experience, and disavowing the notion of objective gatekeeping."[49] Among other things, Holliday's vision included newsrooms that redistributed journalism skills and collaborated with "nontraditional news sources to reduce a scarcity of resources exacerbated by competition." This idea of collaboration lifting all boats and nurturing a larger local news environment was frequently referenced by NICE staff.

The way staff working with the NICE project attempted to walk a line of being apolitical while simultaneously expressing a desire to embrace practices that challenged dominant norms of distanced objectivity points to a larger tension of doing work that challenges legacy structures from within them. Staff members did have an analysis of the problem NICE sought to address, as they explained to me: "We know, traditionally, mainstream news organizations have been predominantly white-male-led organizations. This has left a lot of our community out of the conversation." NICE aimed to intervene into this local journalism conversation by supporting its network of partners who were already working as grassroots media organizations or as individual influencers to serve the information and representation needs of their communities. It also sought to challenge assumptions about who gets to participate in conversations taking place in WHYY's own programming by inviting partners to contribute in various ways. Through this, NICE offered the possibility of injecting more BIPOC-centered narratives into local storytelling networks, both by supporting partners as local media actors with their own network ties and by occasionally amplifying the partners' work through WHYY's network.

BUILDING TRUST IN A GRASSROOTS NETWORK

One of the strengths and challenges of the cohort the NICE project brought together was its considerable breadth. They not only worked in a range of mediums (print, digital, podcasts) and languages (English, Mandarin, Spanish, Vietnamese); they also had different needs in terms of financial and editorial skills, content, and access. Some, for example, were skilled in securing local advertising but needed more local content. Others had content but wanted to reach larger audiences. Partners also had a range of resource needs. WHYY staff arranged regular professional development trainings on things like grant writing or measuring impact. But they acknowledged that the range of the cohort meant they had to take an "almost à la carte approach," working to respond to needs that arose from individual partners—everything from video production skills to helping partners get press passes.

WHYY staff explained they were attempting to collaboratively build the project from the ground up in order to get away from "this hierarchical structure where these legacy organizations, news organizations, tell community members or tell these content creators what to do." They acknowledged that their intentionality about power dynamics could sometimes slow down the process as they sought to avoid "bigfooting" grassroots content creators and to move "at the speed of trust": "We didn't ask for anything from them upfront other than their participation and their time. And we started with a needs assessment—asking them what they need rather than telling them what we need." WHYY staff observed that partners had responded to their approach to trust building in varying ways: "There are some who have jumped in with both feet, and they're running full steam ahead. And there are others that are slowly coming to trust WHYY and that it truly will be mutual aid."

Conversations with NICE partners reflected some lingering skepticism about WHYY's motives and goals. Some shared concerns that they did not want to be used for virtue signaling or as an "extra arm for promotion in the hood." Others felt hesitant when WHYY requested they share information on community members they had cultivated relationships with so that they could potentially be used as sources for WHYY. NICE organizers suggested that many partners had been happy to help such community members get "a bigger spotlight or a bigger platform," and they said WHYY occasionally shared sources with partners as well. But they acknowledged that they looked at developing sources through NICE as a possible metric to measure their success: "How many of these sources that we've learned about have actually been used to enhance our [WHYY's] journalism?"

OBJECTIVITY AND REDEFINING "REAL JOURNALISM"

Another area where expectations sometimes diverged or lacked clarity was around on-air opportunities at WHYY. NICE organizers emphasized that the project sought to help partners strengthen their respective outlets, not to broadcast their content on WHYY. Nevertheless, early in the project, many partners expressed an expectation that participating in NICE would lead to opportunities for their work to be broadcast on WHYY television, radio, or online. Some were clear about what success would look like: "Can I really have a TV series on WHYY, or are you just shitting me?" Expectations were raised by the fact that some partners did produce content for WHYY. Two of these had started as freelancers before or simultaneous to the launch of the NICE project, three others became contributors after the start of the NICE project, and others were featured as participants in panel discussions.

WHYY staff explained how it sometimes took months of mentorship and feedback to help partners produce content. Most partners did not have a professional journalism background, and WHYY staff often worked with them to revise pitches, encouraging them to stay true to their own voices and not construct on-air persona they "thought we wanted to hear." One partner shared their surprise: "Wow, they really want my organic stuff." While WHYY staff were clear that producing content for WHYY was not a primary aim of the project, they did speak of those contributions as a measure of success: "Being able to bring somebody into the space and integrating their knowledge and assets into our workflow and programming is really a way of measuring community involvement and participation."

Tracking how content produced by NICE partners was being received by WHYY audiences and the extent of its potential to connect with communities more broadly was complicated. WHYY's internal metrics suggested some of the projects that grew out of their community engagement work actually had a low "return on investment," given that other stories that took less time generated bigger audiences. One staffer shared the example of a NICE-partner-produced bilingual English-Spanish series *The 47: Historias Along a Bus Route.* These were highly produced stories that wove together sound, voices of community members, and the narration of a host who was a native Spanish-language speaker. The staffer suggested that while these stories were excellent journalism, limited audience metrics meant they were a "loss leader" for WHYY: "It helps us build our bona fides, it helps us cultivate sources, and it helps us put a stake in these communities so that then over the coming months, if we persist with that, then we're going to start to actually begin to cultivate real audience there and begin to generate some actual traction."

I shared an example from *The 47* with some community focus groups. Participants were largely appreciative after listening to one of the stories about a youth soccer program. As one participant said, "I can't hear this story anywhere else that I go for community news, and I can rely on WHYY to tell these stories." At the same time, concerns were raised that the story "may not play well for [an NPR] audience":

> *Participant 1:* I think that was a nice story. I think that it could use a little editing. . . . Just it was a bit long. I don't know if we needed all the dialogue of the man, to hear that in Spanish. I think it just could've been edited down a bit, maybe not quite so verbose.
>
> *Participant 2:* I kind of agree that the extended audio clips in Spanish to someone who is tuning in for a quick headline recap on their drive home, that might seem a little verbose, a little long-winded, but I also think that it's pretty smart, strategically, being that Spanish speakers can be difficult to reach out to in traditional news avenues. And then, if they are flipping through channels and they hear this, they hear their own stories being told in a way that is not

framed by a crisis at the border or anything to do with immigration or anything like that. It's nice to hear that story about something so positive in our own community.

Other community members suggested that broadcasting a story like *The 47* was more *about* Philadelphia's Latinx/e community than *for* them: "I think it was more for the people outside of the community to give them a glimpse at something positive that's going on in the community." Participants who identified as Latinx/e in a Spanish-speaking discussion group expressed their appreciation for the story. At the same time, they did not independently bring up WHYY when talking about how they found news and information about their community. This example suggested that the narratives being shared by this NICE partner on WHYY were centering BIPOC experiences and challenging whiteness norms (and English-language dominance) at least in some ways, but it was less clear to what extent they were offering a meaningful service to BIPOC communities.

In addition to the NICE-partner-produced *The 47* series, I also shared examples from the *Mad or Nah?* series mentioned earlier. Interestingly, while this series had stronger audience metrics on social media, focus group participants raised a number of concerns with its style and substance. After listening to an episode about responses to gun violence, some said they found the production style "distracting" and "videogame-ish." One participant noted that the sound effect of "the cocking of a gun as a transition from one speaker to another seems very unnecessary and harmful, potentially, to the purpose of the story." In a focus group with Black residents of the West Philadelphia neighborhood where the presenter was from (some of whom identified as WHYY listeners), participants who were older than millennials suggested that there was a generational disconnect in how the piece was structured. One person critiqued the host for inviting adults to answer a question using vernacular most commonly used by teenagers: "Don't ask me if I'm mad or nah. I'm not twenty. I'm not eighteen, nineteen. I'm not no sixteen-year-old. Talk to me like you got some respect." Others said they saw the series' emphasis on anger to be frustrating and sensational: "This goes back to what I was saying about journalism trying to work us up all the time." Some participants said they wanted more exploration of root causes of problems as well as more solutions-oriented angles: "It could've been like, are you mad and upset and what would you do about it? Right? Because the one guy was like, 'Well, there are a lot of straw purchases going on. They should have people who are doing straw purchases have to list every gun that they've purchased.' I'm like, 'That is a really good solution.' So the community members have a lot of the solutions. So if you're going to poll the community, ask them for how they would start to fix the problem."

In a demographically mixed group of Philadelphia residents, discussion about the *Mad or Nah?* format turned to whether the program constituted "journalism":

Person 1: There's no hard numbers. There's no people who have any kind of authority on this issue speaking about it. It's just people who seem despairing and that they don't know what to do about this issue, but then the journalist themself offers nothing about what to do. There's mention of straw purchase, but other than that, there's no framing of the actual issue or framing of what is to be done about it.

Person 2: Yeah. I mean, I'm not sure what asking if someone's mad about something is—if that's actually journalism or not. It's not looking for answers.

Person 3: I'm also not expecting the journalist to have answers because they're a journalist. They're posing a question, and they're asking for reactions. I don't think that a part of what the journalist's job description is is to have the solution. I think it's to highlight the issue. It's to highlight the problem. It's to highlight the anger and the frustration and the fear that people are feeling around gun violence. And I think because it may not have been soft on the ear is no reason to discount the actual story within the journalistic attempt.

WHYY staff working to bring NICE partners onto WHYY broadcasts positioned this work as a challenge to dominant assumptions about who gets to be part of "real journalism": "What does a "real journalist" mean? Someone who just has a journalism degree, or someone who has the trust of the community and provides news? I would say it's the latter. And the idea that 'I'm not objective enough.' No quote-unquote real journalist is objective, right? You get into journalism because you want to solve problems and you want to take an issue and make sure that it's right and bring light to it."

Another WHYY manager suggested that the NICE project was attempting to disrupt a journalism system that reinforced whiteness by working with grassroots and nontraditional journalists. They explained that dominant norms of distanced objectivity and practices around professional gatekeeping often had the effect of forcing BIPOC journalists to justify their own legitimacy: "The assumption is always that the white journalists told it the best, right? . . . And then the rest of us who got into journalism because we have seen our communities, our families, ourselves left out of journalism—the rest of us have to not just defend our 'objectivity'—are we able to really discern if somebody is using us? If somebody is telling us something that's not true? We not only have to defend our journalism; we have to defend ourselves."

For these WHYY staff, by expanding who is considered a "real journalist," the NICE project complemented WHYY's broader work to expand who gets to tell local stories and to be heard on the public media airwaves. In this way, the project was influencing who had agency over the narratives circulating in the local storytelling network, while also creating a structure to support grassroots community media makers and connect them with WHYY.

FROM PROJECTS TO PROCESSES

Before starting the NICE project, when she was wrapping up the official grant period for the "Creating Culturally Competent Newsrooms" project, Sandra Clark was adamant that WHYY's work was not "finished." Her goal was to institutionalize the work of cultural competency more broadly and extend it beyond the timeframe of a grant cycle. To this end, she and her team could point to some initial accountability infrastructure that sought to move the station toward antiracism. This included a system for teams to monitor and track the diversity of their sources on an ongoing basis, the integration of DEIB goals into performance reviews, and the standardization of including DEIB or "cultural competency" questions in newsroom job interviews. Staffers I spoke with were able to point to a number of examples where they had challenged practices that had allowed colorblind framing to flourish and contributed to a white spatial imaginary.[50] For example, they now required freelance photographers to work to ensure that their photos reflected the diversity of the events they covered. They noted ways WHYY had begun to feature more BIPOC voices in stories and as storytellers—suggesting that using a communication infrastructure theory (CIT) framework, this intervention could be having some influence on the narratives circulating in the local storytelling network. As the NICE project got underway, Clark also noted how she wanted to continue to deepen WHYY's relationships to BIPOC communities in the area, indicating that more work would be done to strengthen ties between CIT storytelling network actors. In chapter 3, I will return to how WHYY's community engagement and DEIB work has been received within the organization and explore the extent the initial changes introduced by the "cultural competency" project were institutionalized beyond the leadership of Clark as an individual. But first, I will shift to another majority-white newsroom that took a different approach to accountability infrastructure as it grappled with its legacy of structural racism, the *Philadelphia Inquirer*.

2

REPAIRING AND REIMAGINING AN "ANTIRACIST" LEGACY NEWSPAPER

It's almost like the little bit that I can do is almost window dressing on an institution that basically disrespects, dishonors Black life. I'm just talking about Black life because that's what I care most about and pay most attention to. There are other communities that can say the same thing.

—BLACK *PHILADELPHIA INQUIRER* STAFFER, AUGUST 2020

n August 2020, I began a series of conversations with journalists at the *Philadelphia Inquirer*. The metro daily newspaper had just gone through a very public confrontation with racism in its coverage and institutional culture. Two months earlier, they had published a headline about damage to buildings caused by looting during Black Lives Matter protests titled "Buildings Matter, Too." Scathing criticism of the headline followed on social media, and within a week, the paper's top editor had resigned. In the months that followed, the *Inquirer*, whose staff at the time was 74 percent white, acknowledged the headline was racist; a massive diversity, equity, inclusion and belonging (DEIB) initiative called "*Inquirer* for All" was launched; and an independent "diversity and inclusion audit" of coverage was undertaken.

None of these actions, apart from the headline, would have happened were it not for the organizing and advocacy of the paper's journalists of color. In the days immediately following the headline, BIPOC staff organized a protest where they called out "sick and tired" and collaborated on an open letter that called on the paper to "do better," noting: "Your embarrassment is not worth more than our humanity."[1] These journalists were responding to more than a headline. They were responding to layers of history, norms, traditions, and power dynamics that contributed to racist coverage and a toxic newsroom culture, and they were doing so in the context of previous DEIB initiatives that were seen by many to make modest gains but end largely in disappointment.

The *Inquirer*'s journalists of color were also responding within a particular moment. In 2020, the *Inquirer* was among a number of U.S. news organizations facing a "reckoning" with systemic racism. Across the United States, from Los Angeles to Pittsburgh, multiple news outlets grappled publicly with racism embedded within their past and present coverage, as well as within their newsroom practices and treatment of BIPOC journalists.[2] This included WHYY and other public media outlets mentioned in the previous chapter, but cases of metro newspapers were even more widely discussed. These cases raised larger questions around whether it was possible for legacy news organizations steeped in structural racism from their earliest days to repair and to create transformative change from within.

In this chapter, I examine this and related questions from the perspective of an outsider given an opportunity to observe the *Inquirer*'s attempt to move from a moment of crisis toward a goal of transformation. After BIPOC staff shared a list of demands that among other things called for the *Inquirer* to "undertake a comprehensive review of our coverage, past and present, and commit to more equitable treatment," Temple University's Klein College's Dean David Boardman put together a team of faculty and staff, co-led by the late Bryan Monroe and myself.[3] We were tasked with conducting an independent diversity and inclusion audit.[4] Monroe was a highly regarded former head of the National Association of Black Journalists and leader in advocating for DEIB in journalism, and he had past experience with audits of print publications. I was invited to co-lead thanks largely to my work with WHYY on its source diversity audit efforts.

I admit that I accepted this opportunity with trepidation and some skepticism. Unlike WHYY, where managers had begun their push toward antiracism in 2017 as a proactive initiative, the *Inquirer's* effort felt like reactive crisis management. I was wary of investing in an initiative that might only confirm assumed deficits and potentially unearth trauma, if no action would be attached. As an outsider relatively new to Philly and never having worked for a metro newspaper—and as a white researcher—I also was concerned I might have difficulties building the trust needed with staffers to get an understanding of possibly sensitive dynamics around journalistic practices and workplace culture. It was a moment of palpable frustration and pain that had taken a deep toll on journalists of color in the United States, and it was clear that tensions within the *Inquirer* newsroom were high. These reservations, however, were outweighed by a sense that not trying to contribute to the initiative called for by the *Inquirer's* journalists of color would be worse. The *Inquirer* played a critical role in the local news built environment, and anything that could nudge their work in the direction of antiracism seemed inherently valuable. And thanks to the sterling reputation of Monroe and our team of Temple faculty and staff who had deep ties to the *Inquirer*, Philadelphia journalism more broadly, and local BIPOC communities, we dove into what would become a somewhat massive quantitative and qualitative "audit."

The quantitative side of our audit revealed stark if unsurprising truths. In the nearly three thousand stories we looked at, 60 percent of all of the people featured were white, and 90 percent of staff stories included at least one white person (in a city that is only 34 percent non-Hispanic white).[5] To contextualize this quantitative snapshot of the *Inquirer's* content, I led a qualitative study where *Inquirer* staffers were invited to reflect on norms and practices around sourcing, editing, placement/promotion, engagement, and workplace culture issues.[6] Throughout this work, I acted as a participant observer, periodically discussed aggregated findings with the *Inquirer*'s staff, and offered input on their follow-up planning. After the initial audit, I conducted a second study with focus groups and interviews six months later, followed by periodic update interviews to track progress.[7]

In this chapter, I explore what I learned from these conversations and observations of the *Inquirer* for All effort. In the sections that follow I'll first review how norms around "objectivity" and the influence of colorblind ideology influenced the *Inquirer* as a node within the local storytelling network—reinforcing the influence of whiteness in the reporting and editing processes and the narratives they circulated as a result.[8] I'll also look at how colorblind ideology and daily journalism norms acted as a barrier to community engagement as well as newsroom opportunities for BIPOC journalists—in effect limiting who connects to and participates in the local storytelling network. I'll then examine how some were attempting to shift practices in the direction of antiracism both individually and through institutionally supported infrastructure and note lingering questions about the *Inquirer*'s business model and connections to communities as it navigates a pursuit of antiracism.

"INQUIRER FOR ALL" IN CONTEXT

I focus on the *Philadelphia Inquirer* not only because of the highly public nature of its DEIB efforts but also because of the key role it plays in the region's news and information built environment. As discussed in the introduction, Philadelphia is home to a rich network of local news outlets, as well as other organizations and actors that circulate stories about the region in what communication infrastructure theory calls local "storytelling networks."[9] The *Inquirer* has a long history, operating since 1829. Since 2000, its history has been tumultuous, with multiple owners, layoffs, and mergers with the *Daily News* and Philly.com. It went from a newsroom of some six hundred journalists to just over two hundred.[10] Despite this, it continues to have the city's largest newsroom.

As the journalist Wesley Lowrey documented in an article the *Inquirer* commissioned to reflect on its history with racism and exclusion, the news organization also has a long if imperfect history of DEIB initiatives. Looking across its history, Lowrey noted some familiar-sounding patterns going back to the 1950s and 1960s of protest and unrest creating "crisis that required newspapers of record to cover parts of their cities they had long ignored—and to hire people whose lived experience could help them gain entry into those communities."[11] The 1970s and 1980s saw more hires of Black journalists but a climate where "opportunities for advancement seemed limited, and where no one seemed especially invested in their success."

Hires in the late 1980s and 1990s were more significant. My colleague Arlene Morgan, a former *Inquirer* editor, noted that this era included a range of diversity and inclusion efforts, including internships and residencies for journalists of color, a high school workshop program, and an audit of coverage.[12] However, many of the BIPOC journalists who joined in the 1990s were the first to lose their jobs when staff cuts hit in the 2000s, as union regulations required recent hires be the first to go.[13] In more recent years, before the "Buildings Matter, Too" furor, DEIB initiatives had also been tried. Multiple staffers described DEIB committees that primarily consisted of small groups of BIPOC staffers "huddled in a room somewhere"[14] working on recommendations that were not implemented in a meaningful way. It was within this historical context that the *Inquirer* for All initiative was announced. And it was because of this history and the deep skepticism it engendered, that management set out to make this DEIB effort look very different—and to include many more people, including veteran white editors, huddled in many more (virtual) rooms.[15] All told, the *Inquirer* for All initiative would involve some eighty staffers in a steering committee, five working groups ("voice," "coverage," "process," "culture," and "audit"), and several related committees, all with regular meetings. I will return to the substance of their intervention, but first I'll offer more context on the challenges this work sought to address.

CONFRONTING "COLORBLIND" SOURCING NORMS

"It's never been something that anyone really talks about," an *Inquirer* reporter explained, reflecting on how reporters and editors do or do not consider the demographic backgrounds of the people they include in stories. "The levels and depths of sourcing are so varied because it really is just up to the reporter to get it done as part of the reporting process."

There were many parallels between how journalists at the *Inquirer* and at WHYY spoke about sourcing. As with WHYY, at the *Inquirer*, there was no written list of do's and don'ts for determining whom to interview for stories. But as we conducted interviews for our audit, the way that journalists reflected on their practices suggested similar norms at play, many of which connected with the dominant interpretation of "objectivity" as meaning neutral and unbiased reporting, as discussed in the introduction.[16] These included using authoritative sources representing two sides of a political or policy issue, while keeping community organizers and activists at arm's length, which often had the effect of overrepresenting officials who are more likely to be white and male.

As alluded to by the reporter just quoted, one of the most common ways that journalists acted to reinforce sourcing norms was by not talking about the race or ethnicity of sources in the process of pitching or editing stories. Many *Inquirer* staffers, both white journalists and journalists of color, said they only discussed the background of sources when it was "directly related to the subject matter of the article," referencing examples such as stories about Black Lives Matter protests. A number of staffers, mostly white, also reinforced sourcing norms when they used the language of colorblind ideology, saying they didn't care about race or ethnicity as much as getting the "best people."[17] Listening to their perspectives, I was reminded of conversations I had heard WHYY staffers have with NPR's Keith Woods a few years earlier. An *Inquirer* editor explained, "I never ask for background, color of the skin. . . . It's just not part of how we do what we do." A reporter said they wouldn't feel comfortable explicitly asking a PR person to find them an expert source of color. Others said they expected source diversity to occur "organically" or to "naturally bubble up." One editor noted how a reporter of color "naturally" had a diverse group of sources. While well intentioned, this language of diverse sourcing happening "naturally" under-values the labor that must be invested into developing relationships and contacts.

While listening to white journalists sharing these perspectives, I did note a pang of familiarity. Early in my career as a journalist in the early 2000s, I recall being pleased when the people I reached out to turned out not to be white men, but I also remember being reluctant to directly talk about race or gender as a factor in the selection of sources. Even when I did attempt to seek out people with BIPOC backgrounds, I usually avoided talking about it overtly in the process of reaching out to interviewees. This prac-tice of not talking about race or of assuming nature will take its course rein-forces sourcing norms where white perspectives are overrepresented because it means explicit effort is unlikely to be invested into building rela-tionships with sources of color. In this way, colorblind ideology was shap-ing practices at the *Inquirer*, a node in the local storytelling network, and influencing the narratives they in turn distributed through the network.

Of course there were journalists at the *Inquirer* who took initiative as individuals to modify or challenge sourcing norms by acknowledging race, either at particular moments in time or as a guiding practice. Most of the BIPOC journalists who participated in interviews said they did work to include more sources of color, such as developing their own lists, and that they did talk about the background of sources with editors, though they noted that this constituted "invisible labor" that they had to initiate "pretty much 100 percent of the time." However, some editors, both BIPOC and white, also shared experiences of working with reporters to encourage greater representation of BIPOC sources. Some, like their counterparts at WHYY, suggested they allocated additional time to the sourcing process to "make sure that we have a lot of different voices in place." Several of these same editors, however, were reinforcing the norm of not speaking about race with their reference only to "different voices" rather than speci-fying the racial or ethnic background of sources. In addition, it would seem more journalists were actually reinforcing sourcing norms that prioritized timeliness over diversity, given the frequency with which productivity concerns were raised by interview participants. Several journalists shared examples of how an emphasis on productivity and speed prevented them from building relationships with new sources outside the context of story production: "I'd come back from a coffee or lunch with someone, and then my editor would say, 'What's the story?' And you're like, 'Well, actually, it was just a conversation. No concrete story came out of it.' . . . And so that kind of makes you more selective about who you reached out to talk to."

Finally, for many, the dominant norm of objectivity was reinforced by ideas of what made a source "good" and "authoritative"—assuming they were limited by traditional understandings of expertise, where official title holders, especially on particular beats, tended to be white and male. Some did share with me how they wanted to think more expansively about who was included in stories beyond the "expert" role. One journalist of color explained: "I would appreciate the opportunity to work with my editors to think of ways to broaden my sourcing. . . . We have to find other types of expertise, and that's not a conversation that is happening right now." For some, a desire for such conversations was paired with a desire for systems to incentivize more diverse sourcing: "I think it needs to be tracked, and it needs to be a regular thing. I think that there is an attitude that diversity matters on certain stories and not every story." While some voiced a desire for accountability infrastructure to support more diverse sourcing, and our audit shared this as a recommendation, the process of implementing this would require many more conversations.

CHALLENGES ON THE ROAD TO SOURCE TRACKING

Following up on recommendations by staff and our audit to regularly track who is represented in stories, the *Inquirer* for All's steering committee tasked an "audit committee" to develop a system for ongoing source tracking. While they made both source tracking and the establishment of a more inclusive source database a goal, eighteen months later they had still not implemented either newsroom-wide. Unlike WHYY, where one or two people developed, launched, and mandated a process, the *Inquirer* for All audit committee involved many more staffers and months of deliberation. While this arguably led to a more considered process with potential for greater investment across the organization, it also introduced inherent inefficiencies. As with all *Inquirer* for All committees, audit committee staff were volunteering their time, and the committee had turnover in membership and leadership. This is not to say committee members were not dedicated to their efforts. When I spoke with them, they shared the meticulous steps they were taking to survey industry best practice and consider the strengths and weaknesses of various systems. They deliberated what data to collect, whether elements of the process could or should be automated, and how it could interface with existing workflows and tools (for example, whether to include it in the existing content management system or to keep it separate). They also grappled with how to ensure that reporters and editors on different desks would feel invested in the system and find the data meaningful. They conducted newsroom surveys and planned to organize workshops and pilot efforts with particular desks before sharing with the newsroom as a whole.

In the meantime, some desks undertook their own experiments in tracking their work. For example, one desk had reporters track sources on a basic spreadsheet by asking them how they identified in an open-ended fashion and then held a series of follow-up, one-on-one discussions between reporter and editor and then across the team. Despite the initiative of particular desks, members of the audit committee expressed some frustration that the process of getting a system adopted newsroom-wide was taking longer than anticipated. Some explained that what they were hoping to do, for a newsroom of their size, was actually more ambitious than the ongoing source tracking they had seen at smaller news organizations including WHYY. It required overcoming resistance from those who were uncomfortable talking about race and multiple logistical barriers. As they got closer to implementation, more questions arose that required more deliberation—for example whether the data collected for source tracking could be referenced by reporters in their stories. But their biggest outstanding worry was how they would navigate a perception that they were adding additional labor to already overstretched reporters and what this would mean for adoption. While there were real lingering challenges, committee members were working with the backing of the institution to put tracking systems in place that could make patterns in sourcing more visible. And as one manager explained, having data on sourcing could be a first step toward instituting accountability infrastructure in the organization to encourage more antiracist reporting and editing.

WHITENESS IN THE EDITING PROCESS

As the community members I spoke with in the introduction illustrated, whiteness shaped coverage not only when BIPOC voices were omitted but also when stories were constructed and framed to appeal to a white audience. In conversations for the *Inquirer* audit, I spoke with staffers who also saw this as a concern and suggested that the editing process, and how editors deployed the norm of objectivity, played a role. At the time, thirty-five of the forty-seven editors were white, and conversations suggested it was not uncommon for editors to reinforce objectivity norms by failing to acknowledge their own positionality and subjectivity. This was pointed out frequently by journalists of color who wanted to challenge these norms but believed that white editors were using the language of objectivity to mask assumptions informed by whiteness, even if unintentionally.

"If you're white and you get killed, woo woo! If you're Black, a line or two." This assessment of the *Inquirer*'s homicide coverage sounds like it could have come from one of several community and advocacy organizations that have been publicly critical of the paper's crime and justice coverage. Instead, the critique came from inside the *Inquirer*, from a BIPOC journalist who said they had observed more resources going to stories about white victims than BIPOC victims. Others shared examples of how stories about people of color were held to a different standard than stories about white people. For example, they said they were asked to include reporting on criminal records or code violations in scenarios they would not have expected to be included in equivalent stories if the subjects were white. Reflecting on such approaches to coverage, a BIPOC journalist concluded that the editors making these choices were "not bad people" but that the assumptions they made had the cumulative effect of devaluing Black life.

Another BIPOC journalist said these cases illustrated how journalistic standards like "objectivity" were not applied consistently:

> Editors who have been there for a while will essentially invoke journalistic standards as if journalistic standards don't change from story to story. I mean, there is a lot of unwritten rules of baseball that journalists lean on, right? . . . A lot of times people will be like, "Oh, well, we have to because of how we do this and out of the interest of fairness, include this on this group," or whatever it is, without recognizing that that's not actually how we might do it in a story if they were white.

Journalists interested in challenging these norms also shared examples of their editors reinforcing them in the process of pitching stories. For example, a journalist of color explained that when they reported on a community of color they had to change the framing of the story so it was legible to their white editors: "I have had to pitch an idea, if it's not understood do some reporting, come back again and try to pitch it again. And if it still doesn't get across, then I have to change the focus of the story so that it gets past the editor. . . . I just intertwine the mainstream with the community focus in some way." They explained that through this process, the story becomes a "monster of two worlds" and aligns with neither the editor's "mainstream" expectations nor what communities were expecting: "It's either this or there's no story, and then the community's not going to have any trust in me."

I had many conversations with BIPOC journalists where they shared specific examples of the additional labor they had to do given white editors' lack of understanding of communities of color. I cannot share the details of most of these as they would jeopardize anonymity, but they often included a case where a white editor was unaware of a major event, issue, public figure, or institution that was widely discussed within

BIPOC communities. This theme was one of the most recurrent in my conversations—it came up in early interviews in 2020 and then again in later ones in 2022. While some gaps in knowledge are inevitable (and there were certainly cases where I had to Google someone mentioned), BIPOC journalists pointed out that these white editors did not see it as their responsibility to educate themselves about a large population in the city they claimed to cover. Rather, these editors reinforced whiteness in the editing process and the narratives they produced by expecting reporters of color to explain issues or avoid stories that were complex from their vantage point, as one BIPOC journalist explained: "I've had editors tell me that my stories take too long to edit, because they're kind of complicated issues. . . . My editor reading it would tell me, 'I've never heard of anything like this.'"

Evoking Lipsitz's white and Black spatial imaginaries, some white editors expressed reflexivity about a "daily gulf" between reporters of color and what they called "a veteran editor class."[18] One editor summarized what they imagined their veteran editor peers believed made a story worthy of publication: "An *Inquirer* story is the story that I think is good. And, what I think is good is basically what my neighbors think is good." Similar to Nelson's findings regarding *Chicago Tribune* journalists viewing neighbors as proxies for audience, the editor noted that these other editors' points of reference were others within their white, liberal, financially well-off neighborhoods or suburbs.[19] As a result, they reinforced whiteness by asking for explanations of concepts that were seen as outside the boundaries of understanding of an assumed white audience; in doing so, they signaled to BIPOC audiences that stories were not intended for them.

Some journalists, including some white editors, were attempting to question these norms around what makes a good story. This included some white editors who said they had been working to reflect more on their own positionality when considering story ideas, asking, for example: "Is this not a story to me? Or is it really not a story?" In addition, a number of BIPOC journalists were attempting to manage up or laterally to encourage white editors to cultivate reporting that offered context and specificity that was meaningful to the communities of color they reported on: "I think that we can help them understand, to grasp that the viewpoint from where traditional mainstream media covers these communities is othering." But sometimes these individual efforts backfired. Another BIPOC journalist seeking to challenge the whiteness of editorial priorities shared their experience of pointing out a gap in coverage on an issue important to a community of color. However, the editor they shared this with reinforced existing norms by suggesting the journalist provide ideas to fill the gap even though it was not within their beat: "I am bringing this to you, and you don't care because your response isn't, 'You're right. We'll fix it. Can't believe we missed it. There's a blind spot. Let's fix it.' Your response is, 'You fix it. If you care so much, you fix it.' And so that told me, I don't matter to the *Philadelphia Inquirer*."

One of the complications of attempting change to the structures of distanced objectivity and the whiteness it supports is that the very journalists of color who are harmed by existing structures are often expected to be the ones to undertake the labor of changing them. A number of BIPOC journalists expressed a sense of frustration and exhaustion from expectations that they be the ones challenging and modifying structures, when so often these structures were being reinforced by senior white journalists. Some spoke of a frustration that even well-intentioned white editors assumed that journalists of color would be the ones to bridge gaps of cultural competency: "I know it's difficult for someone to understand because they haven't walked these shoes. . . . But at the same time, it's like, be decent and do the work." Another BIPOC journalist pushed back on the idea that Black journalists should be the ones to prevent problematic content from getting published: "If a headline gets in that's outrageous, and nobody Black's around for you to check it with, that's on you. You have to claim that."

ACCOUNTABILITY INFRASTRUCTURE
TO SHIFT EDITING NORMS

Even before the audit was released, the *Inquirer* was taking steps to build off the suggestions of journalists challenging editing practices that reinforced whiteness. Through the *Inquirer* for All initiative, various working groups were tackling elements of the reporting and editing process and attempting to institutionalize policies and processes in response. This included the development of a "Content Consult" Slack channel and efforts to revise the *Inquirer*'s style guide. Later, committees undertook initiatives such as an antiracist workflow guide, which addressed norms and practices within editing, and began developing a mechanism for postpublication feedback.

CONTENT CONSULT CHANNEL

In my many conversations with *Inquirer* staffers after the audit, the initiative most frequently and enthusiastically noted as a concrete DEIB intervention was the development of a "Content Consult" Slack channel. This was one of the *Inquirer* for All's earliest efforts, led by the process committee. The channel offered a prepublication space for staff members to raise issues or seek advice regarding stories that could be sensitive or problematic. Some spoke of this as a way to prevent the publication of offensive content such as the "Buildings Matter, Too" headline. The channel also aimed to address the other side of that spectrum, where staff members recounted examples of how stories seen as potentially "too fraught" had been halted out of fears of getting it wrong leading to a "paralysis" in coverage. The channel developed followed a similar concept as a channel implemented by the *Seattle Times*, where volunteer staffers were available to offer input on questions as they arose.[20] It sought to shift away from informal pathways—where white journalists had often sought out the input of BIPOC journalists, imposing additional uncompensated labor.

In March 2021, the Content Consult channel launched. Its operating manual illustrated the rationale and ambitious expectations for this intervention: "Our current gatekeeper hierarchy of editing is too narrow and defaults to a white-centric filter for both processes and content that can lead to a lack of sensitivity, and to offensive, demeaning, or racist language. Getting guidance from the broader newsroom on specific stories or approaches can help prevent mistakes before they are published, accelerate everyone's awareness and understanding, and better serve, grow, and retain diverse audiences." The user guide goes on to explain that the staffers should use the channel to ask questions and seek feedback "without fear of retribution when they recognize a blind spot or potentially racist element in their work." The guide suggests the channel seeks to provide infrastructure to shift the *Inquirer*'s editing processes: "[Getting feedback through the channel] should be as normal in our workflow as workshopping a headline, making a photo request, or reviewing budget lines in news meetings."

By providing an infrastructure to discuss content, would the Content Consult intervention support a structural shift in editing practices? The *Inquirer* reported that from March to June 2021, the channel received 110 submissions, roughly one per day, including weekends. Reporters and editors, mostly white (fewer than 10 percent identified as BIPOC), submitted stories (mostly their own but occasionally others) to the channel, which, at the time, was moderated by nine volunteers: two who identified as men and seven as women, five who identified as white, two as Asian, one as Black, and one as Latinx/e.

Staff members who used the channel reported a mix of appreciation and anxiety about the process: "I've dropped one story in there and really like getting the feedback before it published. I'm going to drop another one in there this week and I'm terrified, but I think that that's good. I'd rather have it drop in there first than just go out to the public." While most staff suggested discussion in the channel was constructive, some also admitted there was a stigma associated with having one's work discussed in the channel, suggesting participation had yet to be normalized. As one editor said, "That's not a place I want any of my stories appearing." A reporter similarly shared that their first reaction to their editor volunteering their story for the channel was "Wait, what's wrong?"

Another editor suggested the channel "has potential to bring us together and it has potential to divide us," adding that their reporters expressed a range of sentiments about participation. The editor expressed reservations "because it's like, wait a minute, are we editing by committee?" They said that while they often made use of the guidance offered by the channel, they did not feel beholden to change their stories based on it. Their reflection suggested an openness to the new infrastructure's intervention within the editing process—but only up to a point.

The channel was also designed to offer an infrastructure to supplant informal processes that had historically burdened BIPOC journalists with educating white peers on their cultural blind spots. Some, including this BIPOC journalist, suggested the channel was meeting this goal: "I think our Content Consult channel has been very, very helpful, especially for those of us . . . who kind of felt like we were on the racial help desk. It's like, 'Okay, line two, how can I save you?'" Others were less confident that the channel, staffed by a majority of white volunteers and drawing more broadly from the insights of a largely white newsroom, would be an effective "gut check channel," the channel's initial informal title. As one BIPOC journalist pointed out, "With a lot of really sensitive areas, the *Inquirer's* newsroom is not where I would ask the room." Some pointed to articles that were published and had not been discussed in the channel but were nevertheless offensive to BIPOC audiences: "If your gut is not telling you that that's obvious, then you're not going to put that in the Slack Consult channel." Because of the lack of diversity among participants, there was a risk that the channel would "basically affirm rather than interrogate whether we're doing the best thing" or, as another staffer put it, be a space for "unburdening of guilt" without substantive feedback. Others suggested that many approached the channel in the spirit of "CYA" ("cover your ass") or "let me make sure I don't get myself in trouble," as opposed to considering it a more substantive learning or dialogue opportunity.

The channel's own operating manual suggested periodic reevaluation, and management expressed an awareness of the need to consider the sustainability of the channel's all-volunteer structure. Nevertheless, while the Content Consult channel had significant limitations in its ability to shift editing structures, it did present some potential disruption to uncritical editing practices that were skewed by whiteness and contributed to racial inequity. Additional adaptations, like ensuring BIPOC perspectives were represented through compensated labor and integrating the channel into a larger infrastructure of pre- and postpublication reflection, could increase its impact.

STYLE GUIDE

The *Philadelphia Inquirer* had long had a style committee, but over the course of this study the committee undertook a number of efforts that complemented the work of the *Inquirer* for All committees and sought to intervene in standard editing practices. In June 2020, around the same time the Associated Press and others made a similar change, the *Inquirer*'s style guide was updated to capitalize the *B* in Black. In addition, the style committee had been discussing how African American Vernacular English (AAVE) was edited. As one journalist explained, the *Inquirer* had been following a practice of "whitewashing" AAVE—for example, rewriting the quotes of AAVE speakers:

> A lot of people think that it's ungrammatical and don't realize that African American English has its own grammar. . . . Basically, people were revealing that they did not know enough about the language to make the editorial decisions that they were making. So someone said to me, "Yeah, but if someone says, 'I be walking my dog,' we have to change it to spare them, and we have to just say 'They walk their dog.'" And I had to explain to them, "Well, then you did not accurately paraphrase what they said. When someone says 'I be walking,' that means that they're doing it relatively frequently and repeatedly. And if you are going to paraphrase it, you would need to include something like that."

While the style committee acknowledged the need to revise this practice, the journalist explained, they did not have enough editors fluent in AAVE to implement the change. In these instances, journalistic agents attempted to institutionalize their challenges to stylistic norms within the editing process; however, they were not able to significantly shift the structure given the lack of Black editors.

A year later in 2021, style committee members explained how they were working on a complete audit of their stylebook, which included updating and rewriting entries to synchronize it with the *Inquirer*'s antiracism work. Members of the group explained that they hoped this went beyond creating a dictionary to creating new "standards, best practices, and policies" within the editing and reporting processes: "So if our standard needs to be, you ask people about how they want to identify. If they identify as a woman, if they identify as Black, how do they want to be called? How do they want their surnames to appear on second reference? That should be our standard, as opposed to our style."[21]

The committee also attempted to create infrastructure to facilitate adoption of these standards and to encourage the broader newsroom to feel invested. They created a Newsroom Style Slack channel to offer "language consult and guidance." They also attempted to be more transparent about the research that informed their policies and to allow staff to share input on style changes. The style committee's intervention was likely to be less dramatic than the Content Consult's potential to catch racist headlines, and it was still in progress at the time of writing. However, the fact that style rules had to be adhered to across the newsroom and that adhering to these rules in turn influenced practices meant efforts to create an antiracist style guide could offer a meaningful intervention within editing structures.

ANTIRACIST WORKFLOW GUIDE

On its face, the intervention with the most comprehensive potential to disrupt norms supporting whiteness and colorblind ideology in traditional editing and reporting structures was the *Inquirer*'s "Antiracist Workflow Guide."[22] The digital guide, which was developed by the voice committee, explicitly sets out to encourage more reflexive reporting and editing practices by inviting staffers to answer a series of questions designed for different stages in the process of story production—from story development to postpublication reflection. Some questions apply to all roles, such as, "Whom am I centering in this story?" or "Does this story engage a community, or is it about one?" Other questions focus on issues more relevant to particular job roles, such as print coordinators or producers.

Shortly after the guide's release, I spoke with staffers about how it was or was not being adapted into day-to-day work across teams. Some journalists did share experiences with the guide, such as a reporter whose editor asked questions from the guide as part of the editing process: "I ended up getting some really great additional information that I wouldn't have otherwise got because of the questions. To see [the editor] actually using the guide, I think, was really great." Others had not encountered the guide, though it had been digitally distributed across the newsroom and discussed in a number of meetings. One reporter told me they appreciated the guide but hesitated to "get lost in the middle of an editing process in all these existential, fundamental questions. And then it's like, 'Ooh, okay. We've still got the print deadline.'" The reporter's referencing of deadline pressure speaks to a significant barrier to this intervention's functionality as accountability infrastructure. Not only did staffers note productivity pressures trumping good intentions (as they did with sourcing); it also was difficult to know whether the guide was being used or not and by whom.

Roughly a year after the guide's release, however, enthusiasm for it had waned among some of the staffers I spoke with. One manager reflected: "The guide itself is universally applauded and really well done. My hunch, I don't have any data to back this up, it's just my gut, the people who use it are the people who would also already do this well. And the people who don't use it are the ones who need to use it the most."[23] Another manager similarly found it frustrating to see the lack of adoption of the workflow guide: "I don't think anybody would say that we've succeeded in actually getting people to ask those questions as they go through the process." Drawing on their observations of other workflow guides on different topics, they attributed this less to a failing by *Inquirer* for All in particular than to "baked-in human inertia that is hard to overcome."[24] Another staffer pointed to a limit to this intervention as infrastructure: "I think anything that is content that requires people to pull it to use it I think will always be an obstacle for us." They suggested there needed to be other ways to hold editors accountable for applying the guide or its practices, but they struggled to offer specific mechanisms.

RETROSPECTIVE FEEDBACK PROCESS

Reflecting on the antiracist workflow guide's shortcomings as accountability infrastructure, one manager suggested that a new postpublication feedback process they were developing may help address the problem of needing editors and reporters to opt in. By offering a regular system for stories to be discussed, they reasoned, even those who didn't participate in the prepublication Content Consult channel or use the workflow guide may be compelled to look critically at their work. Indeed, one of our initial audit recommendations to make editing practices more inclusive was: "Organize or participate in monthly postpublication accountability conversations with community stakeholders to discuss both stories that have problematic elements or concerns as well as stories that have been particularly inclusive."

Our audit argued that the *Inquirer* should facilitate opportunities to discuss whether stories had "effectively included diverse perspectives and framing" and that they could normalize a process of talking about DEIB goals by making these conversations about stories that were not necessarily noted as exceptionally excellent or problematic.

In conversations at the time, *Inquirer* staffers mentioned that they had considered a postpublication "story autopsy" process. Over a year later, this idea had still not been implemented, but it had been rebranded as a "Retrospective" process (like the Content Consult, née "gut check" channel, it had shifted away from a more visceral name). The initiative was being organized by the same *Inquirer* for All process committee that had launched the Content Consult channel. While it had yet to begin at the time of writing, managers explained that the process committee would organize formal meetings at the desk level with editors and reporters to evaluate past content. These would be an opportunity "to sit down and say, 'Let's look at our coverage for the last three months and talk about what's going on. What do we need to do differently? What are some communities we know how to cover well?'"[25]

As one manager explained, this process would build upon a retrospective process they already did to review major breaking news events. For those past retrospectives, staffers involved in coverage were surveyed ahead of time to ask what could have been done better as well as what they saw as "wins." This input was then used to inform a discussion. They emphasized that the new retrospective process would be "routine" and "recurring" and that while *Inquirer* for All "concerns" would be prominently featured, the feedback would also include discussion of "other areas for improvement in the storytelling and the reporting." They hoped that framing the process this way would encourage greater investment and "make it feel perhaps less like an inquisition, because it's something we're already doing and because that process has been pretty helpful so far."

While these plans connected with our recommendations from the audit and offered some potential to influence narratives circulating in the local storytelling network, they were notably different in a key respect: the absence of community participation. The *Inquirer* was not considering including community feedback in this process. When asked, staffers mentioned community feedback as something that could potentially be sourced through separate mechanisms. In this way, retrospectives would offer some internal accountability infrastructure, but following a theme of many of the *Inquirer* for All measures, it would be dependent on the people already in the newsroom. Community input was not integrated into newsroom accountability infrastructure designed to make editing or reporting processes more equitable.

ACCOUNTABILITY TO COMMUNITIES?

Perhaps what most directly confronts dominant objectivity norms and the related practice of keeping communities at a distance is the idea that journalists have a responsibility to undertake community engagement and build relationships with the communities that they cover. In the United States, the concept of community-engaged journalism has increasingly gained traction in a number of newsrooms and philanthropic circles.[26] This practice can be interpreted in many ways, but here I refer to "an inclusive practice that prioritizes the information needs and wants of the community members it serves, creates collaborative space for the audience in all aspects of the journalistic process, and is dedicated to building and preserving trusting relationships between journalists and the public."[27] In practical terms, this could include a range of online or face-to-face activities, from inviting the public to submit story ideas or ask questions for journalists to explore, to participating in discussion forums, to acting as community advisors on in-depth stories or for newsrooms as a whole. In communication infrastructure theory terms, engaged journalism offers the potential to strengthen the storytelling network link between local media and residents.

In my conversations with *Inquirer* staff, a lack of community engagement was occasionally referenced as a possible explanation for gaps in the organization's coverage, while the practice of engagement was sometimes raised as a potential strategy to improve coverage, particularly of underrepresented or stigmatized communities. These sentiments were consistent with calls coming from external stakeholders. In the immediate aftermath of the "Buildings Matter, Too" controversy, the organization Free Press released an open letter signed by twenty-nine community and media organizations and twenty-six individual community leaders and media experts calling on the *Inquirer* to "work with local residents to implement a community-first approach that would enable the newsroom to actively engage with the public and build genuine relationships that center community perspectives."[28] The letter offered a series of recommendations including creating practices that would facilitate public accountability for coverage, challenge narratives that centered police and other power holders, and address internal power dynamics by addressing gaps in representation in leadership and via a community advisory board. While many of these recommendations resurfaced over the course of our audit and in subsequent conversations with *Inquirer* staff, as noted with the retrospective initiative discussed earlier, who was responsible for community engagement and whether community perspectives would be welcome into the organization's accountability infrastructure were less clear.

Despite external advocacy urging the *Inquirer* to connect with communities and the increased adoption of engaged journalism practices in many newsrooms, including at WHYY, journalists seeking to adopt such practices at the *Inquirer* shared experiences of encountering resistance from colleagues who either directly took on the role of reinforcers of objectivity norms or indirectly presented barriers to their work. Nevertheless, a number of (mostly BIPOC) journalists shared with me experiences of challenging distanced objectivity norms by organizing meetings with community members or hosting public pop-ups to talk to people about issues they cared about and to "educate people about what newspapers, or what reporters, do." As they explained, they did these activities not just to get story ideas but to establish better relationships. However, these journalists also reported they largely were taking on this work without institutional support. "I begged for support there, and I didn't get it. But I keep doing it because I felt like it was worth it for my job," noted a BIPOC journalist. They shared stories of having to buy their own pens and candies to hand out at public events and of feeling scrutinized by editors, who were skeptical of any time use that was not oriented toward a particular story.

Conversations with staff revealed a lack of consensus on how the work of engagement aligned with standard roles of reporting and editing. For some editors, community engagement was simply seen as thorough reporting—"talking to as many people as possible"—and, in pre-COVID times, being out in communities rather than only on their phones and computers. Their ideas about engagement still fell within a more extractive model of connecting with people to get their stories and then to leave. For those who sought a more relational approach to engagement, this was discouraging. One BIPOC reporter shared their frustration with an editor who did not see engagement as the work of reporters: " 'That's more than what a reporter does.' But the thing is, the cookie-cutter understanding of reporter goes out, ask questions, comes back, write the thing, and it goes out to the paper, that does not exist anymore. . . . That's not what the [community is] expecting from their reporter either."

Others shared concerns that management had historically sent mixed signals about what engagement meant and whether they supported it. The responses of some editors and managers suggested that indeed some were still attached to dominant objectivity norms: "I still have an old school bias though. . . . There's a trend, the thing called citizen journalists, which as a journalist for [several decades] annoys the hell out of me. It's like if you have brain cancer do you want a citizen surgeon to operate on you? . . . It seems advocacy journalism, and I never want to seem like we're advocating one view over another."

Most staffers I spoke with were neither stridently opposed to engaged journalism nor ardent supporters. Perhaps unsurprising given a lack of clear messaging, many expressed a vaguely positive sentiment about engagement but were not certain about what it meant or whose job it should be. There was no clear narrative regarding whether and how community stakeholders could or should fit within accountability infrastructure seeking to promote antiracism.

CREATING COMMUNITY-CENTERED ACCOUNTABILITY INFRASTRUCTURE

While few newsroom workers had clarity about community engagement goals, the *Inquirer* did outline plans for several community engagement initiatives following the conclusion of our audit. This included following up on some earlier work convening online discussions meant to inform coverage and offer insights into questions and concerns shared by residents. But it also included a new series of objectives, including creating a community desk, creating a community advisory board, and holding accountability conversations with external community stakeholders.

COMMUNITIES AND ENGAGEMENT DESK

One of the *Inquirer*'s most debated initiatives has been the communities and engagement desk (sometimes called the "community news desk").[29] The desk was officially announced in May 2021 by the Lenfest Institute, who provided it a $600,000 grant. The desk, they stated, would consist of "a new team of journalists focused on amplifying diverse voices and strengthening relationships with underserved communities."[30] According to an *Inquirer* for All update by the coverage team, in addition to reporting, the new desk would include "direct community engagement initiatives."[31] The senior editor for the team, Sabrina Vourvoulias, was hired in October 2021.[32] While she quickly got to work undertaking a community "listening tour," the desk was not fully staffed and launched until August 2022.

For *Inquirer* staff committed to community engagement, the new desk was viewed with both hope and concern before its launch. One staffer explained they were excited about the desk but feared it would be used to excuse other parts of the newsroom from doing engagement: "My fear is they're going to say, 'Oh, well, that's their job.' Everybody has to do this." Others said they'd already heard similar sentiments and feared the desk had potential to silo off the competencies of community engagement, when they should be seen as a basic element of good reporting for all reporters: "It's not a supplement to the job, it's not just going the extra mile." Finally, some were skeptical of how the desk would function as part of the newsroom. One staffer said they wouldn't want to be a reporter on the community desk because they imagined they would focus on covering positive stories and then as soon as a major news story broke they'd be displaced by the investigative team or reporters from other desks. Managers acknowledged that the silo risks "were real but that the potential rewards of a dedicated team outweighed those risks." They suggested they did seek a future where engagement was "baked into what everyone is doing" but that the community desk structure was a necessary first step.

After an initial period of consultation with newsroom staff and community stakeholders, the desk's new editor created a plan to focus on a combination of identity-based and geographic communities, as well as a number of preliminary partner organizations associated with the respective communities. The team would be expected to devote a day a week to "office hours"–style outreach activities not connected to specific stories. There was also an "audience development strategy" that included a cohort of community leaders the editor had relationships with and a plan to facilitate quarterly "Soapbox Salon" feedback discussions. There was hope, explained one manager, that "as trusted messengers, they come to trust us. And there can be some amplification down the road if we're doing our job right."

There were still a number of areas of uncertainty—for example, how to appeal to a wider array of new readers with an increasingly tight paywall. One manager explained how conversations around this had forced them to grapple with challenges and tension between engagement and business goals. They noted that they planned to test new newsroom products like SMS services and free newsletters with their cohort of community leaders but that this required close consultation with the "business side," which had distinct goals: "It's pretty complicated. I think I underestimated how much needs to go into having this be meaningful and work within the context of the *Inquirer* as a business, and have a good shot at connecting meaningfully with people that it's trying to reach."

How the desk would integrate community engagement into the larger newsroom also remained "the million-dollar question." A manager noted that even before the desk launched, the editor had already begun "raising community concerns on stories that we're covering and stories that we haven't covered." At the same time the silo problem apparently persisted, at least to an extent. In the lead-up to its launch, I spoke with other staffers unaware of the status of the desk or even that positions had been posted for it. A manager explained they were "super acutely aware" of the need to work on the newsroom–community desk relationship and had been doing internal brainstorming workshops in part to determine "how do we avoid either siloing them as the only folks doing meaningful community engagement or just turning them into a glorified community rolodex for the rest of the newsroom. So I think it's going to be hard to avoid but important to avoid."

When I spoke to Vourvoulias shortly after the desk launched, she expressed a commitment that the desk would "take our cues from the community." She noted that while the team reported on a range of stories, "It's as important that you devote the time to sitting down and talking with community members as it is for you to sit down and write a story." She explained that the Soapbox Salon had already begun to act as a feedback loop, particularly via text messages that she exchanged with salon members. These acted as informal information needs assessments—for example, exploring whether communities had adequate information about monkeypox in their preferred languages. Salon members also shared feedback on *Inquirer* content more broadly, and Vourvoulias circulated requests from other desks who were looking for a "diversity of voices" to speak with them about a story. She suggested the communities and engagement desk interacted with various desks in other ways as well, such as when a desk reached out to them to verify something about a community initiative or when her desk posted an invite in Slack for journalists who might want to join them at a community event.

It was too soon to know at the time of writing whether the journalists working on the communities and engagement desk, most of whom identify as members of BIPOC communities, would succeed in their goal of prioritizing deep listening to communities, whether such efforts would position the desk as an outlier in its practice of engaged journalism that acted as a sort of consultant to the larger newsroom, and whether meaningful connections with the desk could contribute to culture shift over time. The structure of the desk was already making some challenges to dominant interpretations of objectivity by partnering with a rotation of Soapbox Salon members' organizations for "deep dives" consisting of eight weekly meetings exploring past coverage and neighborhood dynamics. Traditionally, the dominant interpretation of objectivity norms had made journalists allergic to establishing collaborations with community organizations. By establishing a structure to build ongoing relationships with these organizations and other community leaders, the desk had the potential to make an intervention into what communication infrastructure theory calls the local "storytelling network," strengthening ties between local media and community stakeholders—not only residents but also community organizations. The Soapbox Salon also held some promise to encourage two-way feedback loops and potentially offer some accountability infrastructure, though it was too early to know whether they would be empowered to do so in a meaningful way in practice or whether there would be any public transparency.

COMMUNITY ADVISORY COUNCIL

Another area of contention at the *Inquirer* was whether it would follow up on its plan to launch a standing "community advisory council" that aimed to contribute to company-level priorities. These included not only offering perspectives on coverage and its impact but also on the company's diversity, equity, and inclusion strategy and marketing and subscription goals.

When I checked in sixteen months after the initial audit, I was told that work on the council had been complicated by the initiation of multiple community outreach efforts and a desire to ensure synergy between them. In addition to the communities and engagement desk's Soapbox Salon, there was also a community engagement initiative run by a community marketing manager focused on reaching new audiences and determining "who are the influencers in the city that we should have relationship with or who are the partner organizations that we should be sponsoring and giving funds that are really meeting community needs?" With multiple actors and departments involved, they were trying to synchronize their efforts: "We've just got to figure out how they all tie into one another, and what spaces are we duplicating the efforts? Or should we just take something that one of us is already doing and put a new branding over it because it serves the original intent and purpose behind what the community advisory council is?" Adding to this complexity, there was turnover in the team managing DEIB work. Kendra Lee joined as the new vice president of diversity, equity, and inclusion in August 2022. In October 2022, she replied to my query about the council by explaining: "In the beginning, we had discussed the possibility of creating an *Inquirer* Community Advisory Council with outside groups as participants in the planning. In the end, a mutual decision was made to defer until the communities and engagement desk fully evolved and we completed our broader DE&I community strategy."[33]

This answer in some ways raised more questions than it answered for me—what would it look like for the communities and engagement desk to be "fully evolved"? And, more critically, would there be a time when a "DE&I community strategy" would be "completed"? This seemed to vary from previous statements that emphasized that this work would be ongoing (and of course, the work of antiracism is not something that can be "completed" in a majority-white newsroom). The statement continued, noting that "the Communities & Engagement Desk's Soapbox Salon is, in many ways, a working pilot for the community advisory council." This was notable, for while the salon had the promise of creating feedback loops, it did not seem to have a function of offering transparent public accountability.

When I spoke with outside observers of the *Inquirer*'s work, many expressed frustration about a lack of clear public messaging regarding plans for the community advisory council. Some had publicly advocated for some sort of external community-led board to offer an accountability infrastructure for the *Inquirer*'s coverage and DEI goals. Free Press's Tauhid Chappell shared how, in the absence of such a group, he and others had been developing a new external accountability body, the Philly Journalism Accountability Watchdog Network, or Philly JAWN.[34] While the shape and emphasis of Philly JAWN was evolving over the course of my observation, and I will return to developments in its work in chapter 6, early proposals envisioned "a local coalition of media equity organizations" that could act as a "bridge between the newsroom and the public it intends to serve" for the *Inquirer* and potentially other area newsrooms as well:

> The board would act as a public watchdog, holding the newsroom accountable for coverage and providing ideas for future stories. This would be a call to invite Black and Brown neighborhood leaders—not white corporate leaders, politicians, people with financial privilege or people who run majority-white organizations—to the table. This board would begin to help change the way the newsroom listens to the public and centers people's information needs.[35]

The Philly JAWN project was driven by a collaboration between the media equity organization Free Press and associations representing BIPOC journalists, including the Philadelphia Association of Black Journalists and the Philadelphia chapters of the National Association of Hispanic Journalists and Asian American Journalists Association.[36] JAWN leaders explained that they intended to develop their membership to include other community stakeholders in the future. While such a body's composition would likely be more journalist heavy than a traditional community advisory board, Philly JAWN outlined plans to create programming that would connect and facilitate conversations between community members and journalists.

With all of these potential plans both within the *Inquirer* and externally, a year and a half after our initial audit there was still a lack of clarity around what form the accountability infrastructure was going to take to ensure the news organization was undertaking meaningful two-way communication to hold itself answerable to local communities.

ACCOUNTABILITY CONVERSATIONS

Finally, to extend two-way communication to a broader range of community members, we had also recommended in our audit that the *Inquirer* undertake accountability conversations with community stakeholders. The idea was to facilitate opportunities for community participants to share perspectives on existing and future coverage outside the context of the reporting process. Given the lack of community participation in newsroom accountability infrastructure such as retrospectives, we argued that there needed to be dedicated channels for convening. As discussed earlier, the *Inquirer* was planning some outreach activities via their communities and engagement desk and community marketing team. But there were no set plans for the newsroom more broadly.

Over the course of my observation, *Inquirer* staff did participate in a series of meetings with community members organized by the media equity organization Free Press News Voices in collaboration with the multiorganization Shift the Narrative Coalition.[37] These meetings included community members directly affected by police violence, gun violence, the criminal legal system, and related media coverage. Meetings were intended to inform newsroom guidelines at the *Inquirer* regarding crime and justice reporting and to build relationships with affected communities. Following these, Free Press suggested that they hoped to continue the partnership but that there was also "a need for deeper trust to be built."[38] On the *Inquirer* end, one participant suggested that the conversation was notable for including coverage decision makers, including key editors, as opposed to just reporters. They said they hoped to gather more input as they worked to rethink their justice and injustice coverage and to get community feedback more generally: "I think it has created an appetite for doing more of this, but with perhaps a broader spectrum of groups or figuring out a way to talk to a broader spectrum of people or viewpoints at a given engagement." Another manager explained that while they were no longer engaging in these meetings, they had informed the development of coverage policies, such a right-to-be-forgotten policy they were currently finalizing.

* * *

Navigating how to establish and maintain channels of communication with communities that historically have felt harmed by distorted or absent news coverage will require active and ongoing work, work that challenges objectivity norms that hold communities at arm's length. At the time of writing, the *Inquirer* had a number of potential plans in motion that could lead to the establishment of accountability infrastructure that integrates community perspectives. It was not yet clear whether this infrastructure would be truly community centered, meaningfully share power, and be synchronized with the larger operations of the newsroom. This work has the potential to be central to efforts to transform the *Inquirer* into an antiracist newsroom. Its success will require relationship building to become a crosscutting feature of what it means to do "good journalism" rather than work segmented off to people with the terms "community" or "engagement" in their roles.

This is not to say this is easy work. Indeed, my own experience in the researching of the *Inquirer*'s audit project illustrates how good intentions alone do not guarantee adequate communication and power sharing with community stakeholders. When our audit findings were released, Ernest Owens, the president of the Philadelphia Association of Black Journalists (PABJ), critiqued the audit and the *Inquirer* for All initiative for a lack of community input. Our project was co-led by a former president of the National Association of Black Journalists, my late colleague Bryan Monroe, and in the early phases of the audit I had conversations and interviews with several members of PABJ. But neither my colleague's sterling reputation nor my limited efforts to solicit input were a substitute for proactively engaging with PABJ. Owens noted that he and other community stakeholders had participated in meetings with the *Inquirer* where they announced their plans for the audit and for their *Inquirer* for All initiatives: "They were talking *to* us, instead of talking *with* us. We were not included in the planning or implementation of any efforts to repair the wounds caused by the *Inquirer*'s practices but rather told after final decisions were made."[39]

We as an audit team did not have authority to force the *Inquirer* to consult with community stakeholders when developing their *Inquirer* for All plan. However, we could have done more to formally engage with stakeholders like PABJ to get input on our audit framework from the beginning and, ideally, used this as an opportunity to encourage the *Inquirer* to do the same. As Owens later underlined in a conversation with me, "If this is going to be on behalf of us, it can't be done without us."[40] There are no shortcuts to meaningfully and systematically engaging community stakeholders, and this instance illustrates how easy it is to get this wrong—or at least to miss an opportunity to build trust.

ACCOUNTABILITY INFRASTRUCTURE FOR WORKPLACE EQUITY

The influence of structural racism on access to opportunities in journalism as a whole, and on the *Inquirer* in particular, was evident given nearly 75 percent of the newsroom's staff were white at the time of our initial audit (in a city where only 34 percent identify as non-Hispanic white). As the *Inquirer* set goals to move toward antiracism, they included goals to increase the representation of BIPOC employees in the newsroom, address pay equity, and institute DEI and engagement goals into performance reviews.

HIRING AND RETENTION GOALS

Inquirer managers explained that over the past three years roughly half of the journalists they hired were journalists of color. However, as one acknowledged, their progress was limited by their very white starting place and limitations on hiring and firing: "It's constrained hugely by the fact that we're getting smaller, by the fact that we are in a very strong union shop, and there's not a lot of people who leave based on performance management. . . . So, you're trying to create radical change when you can only do modest changes to the staff itself."

Following the initial audit, the *Inquirer* set a series of goals to fill new positions (both new hires and promotions) with 60 percent or more journalists of color, 50 percent women, and at least 35 percent BIPOC journalists in leadership roles in the newsroom (to increase it from 24 percent). In June 2021, they reported 61 percent of all new positions filled in the newsroom were with individuals from BIPOC communities and 44 percent identified as women. Some external critics suggested that given challenges with retention of BIPOC staff and with the overall low starting numbers of BIPOC staff, target quotas for overall representation would be more helpful than simply looking at percentages of new hires. When I checked back with them in 2022 they had come to the same conclusion, noting that they were focusing on percentages within the newsroom—and that they had gone from 20 percent BIPOC staff in 2021 to 31 percent at the start of 2022. They also noted that newsroom management would be over 45 percent BIPOC managers by the end of 2022.[41] Despite this, I spoke with both internal and external critics who argued that it was important to segment BIPOC hires to understand representation by race/ethnicity—and in particular, representation of Black journalists. They pointed out that much of the June 2020 protests and the *Inquirer* for All response grew out of frustration with the lack of Black reporters and editors in a city where 41 percent of the population identifies as Black. Some noted a lack of Black reporters among the new hires and the challenges of retaining Black and Brown reporters on staff.[42] When I asked the *Inquirer* for newsroom demographics segmented by race/ethnicity (so it would be possible to know change within the percentage of Black staffers), they did not share this information and instead repeated the same aggregated BIPOC percentages.[43]

Reflecting on recruitment efforts, an *Inquirer* manager explained to me that they had faced difficulty trying to hire BIPOC editors in particular: "We may send out offers, and they have ten competing offers." Others suggested management was actually reinforcing structural racism by not doing more to reach Black journalists in particular, suggesting they could do more to recruit from historically Black universities and associations. In addition, there were critiques of where BIPOC journalists had been positioned in the newsroom—with few in heavily promoted desks like breaking news or the investigative team.

As with my conversations with WHYY staffers, BIPOC *Inquirer* journalists shared concerns not only about hiring but also about whether they would be given opportunities to advance their careers and encouraged to stay. Some *Inquirer* managers claimed to be aware of the importance of ensuring people "feel valued and are given the space to, to speak and influence things the way that we say we want them to." However, some journalists of color suggested managers were actually reinforcing whiteness in the workplace by not distributing opportunities fairly—for example, repeatedly giving "the same five or six reporters" the "best stories." They suggested this contributed to frustration and turnover as well as to the lack of diverse sourcing. Others referenced a failure to foster a culture of mentorship or "grooming" BIPOC journalists to become editors. Notably, the *Inquirer*'s parent institution the Lenfest Institute for Journalism had started a mentorship program in response to such concerns.[44]

Of the staff that left in the first six months after audit, just under half were BIPOC journalists. Many staff members suggested these departures were disheartening. As one said, while the losses were statistically fairly well distributed and they believed hiring was going well, "What it feels like is we're bailing water." Other managers minimized the significance of BIPOC journalists in particular leaving, applying a colorblind analysis suggesting it was a volatile moment for all journalists and that many of the *Inquirer*'s journalists were being poached. A year later, some acknowledged "we were losing people" and that turnover rates were significantly higher for employees who had been at the organization for five years or less, and even more so if they were BIPOC employees. This contributed to management's move to reformulate their goals, shifting from new hires to looking at the overall composition of the newsroom.[45] While tracking this data and using it internally does have value as an accountability infrastructure, it could be an even more powerful one if the *Inquirer* communicated what it learned publicly.

PAY EQUITY

Pay equity was a key concern raised by staffers we spoke with for our audit. Many shared anecdotes of BIPOC journalists learning they made less than white journalists in similar roles. The *Inquirer* did attempt to respond to these concerns with a pay equity study and as a result made pay adjustments to about fifty-eight employees, though staff satisfaction with the study was mixed. Some of the longstanding disparities were connected to the *Inquirer*'s merger with the *Philadelphia Daily News* and Philly.com in 2016, when the newsrooms were combined and more than forty staffers were laid off as part of the larger Philadelphia Media Network restructuring.[46] As one former *Daily News* staffer told me, this was less a merger than a "takeover," where *Daily News* employees "were told basically to get a box of stuff and go and find a place to sit. . . . It's like walking into your big sister's room who doesn't want you in there really." The *Daily News*, which, many stressed, had comparatively more reporters and editors of color and a reputation of appealing more to BIPOC communities, also had positions that were paid less than colleagues in similar roles at the *Inquirer*. Following the pay equity study, some staffers who had these legacy salary disparities received pay raises. However, others shared examples of BIPOC staff hired at lower rates than white colleagues even in the postaudit period, and the same week the *Inquirer*'s publisher released a letter apologizing to Black communities and Black journalists for past neglect or harm, the *Inquirer*'s trade union, the NewsGuild of Greater Philadelphia, filed a discrimination grievance[47] alleging a Black journalist was paid less than a white journalist in the same position. For many of those I spoke with, efforts on pay equity were appreciated but greater transparency was desired. Here again the grouping of journalists as BIPOC or journalists of color and saying there was no overall disparity was seen as masking disparities that affected Black journalists in particular. This left one staffer to conclude, "They're playing games."

PERFORMANCE REVIEWS

When I spoke with *Inquirer* staffers about how they might incorporate DEIB and community engagement goals into their performance management process, as WHYY did, the frequent reaction was "what performance management process?" To their own admission they had long been trying to rework how they did annual performance reviews, so working in new goals had to be tackled as part of a larger systemic configuration. That said, managers did take the audit's recommendation to do this on board. As one editor explained: "If you can't diversify your team or your stories, then why are we giving you raises and bonuses?"

The performance management system sought to incentivize all editors to meet goals for representation in their content and for integrating DEIB processes into their desks' workflow. As one manager explained, the aim was to create a situation where white editors who were "not on board with antiracism being a core value" would face ongoing questioning of their work: "When you start to experience those things over and over and over again, and they become pain points in your day-to-day job, eventually one of two things happen. Either you change or you opt out, right?" They said either outcome "gets to the end result that I think we're looking for." In this way, the managers pushing toward antiracism were attempting to create a space of productive discomfort for colleagues who had been reinforcing structures of whiteness. While I was not able to verify that any staffers had left explicitly because of discomfort with the *Inquirer*'s antiracism initiatives, I did hear anecdotes from staffers about white veteran reporters choosing to leave journalism entirely after sharing that they did not feel they "belonged" or knew "how to do what I'm being asked to do." They said these sentiments

were multifaceted and connected to discomfort around digital transformation as well as the *Inquirer*'s legacy on race.

Complementing performance review goals around DEIB, managers also
talked about inserting community engagement goals into the performance
management system for several desks, including features and visuals. Goals
were to encourage managers to consult with their staff, brainstorm three
possible engagement ideas, and then select one to begin that year. When I
circled back with managers a year later after their first attempt at performance management, however, the process had not gone as smoothly as
hoped. There were some achievements—first, that they happened at all,
and second, that they had been able to reward "robust participation" in
Inquirer for All groups. But, managers admitted, there were many things
that "did not go well" or were "overcomplicated." As one explained: "What
I don't think we could figure out how to do was how to penalize someone, if you will, for failing to participate in something that is, I think,
appropriately a voluntary program. . . . It seems quite attainable to me to
articulate how somebody's excelling there and pretty fraught to say how
somebody's not—legally fraught, fraught from a Guild point of view, and
just challenging. . . . I don't think we have the structures in place to quantitatively call out lack of progress." They suggested DEIB goals might be
more effective if the organization developed better messaging around
them and if they had quantitative metrics such as from a source diversity
tracking system. Efforts to hold staffers accountable for community
engagement goals were dropped completely. A manager explained that the
editor championing community engagement changed roles, resulting in
"inoperable goals" because "the person who was driving it was no longer
driving it." This latter situation underlines the limitations of institutional
progress on community engagement when it is seen as a niche passion
project rather than a cross-cutting journalistic competency.

The lack of a mechanism to assess staffers who were not active participants in *Inquirer* for All initiatives made it challenging for managers
attempting to gauge who was "on board" with efforts to move toward antiracism. As one manager said, there was "a group of people who are out of

sight"—they did not participate in company activities or meetings and only knew they still worked there by seeing their byline: "That's the group that concerns me most. What's going on? What's the status? Where are you, temperature wise? Are you just on board with all of this, so it's passive support? Or is it passive resistance? That's the piece that I can't tell."[48]

Performance management has the potential to act as a critical accountability infrastructure to push the workplace in the direction of antiracism, to give teeth to stated institutional ambitions and values, and to create an environment nurturing those who embrace these values—and productively uncomfortable for those who do not. But it will take considerable political commitment and imagination to reconfigure a system that has never been used to measure goals that are inherently difficult to quantify in a bureaucratic environment where quantification is seen as essential. Without systems set up, the only functional accountability came from spaces of "external pressure," as one manager explained—meaning "the Twitter-sphere, but also colleagues and town halls and not wanting to get called out." While that kind of accountability had value, they argued, it was not sustainable.

LIMITS OF REPRESENTATION

Reflecting on overall efforts to reshape who was represented in the newsroom, some expressed a feeling of promising if incomplete progress. As one manager expressed, "We're swapping out staff as fast as we can, and, and putting in senior leaders, who are from much, much different viewpoints than the previous regime." Others cautioned that these changes did not necessarily equal a structural shift toward antiracism and that accountability infrastructure would need to be adjusted to make the ongoing work needed sustainable.

One staff member said there were positive hires and promotions of staff taking place, "But if the top level still just stays exactly the same, I don't know if you can kind of fill the ranks beneath you with more thoughtful folks and then have much change." *Inquirer* managers pointed out that the masthead had seen considerable change since the start of 2020 and that non-Hispanic white men were for the first time in a minority. Many noted the promotion of Gabriel Escobar to the top editor position after the previous executive editor resigned following the "Buildings Matter, Too" controversy.[49] Escobar, who had previously occupied the number-two editor position, identified as Latino, having been born in Colombia. But some observers internally and externally questioned whether his promotion could be an indicator of meaningful change: "He was a part of the previous system that had the diversity inclusion issues. So you all promoted him and used identity politics as a way to try to act like there was progress."

Other staffers suggested hiring BIPOC staff, and editors in particular, was a necessary but insufficient step to building an antiracist newsroom: "I don't think that representation is enough. I think if you hire editors of color who've also been trained in the same systems and aren't deeply interrogating them, and also might be in a position where they again are also answering to their bosses and dealing with those dynamics, it just feels like there needs to be more considerations than just simply bringing in more editors of color to have the changes that we would want to see."

Having more BIPOC journalists in the newsrooms does increase the likelihood that more life experiences will be represented that can cumulatively challenge assumptions steeped in whiteness. It could also help challenge a climate where microaggressions[50] (which, as staffers shared with me, were not uncommon) are expected to be tolerated. Staffers suggested this would be helped further by considering intersectional identities beyond race and gender—factors including class and geographic origin. Nevertheless, as a staffer pointed out, a journalist identifying as BIPOC does not guarantee that they will challenge structures that support whiteness in the newsroom. As discussed in earlier sections, orientation toward journalistic norms like objectivity, particularly as it relates to reporting, editing, and community engagement work, can shape how newsroom staff either facilitate or resist moves toward antiracist newsroom practices. The reflections of staff members at the *Inquirer* illustrate how some journalists who would not think of themselves as contributing to systems supporting whiteness may unintentionally do so. For these reasons, accountability infrastructure was needed to support the creation not only of a more diverse but also a more equitable workplace and work culture.

RESOURCES FOR ANTIRACISM IN
AN ERA OF SCARCITY

It's never "What more should we be doing?" or "What should we be doing that we aren't doing?" That's never the question alone. It's "What should we be doing that we aren't doing and what can we stop doing in order to do that?"

As this editor's reflection illustrates, the latitude managers at the *Inquirer* had in deciding what coverage to prioritize was constrained by financial limitations. Like many local and metro newspapers, the *Inquirer* faced huge financial challenges. Over the past ten years, with the collapse of the advertising business model, the *Inquirer* went from a newsroom of 380 full-time staffers to a newsroom of 205. These fiscal realities indisputably necessitated complicated choices about how to allocate journalistic resources. For this reason, when considering the *Inquirer*'s vision to reimagine itself as an antiracist journalism organization, it is critical also to assess how this vision did and did not connect with its vision for itself as a business.

The *Philadelphia Inquirer* operated as a public benefit corporation under the ownership of the Lenfest Institute, who had a stated focus on serving diverse audiences and not simply advertising or clicks. As one manager explained: "We are uniquely positioned as an organization that technically doesn't need to maximize profit. That's not what we're here for because luckily, Lenfest owns us. We have a profit-sharing thing. So any money we make goes back to our employees anyway." Indeed, over the course of my observation an employee shared with me that they had gotten an email saying that because of the paper's profitability in 2021, everyone on staff would get a $6,000 raise.

Nevertheless, many of the *Inquirer*'s staff referenced a tension between stated objectives of appealing to more diverse audiences online when half of the newspaper's revenue came from print ads. The dominant narrative surrounding the business model was that the *Inquirer* was dependent on an aging white suburban print readership. During our audit process, some staffers expressed uncertainty about audience demographics, but managers confirmed that print subscribers did skew older and whiter, though digital readers were actually more likely to be suburban than print readers. As one employee reflected, concerns about the reader base created a hesitancy to be perceived as radical: "The readers who are paying your bills today are not the ones that are going to sustain us long term as an organization, and commitments around antiracism, battling oppression, elevating marginalized groups are often at odds with the perspective of people who are paying your bills today."[51] The combination of the organization's funding structure (and real resource constraints) and the dominant narrative about it acted as an impediment to efforts to transform the organization in the direction of antiracism. Staff members seeking to push the newsroom toward antiracism frequently cited two main areas where they found themselves having to challenge this business model and narrative: (1) how the imagined dependency on a white audience affected the editorial process and (2) how productivity pressures led to "race-neutral" practices that reinforced whiteness.

CHALLENGING THE IMAGINED DEPENDENCY ON A WHITE AUDIENCE

As noted in the discussion of editing practices, assumptions about a white audience led some editors to act as reinforcers of editorial practices that bolstered whiteness. Others emphasized the importance of digital and its comparatively younger and more diverse audience or the need to embrace the segmentation of the audience by topic area or author—something that audience data suggested already was happening. For example, one editor explained how they targeted content to segmented audiences such as Black Twitter: "I really think that if you're conceiving content for everybody, you're conceiving it for no one. And so when you do that, the default in the *Inquirer*'s case is a sixty-year-old white man." However, others suggested that their efforts to appeal to audiences of color were either overlooked or received pushback from editors who acted as reinforcers of a model that centered white subscribers: "It's extremely common to hear editors say, 'Sure, but the reader's not going to understand that.' And then you have to engage with them about who they think the reader is." Indeed, some staffers expressed ambivalence about changing the business model because they believed that appealing to more diverse audiences risked alienating the white suburban subscriber base: "We run the risk of appealing to everybody except for the people who we used to appeal to, because they have interests that are different as well, and they are a community also. And I feel sometimes like we're saying, 'Well, you people had your day.'"

Others argued that such concerns were short-sighted and underlined the need to push revenue models and marketing in the direction of antiracism: "You're still worried about these people who are saying that they're not going to buy the paper because they're tired of your wokeness. . . . We don't respond in a way that says our goal, our ultimate outcome, is to be an antiracist organization. If you are not with us, then leave, and we will build our revenue elsewhere." Some editors suggested the dominant narrative around the business model could be challenged by redefining readership goals not based on demographic categories but by focusing on civic characteristics like being invested in making the city better: "The person who gives a fuck in a civic sense. I think that that applies to what you might consider the traditional white Center City lawyer, *Inquirer* subscriber, but also to any block captain in the city."

Others challenged the dominant narrative about the business model by critiquing the assumption that by "going after Black and Brown communities or targeting your messaging in a way that is more inclusive of Black and Brown communities, you somehow have less access to those who will be subscribers to our paper."[52] Another manager argued that it was "reductive and problematic" to suggest that a subscription-based product wasn't "a good fit" for BIPOC communities: "People pay for what they value and, if there is journalism that they value and that speaks to them, I think people will pay for it. So I see tension between the business model and the mission of serving the public as a whole. I don't know that I see tension between our interest in becoming an antiracist organization and the business model."

This view illustrates the belief shared by several *Inquirer* managers and staffers I spoke with who did not think of antiracism as being linked to anticapitalism and class oppression, despite this being a key contention of many advocates for antiracism, as discussed in the introduction. For example, another manager reflected that while they were familiar with arguments linking antiracism and anticapitalism, they did not have a problem with a "more circumspect" definition of antiracism that was "more about representation and coverage and overlooking communities, and actual racist language and quoting racists."[53] This, they argued, was "a big enough job."

These conversations and the back and forth about what an antiracist business model might look like highlight the challenges of undertaking the goal of antiracism from within a neoliberal framework. The challenges staff made to the dominant narrative that the *Inquirer* was dependent on white audiences also underlined the importance for conversations about antiracism to take place not only on the editorial side of newsrooms but also company-wide, including on the business side of news organizations.

CHALLENGING RACE-NEUTRAL RESPONSES TO PRODUCTIVITY PRESSURES

The other area where resource pressures collided with the desire to shift the newsroom toward antiracism was in the tension staff and managers said they felt between wanting to do their work differently, in a way that centered antiracist practices, and the demand to produce a "daily crush" of content with limited resources. The measures staff took to respond to productivity pressures were largely framed as pragmatic decisions that were race neutral or colorblind. However, when such strategies are made without a critical race lens, particularly in a newsroom that is majority white, practices relying on colorblind ideology can reinforce whiteness in coverage. For example, the need to fill inside pages of the print product, as one manager explained, had historically resulted in many newspapers choosing to run crime briefs or content that came from authorities like the mayor's office without a great deal of supplementary reporting. Such content was likely to amplify the perspective of officials in positions of power and unlikely to offer nuanced representations of BIPOC or other marginalized communities. While *Inquirer* managers suggested they were taking steps to change this particular practice, there were other seemingly race-neutral choices like shifting from covering geographic areas to covering thematic beats. Some staffers observed that, while not the intention, this approach resulted in the overrepresentation of communities and voices that the mostly white staffers were familiar with. Overstretched staff tended to cover what they knew.

Staff members also told me about cases where productivity metrics they were evaluated on posed a barrier to investing time in the more antiracist newsroom practices and processes generated by the *Inquirer* for All initiative. As one reporter worried, even if their manager encouraged them to take the time they needed to pursue antiracist reporting practices or to diversify their sources, "There's only so much your direct manager can do to protect you from what you're being judged for." Top managers suggested that productivity demands at the *Inquirer* were actually modest compared with similar newspapers, but staff suggested their perception of pressures were amplified given a climate of resource scarcity that had recently manifested in a series of buyouts.

Only a small number of *Inquirer* staff had the power to directly challenge the company's business model in terms of its actual revenue strategies. However, the reflections of staff illustrated how journalists did have agency in either challenging or reinforcing the dominant narrative about the business model. The *Inquirer* faces complicated choices about how it will manage finite resources going forward. But the range of orientations these staffers shared illustrates the importance of considering what is possible through an antiracist framework that critically explores assumptions about audience and productivity.

CONCLUSIONS: GUIDING VALUES FOR ANTIRACIST JOURNALISM?

Perhaps one of the biggest challenges to structural shifts at this or other newsrooms was a gap one BIPOC journalist pointed out—that it was difficult to discuss how to improve their journalism when there was not a shared understanding about what the core role of their journalism should be. Expressing good intentions about diversity and inclusion or even taking actions toward an antiracist newsroom would inherently be a piecemeal effort if there was no shared positive definition of what values were guiding their journalism. As one editor explained: "Until we have our identity, answering some of these questions is really hard, and it becomes, 'Wait a minute, last week we said this, but this week we said this.' Who is our audience, what is our purpose?"

Transforming the *Inquirer* into an antiracist news organization would require shifts throughout the organization—from how readership is conceived, to what the reporting and editing process looks like, to how relationships with communities are formed and nourished. The conversations I had with staffers illustrated how doing this work required rethinking "colorblind" practices and norms, like the dominant interpretation of "objectivity," that had the effect of masking racism and overrepresenting white perspectives in narratives that circulated in communication infrastructure theory's storytelling network. But these conversations also revealed a desire for a positive understanding of what values and norms should guide an antiracist newsroom and, in turn, the narratives it shares.

The *Inquirer* for All's voice committee decided that in order to develop a shared understanding of what an antiracist voice for the *Inquirer* looked like, they first needed to try to define the principles and values that guided their work. A committee member explained that they were facing resistance from people who associated antiracism with protest and practices that were antithetical to a distanced, neutral view of "objectivity." For example, they felt that if the *Inquirer* were to be an antiracist organization, it had to be able to label something as racist in a story when appropriate, but they faced opposition from colleagues who considered the application of the label akin to advocacy. The group discussed how they had been trained as journalists, including journalists of color, to uphold rules of journalism that were "really allowing systemic racism to grow." They concluded that "it really boiled down to values. And even saying as a newspaper that we have influence." Responding to this, the group developed a list of guiding principles for the *Inquirer* to consider. They attempted to formulate positions on confronting racism, acknowledging the role journalists play in their communities, and recognizing how journalists are informed by their own life experiences. They also sought to tackle challenging conversations around objectivity norms head-on. Critically, they linked each value with related practices and policies under consideration as part of the *Inquirer* for All initiative.

Conversations I had with staff members underlined an appetite for greater clarity around the *Inquirer*'s values. In an exploratory survey and a series of focus group discussions, staffers were invited to rank a list of possible values for journalism, including respect for democracy, care for communities, pursuit of equity, inclusion of a plurality of demographic and cultural perspectives, and discussion between multiple ideological perspectives. The list of values was overlapping and intended as a jumping-off point for conversation, though the rankings themselves suggested some trends. Respect for democracy and care for communities were both consistently ranked high, with white journalists on average ranking respect for democracy higher and BIPOC journalists on average ranking care for communities higher.[54] Discussions underlined a shared sense of flux when it came to the *Inquirer*'s values. Some suggested the institution had not historically prioritized values such as care for communities, but recent DEI work was attempting to shift that. Many expressed concern that management had not articulated what values the *Inquirer* prioritized, and so it was unsurprising that staff did not have shared goals: "I just want somebody to say, here are the values that we operate on, and nobody ever has."

Managers suggested it would be more beneficial for values to come from ground-up processes such as the DEI committee's effort, rather than having it be "handed down on high tablet-like." Some suggested there were unresolved issues to consider around the degree that the *Inquirer* was reporting *for* and *with* communities across its content: "I also tend to think that conversation can be a little reductive and that an entity like the *Inquirer* can be big enough to hold multiple values and different variations on said values." Others who positioned themselves as proponents of antiracist values and who questioned the way objectivity was deployed suggested the *Inquirer* may have the best chance at success at shifting the institution toward more antiracist values with a "trickle-up" process consisting of "a lot of smaller-term shifts in the way we operate that ultimately solve for the bigger ones." They conceded that the direction and pace of this work could be frustrating for some but that it may offer the most strategic path to structural change. Over a year after our original audit, the *Inquirer* for All's voice committee had internally distributed a statement of "antiracist values." But at the time of writing, management still had not allowed these values to be shared publicly.

* * *

The experiences of the *Inquirer* chronicled in this chapter highlight, in communication infrastructure theory terms, the challenges of shifting narratives circulated by a key actor in the local storytelling network. Their various *Inquirer* for All initiatives showed some promise but also the complexity of developing accountability infrastructure to support antiracist journalism, particularly when what is meant by antiracism is not universally agreed upon and when colorblind ideology is often unchallenged. Unlike WHYY, where efforts grew from a proactive vision, the *Inquirer*'s initial move toward antiracism was prompted by crisis in response to advocacy by BIPOC staff and public pressure. Nevertheless, by devoting considerable institutional heft to an infrastructure to support DEIB labor, they may actually be in a stronger place to make their work sustainable—something that is less certain at WHYY. In the following chapter, I will explore how both the *Inquirer* and WHYY are grappling with the need to make accountability infrastructure sustainable for the longer-term work needed to push local journalism toward antiracism and how they are navigating how they see themselves in relationship with other community and media stakeholders.

3

INSTITUTIONALIZING
ACCOUNTABILITY INFRASTRUCTURE

You've got levers that you're pulling, levers that you need to build, then it feels like there are structural forces that . . . I mean that almost in a literal way, that are leaning against all this work.

—MANAGER REFLECTING ON THE *PHILADELPHIA INQUIRER*'S ANTIRACISM INITIATIVE

D uring the week of February 15, 2022, a year after our initial audit, the *Philadelphia Inquirer* published two stories focused on the local journalism scene. Reporters had interviewed me either on the record or on background for both stories weeks and months prior, but I did not know when they would be coming out. Reading them and watching the conversations that unfolded around them underlined some of the complicated realities any effort to make Philadelphia's news and information built environment more antiracist had to grapple with.

First, on February 15, the investigative reporter Wesley Lowrey published the inaugural story for the *Inquirer*'s More Perfect Union series, entitled "Black City. White Paper."[1] As noted in the previous chapter, Lowrey's piece documented the *Inquirer*'s history with racism and past attempts to account for it. The next day, the *Inquirer*'s publisher, Lisa Hughes, published an apology to Philadelphia's Black community and Black journalists.[2]

Then on February 17, a story came out about a wave of resignations in WHYY's newsroom.[3] The reporter had contacted me, sharing that they estimated that nearly half the newsroom had left since the start of 2021, including several BIPOC journalists. They were looking for perspectives on what explained this. When I spoke with the reporter, I suggested this was a volatile time in journalism, though this did not mean WHYY didn't have real problems it needed to work on to improve retention, as I noted in chapter 1. There were now big questions about how this flux would affect WHYY's ongoing efforts around diversity, equity, inclusion, and belonging (DEIB) and community engagement.

While I had been watching the departure of talented staffers with concern, I was a little surprised that the *Inquirer* had decided to do this story at that moment. I had heard grumbling from some about how the *Inquirer* itself was implicated in this exodus—that several of these staffers had been actively recruited, or, in their words, "poached," by *Inquirer* managers. Others suggested the *Inquirer* too had lost a substantial number of staffers, a point the story acknowledged.

Neither of these stories shared news that was particularly surprising to me. However, in the days that followed, they led to animated discussions of both organizations on social media, particularly Twitter. On the *Inquirer* side, the "Black City, White Paper" article drew criticism from across the ideological spectrum, including from some touting narratives of colorblindness ideology and calling the article things like "left gobbliegook [*sic*]." But the article was also critiqued by the president of the Philadelphia Association of Black Journalists, Ernest Owens, who offered this assessment via a Tweet: "So let me get this straight: This week @PhillyInquirer drops a bombshell report about the history of racism at their publication—publisher later apologizes to the Black community & journalists. Today, they publish a tell-all about similar issues at @WHYYNews. Now this . . ."[4] Owens then retweeted the statement made by the *Inquirer*'s trade union, the News-Guild of Greater Philadelphia,[5] about filing a discrimination grievance against the *Inquirer* for paying a Black staffer less than a less-experienced white colleague in the same role. The NewsGuild tweeted: "We wish publisher Lisa Hughes' actions spoke louder than her carefully penned apology Wednesday to Philadelphia's Black residents and communities and to the *Inquirer*'s Black journalists, past and present."[6] Owens later went on to publish an opinion piece for *Philadelphia* magazine calling the *Inquirer*'s "More Perfect Union" article a "self-congratulatory production," suggesting resources could have better served the community if the *Inquirer* would "simply shut up and execute a plan with community voices and input at the forefront."[7] Owen's critiques underlined the need for more transparent engagement and accountability infrastructure to address the deep well of distrust harbored by many community stakeholders and Black journalists.

Meanwhile, while the story about WHYY led many to share concern about the welfare of the station on social media, many also expressed ire toward the station's CEO, William Marrazzo, after he was quoted saying that despite losing nearly half their newsroom staff they had "been able to replace those people in kind and in some instances with people with a higher skill set." He went on to note that despite turnover, their operating margins "have remained super strong because of audience growth." This led a number of current and former staffers to tweet that this was an illustration of how staff were not valued by C-suite managers. Tweets from several BIPOC former staffers were particularly pointed, with some offering expressions of solidarity to current staffers: "To whom it may concern, your skill set is valuable and greatly appreciated. If not where you are, definitely somewhere else. Get yours."[8] Others were more explicit, saying that they themselves had left WHYY "due to the negligence from upper management" and detailing ways they saw a lack of commitment from top management on DEIB efforts.[9] Marrazzo's statement also drew attention from external observers, like Molly de Aguiar, the head of Independence Public Media Foundation, who tweeted that Marrazzo's statement was "truly terrible and unacceptable."[10] Other Philadelphia area Twitter users suggested WHYY's board should be held accountable for improving the situation for its employees.

The discourses that circulated that week about both news organizations illustrate how both WHYY and the *Inquirer* face complex challenges in looking internally at their own leadership and management structures and looking externally at their relationships with communities. Thinking of communication infrastructure theory's local storytelling networks, the controversies within these newsrooms underscored structural weaknesses that impeded progress on antiracism goals both within the local news organizations as nodes in the storytelling network and in the links connecting them with community stakeholders. These episodes highlighted the need for accountability infrastructure but also possible barriers to sustaining them. In this chapter, I will focus on the experiences of both news organizations as they attempted to institutionalize DEIB and community engagement projects. I will follow up with WHYY in the period following their initial grant-funded cultural competency project, and I will look at how the *Inquirer* has attempted to revise how it structures its DEIB efforts. I will reflect on what the experiences of both organizations suggest regarding accounting for leadership and governance structures and the nexus between organizations and the larger news and information built environment.

WHYY: COMMUNITY ENGAGEMENT AND NEWSROOM RESOURCES

WHYY's vice president for news and civic dialogue, Sandra Clark, and her team positioned community engagement efforts as key pillars in their larger work to push the organization toward antiracism and to better represent the region's communities. But, as I began to explore in chapter 1, the connection between WHYY's community engagement efforts and the day-to-day workings of the newsrooms was not always clear.

The station had undertaken a range of grant-funded initiatives, most prominently the News and Information Community Exchange (NICE) discussed in chapter 1, but also other projects focusing on community events, discussions, and collaborations with "community curators" with deep community networks and with partners such as the city's public library system. These efforts were coordinated by a managing editor for community and engagement and other newly hired outreach and engagement staff, rather than the staff responsible for daily news reporting.

Despite this, WHYY managers emphasized that their larger goal was for community engagement to be integrated into the work of the newsroom as part of their larger ambition of connecting WHYY more deeply to local communities. As one said, "Community engagement is journalism—and so I don't like it when it is framed as 'there's journalism and there's community engagement.'" When COVID permitted in-person work, community engagement staff sat in the center of the newsroom, and the editor was invited to participate in regular editorial meetings. Newsroom staff's interactions and awareness varied considerably, however. Some reporters shared anecdotes of how the community engagement staff had reached out to share sources relevant to stories they were working on: "They just have this database in their brains of humans all over the city." Others expressed frustration that there was a lack of timely communication to the larger newsroom about community engagement initiatives, which they saw as operating in "silos": "There isn't always a great understanding about, well, what does the community engagement team do and how can we work with them? And how can we be part of that and participate?"

While general expressions of interest and goodwill for the NICE project poured forth, newsroom staff, engagement staff, and NICE partners all acknowledged a lack of shared expectations when it came to collaborating. A newsroom staffer explained how productivity pressures complicated their desire to work with community partners: "I am being told, 'You need to get the news out now. Fast, fast, fast, fast.' And then they are being told, 'Well, we want community-based journalism.'" News editors and NICE partners had different expectations for pacing, they explained, meaning it was complicated to pair up WHYY staff reporters with NICE partners, who may not be able to "drop everything" to cover a story at short notice. Members of the community engagement team detailed how they were attempting to build connections with newsroom journalists—for example, by inviting them to come to NICE meetings and lead workshops with partners on journalism and media skills. But staffers on both the reporting side of the newsroom and the community engagement side shared frustrations that more needed to be done to build bridges between NICE and other initiatives and ongoing news operations. While expressing support, a newsroom manager acknowledged, "I think it's going to have some growing pains for a while until we figure out the best way to integrate it."

One of the challenges to integrating the NICE project and community engagement efforts more broadly was concerns around resource availability, turnover, and resulting productivity pressures—as noted by the *Inquirer* article mentioned earlier.[11] While positions were being filled, many reporters and editors complained about feeling spread thin and having less time to spend in communities to produce the "slow-cook stories" when the demand for daily turnaround stories had increased. Some staffers said that given this context, there was a perception of resource tensions between community engagement initiatives focused primarily on events and projects with nontraditional journalists versus "boots-on-the-ground" community-centered news reporting: "What is the reasoning behind putting money or funding into community engagement, rather than kind of bolstering up something like what [name of a BIPOC reporter at WHYY] is doing?" said one staffer. Indeed, some BIPOC newsroom journalists sensed that while they had joined WHYY with the intention of strengthening relationships with BIPOC communities, the current time pressures of their job constrained their ability to follow through on their ambitions. Other newsroom staffers voiced concerns that while these engagement initiatives had value, they risked becoming "a performative thing for funders" if they were not complemented by more reporting resources for WHYY staff. A newsroom editor shared the example of how the engagement editor would raise a story idea in a meeting but would not have enough reporters to follow up. They argued that without more reporting resources, they ran the risk of overpromising what they could deliver to communities:

It's disingenuous . . . to go into a community to say, "Yes, we hear you," and then not have the bodies, and to have to constantly rob Peter to pay Paul in order to get equally important stories out there. We're not picking between a story about a white community and a Black community. Many times we're splitting hairs between, okay, we want to do this story in this Latino community and this story in this Latino community, and today we can't do both because we don't have enough reporters. . . . It's not fair to say to people in Willingboro, or Camden, or Upper Darby's Asian community, or Chinatown, "Yes, we hear you," if then we can't back it up with real journalism.

Sentiments like these dampened the enthusiasm and energy some in the newsroom could direct toward projects like NICE. Some staff members said they wished funders would consider how supporting news production and not just outreach and events could help build relationships with communities. But some managers said they appreciated that funders incentivized engagement that demanded a rethinking of what "real journalism" looked like. They hoped this would challenge "the culture of feeding the beast" and encourage colleagues across the organization to center engagement.

WHYY: SUSTAINABILITY BEYOND THE NEWSROOM

WHYY managers and staff working on community engagement and DEIB initiatives often emphasized that in order for their work to be successful, it would have to shift from time-limited projects to institutionalized practices. They also explained that doing this required support and resources beyond WHYY's newsroom. Ultimately the changes many called for involved challenging an interpretation of public radio's funding model, which centered an imagined white core audience and membership and at times attributed regressive attitudes to them without empirical backing. In addition, if institutional transformation were to be genuinely accountable to communities, the organization would need to consider the status-quo-reinforcing tendencies of public radio's governance structures.

While WHYY as an organization had stated commitments to DEIB goals, multiple staff members expressed a sense that the ambitions emanating from the newsroom were not always matched by other sectors of the organization. For example, staffers shared examples of how they felt their efforts to appeal to BIPOC communities and communities of varying class backgrounds were undercut by marketing and membership efforts that seemed to be targeting older white elites with costly events. One staff member called it the "white dinosaur" problem: They worried that membership strategists continued to chase an aging white elite.[12] In a majority-minority city like Philadelphia there was a much greater opportunity to pursue members of color who were more plentiful and would be around after the dinosaurs died out. But so long as membership devoted its resources to courting the dinosaurs, the rest of the public would have less incentive to connect. Some staffers noted that they knew BIPOC residents who had been members of the station but felt like the station didn't invest in appealing to them. Such concerns illustrate the limitations of public radio membership strategies that focus on major gifts, particularly if they are perceived to be focusing on the same limited pool of donors rather than prioritizing a greater number of smaller donations and building relationships beyond existing donor circles.

A number of WHYY staffers, from a range of demographic backgrounds and positions, also suggested there needed to be more commitment to the goal of antiracist transformation of the organization not only at the level of editor and up in the newsroom but also in different parts of the organization—including up through the executive ranks and board. As one staffer said, "You have to have the people at the very top be committed to this thing in order to make it work."[13] One staff member who identified as Black reflected on how they felt a disconnect between efforts within the newsroom and the larger institution: "In one week, I was greenlit two very Black stories that I definitely wanted to do, and in that same week I was called an affirmative action hire." They noted that the latter statement came from leadership outside the newsroom. This and other allegations of racist and sexist microaggressions outside the newsroom suggested the DEIB training the newsroom undertook multiple times during my observation would potentially be of benefit to employees and managers across WHYY and its executive team and board. In addition, doubts about the commitment of top leadership to community engagement and DEIB work led some to question the sustainability of WHYY's efforts: "I really want to believe this is forever, and that this is not trendy, but I haven't really been given a reason to think that it's not trendy." From the start of my observation, some staffers expressed a feeling that the momentum of this work largely hinged on VP Sandra Clark's continuing to act as an organizational champion of this work, though some also expressed hope that the work was not the "flavor of the month" and had the potential to "persist and become part of the structure of the place."

When I spoke with top managers early in the "cultural competency" work, they expressed a commitment to diversity and inclusion. They explained they had done a survey a few years earlier where they had noted respondents in the region said they thought of WHYY as "white and more upper class." When it came to questions of recruiting and retaining staff of color, one of the managers acknowledged that there was work to be done to make sure the workplace was "welcoming." The manager spoke about possible measures such as mentoring. But the station's CEO used a more colorblind framing: "I don't think the rules used to engage any good employee differ depending upon race. I think where we fall down as management is when we don't follow those rules for everybody. I think it becomes more amplified for a person of color who may worry about whether they are welcomed or not to begin with."[14] With regard to how WHYY's digital and broadcast content reflected the community, he acknowledged room for growth: "Traditionally, there are certain age groups, and there are certain races and ethnicity which have not felt comfortable or welcomed within public media. So, altruistically, we have a challenge to improve upon people's comfort level with us."[15] At the same time, the CEO expressed a concern that these efforts should not "prostitute or compromise on the quality of information." As he explained, "I don't think we should dummy down our production value." While he suggested there were other ways to make content more accessible through outreach and engagement, implicit in his reasoning was an assumption that quality was associated with a white middle-class audience.

The head of the station also mentioned that coverage of diverse communities was valuable not just to connect with those communities but to connect with "our white middle-class audiences" who "have a desire to know more about racial and ethnic minority issues." A focus on the interests of progressive white audiences supported the increased representation of communities of color. At the same time, it also explained some of the concerns raised by journalists who felt coverage of BIPOC communities was more *about* these communities than *for* them.

VP Sandra Clark acknowledged that there were still internal tensions about how to approach the strategic imperative to diversify the stories and perspectives represented in coverage: "There's too much of that walking away with this binary choice of, oh my gosh, if we diversify, we're turning our backs on our core audience. Core audience meaning mostly white people. . . . Oftentimes risk is ascribed to turning our backs on people when no one is saying to do that."[16] For Clark, the risk lay in *not* diversifying content and continuing efforts to make WHYY sound more like the city it purported to serve. She and other managers mentioned hearing from core audience members who appreciated this: "We've seen it even in some of our pledge drives, where people will call in and say, 'I'm supporting WHYY because there's a sound that I haven't heard before. There's a diversity I haven't seen before. And we appreciate that.'"

WHYY: TRANSITION AND TURNOVER

In December of 2021—just before the *Inquirer* reported on newsroom turnover at WHYY—Vice President Sandra Clark announced she was leaving WHYY to become the CEO of StoryCorps, a national nonprofit that preserves and shares oral history "stories of everyday people" on National Public Radio and other platforms. Explaining her decision to leave, Clark contended that hers was not "a great resignation story" but rather an "opportunity that I couldn't say no to came to me."[17] It had not been an easy decision, she explained, given how deeply she cared about the continuance of

WHYY's work to become a more antiracist news organization. She emphasized that she believed this work could continue even though she was leaving: "Usually in so many organizations, it's one or two people who are the drivers of this work. And then once they leave, the work gets left behind. So, I do feel positive that there are people in important places, our newsroom leadership for sure, who are dedicated to continuing this work. And again, part of our process was hiring in people who already get it and who don't require buy-in."

Clark pointed to the practice she had implemented of foregrounding DEIB and cultural competency priorities in job descriptions and interview questions. As a result of this work, she noted, people had been coming to interviews prepared to talk about DEIB work and saying: "I want to work in an organization where we are having Neighbors and Newsroom Summits, where we are doing cultural competency work and diversity work, and where it's institutionalized in a way that people feel like the work is real." She acknowledged that maintaining momentum would hinge on continued leadership: "It matters a lot to have people in high, the highest levels of leadership to make this a priority and to understand the work and to understand how hard it is to do the work. And so I think it's important whoever is my successor is 100 percent committed to doing this work." Clark acknowledged that WHYY had challenges ahead with issues like staff turnover. She suggested there was also more that could be done collaboratively across the organization to introduce accountability infrastructure within areas such as performance reviews and job descriptions. When things are difficult, she argued, the key is "not to walk away from the work, it's to see how do we deepen that accountability."

WHYY's management underlined that sustaining their cultural competency and community engagement work was a goal. As CEO Bill Marrazzo stated, "It is a strategic imperative for us to fulfill our mission, to maintain those programs and to grow them." But in the interim period while Clark's replacement had yet to be hired, several staffers expressed a feeling of uncertainty and vulnerability. While community engagement initiatives like NICE continued to advance their work, other DEIB efforts like source diversity tracking were on shakier ground, because efforts like follow-up meetings with teams to review progress were things Clark had led. Staffers said that that component of the work had been put on pause as they waited for Clark's replacement, a gap that would run from January to July 2022.

Another staffer shared how some of the DEIB work that was continuing, in particular the antiracism training facilitated by the Maynard Institute, revealed limits to the progress that the organization had made. They shared examples of some of the anonymous quotes shared by colleagues, such as: "I don't feel like being white is valued in the newsroom." This left them feeling somewhat demoralized: "It was hard to watch because I felt like we were further along than this."[18] They suggested that Clark's presence in the role of VP had contributed to what they called an "Obama effect," where there was a sense that having a Black person at a high level of leadership obscured the racism that existed and gave a false sense of progress: "Because [Clark] was here and she was doing all this work, that was enough. . . . [But] not everybody was doing the work. . . . People thought that listening to [Clark] speak about it equated to education." To this staffer, the answer was not necessarily more training but rather: "Where the work needs to start is from the top, honestly, because it has to feel like it's important to the company at large." They noted that top executives or other parts of the organization such as marketing had not participated in the training and that the station did not have anyone whose role was dedicated to DEIB in human resources or elsewhere.

Other current and former staffers shared a concern that the cultural competency and community engagement efforts undertaken by the newsroom were not matched or supported by other parts of the organization. They suggested that problematic elements of executive management culture and the institutional structure itself jeopardized the sustainability of work toward antiracism. One staffer summarized, "I just think that among executive leadership, there's a lack of willingness to alter the management culture to better support diverse communities."[19] Multiple staffers shared what they saw as examples of micromanagement by the CEO and other top managers outside the newsroom. They suggested Clark had frequently run into roadblocks to her work as a result: "It just puts up a lot of barriers to do anything, to get a raise, to do a new project, to do a specific kind of project." By creating barriers for newsroom managers, the executive leadership was signaling "a lack of trust and understanding." Some lamented that these barriers contributed to the problems WHYY had with retention: "There are so many great people that work or have worked at WHYY. Just let people do their jobs."

Others pointed to what they saw as inequities in how the newsroom and adjacent initiatives were structured. In recent years, WHYY had acquired and absorbed several digital news operations. Some staffers suggested the current setup was unnecessarily complex and inequitable; for example, outlets such as Billy Penn had not been integrated into the newsroom. The editor of Billy Penn reported directly to the CEO and the head of New Ventures and Enterprises as well as the VP for news. As a result, some suggested Billy Penn felt like a competitor. Others suggested the station should "eliminate all the different project verticals and just have a coherent newsroom." At present, "no one has an incentive to work together." A former staffer shared how they did not realize how "dysfunctional" the newsroom was until they left and began work at another newsroom: "I think that the DEI work and the community engagement work cannot be detached from the overall functioning of the newsroom. . . . It was not a healthy newsroom. It's just there's not enough people, there's not enough coordination. There wasn't a sense of equal investment from people. There was a lot of people doing their own thing . . . there's no common goal. And there's no one keeping track."[20]

A number of staffers and former staffers were particularly critical of the CEO and top management for what they perceived as a lack of investment in the newsroom and its people. Pay, as mentioned, was a key point of contention. Despite some progress as a result of union negotiations, many staffers referenced low salaries and a lack of transparency as demoralizing and a barrier to retention. As one former staffer noted, "I do think it's an issue of if you want to keep capable adults in the newsroom you have to be paying a salary that covers their lives." They noted that while the *Inquirer* distributed $6,000 to staffers as part of their profit sharing, WHYY distributed $200. A staffer referenced this as an example of how WHYY's

CEO had seemed out of touch by treating this amount as a substantial accomplishment; the staffer, by contrast, saw it as covering a family's groceries for a week or possibly two days of daycare. "He just doesn't understand," they concluded. Some also noted that they found it particularly galling to be told that the station lacked funds to give the lowest-paid staff substantial raises when the CEO made $740,000 annually.[21] Others suggested: "I don't care how much [CEO Marrazzo] makes, I care that other people aren't making a living wage. I wouldn't care if he made a million dollars if everybody was paid fairly."[22]

While retaining newsroom staffers was a widely cited challenge, looking across the organization at veteran personnel, a number of staffers shared a concern with the opposite end of the spectrum. There were a number of long-time personnel, they noted, who had been in the building "too long" and were "never going to leave," despite a perception that they seemed "miserable" and were subsequently spreading "that misery around." Some also suggested that the CEO role itself was structurally problematic, in that the CEO was only accountable to the station's board. The self-perpetuating station's board included many who were close to Marrazzo, making critical accountability unlikely, particularly when he had been in the same role for twenty-five years.[23]

For some, such concerns around management, institutional cohesion, and equity presented what they saw as a roadblock to DEIB and community engagement—one that posed a particular challenge for whoever was in the role of VP for news and civic dialogue. They reflected on what they saw as the challenges with the "institutional setup" that Sandra Clark faced in that role:

> There were a lot of really important efforts that were being put forth, but none of them got the investment that they needed to be scalable and to be long-term. There is a lack of long-term investment in this from the top of the organization. And that is the barrier. Until the leadership fully understands and invests in this work, it's not going to be able to transform the newsroom. And that failure to do the DEI work and engagement work in a successful way has ramifications. It's not DEI for its own sake. It's you lose a lot of talent. General morale is low. People don't feel

good about the place where they're working. People feel confused, and now the organization is in crisis.[24]

Others voiced concern that so much hinged on who was in the role of VP for news and civic dialogue and that the sustainability of WHYY's DEIB and community engagement work relied on that role not only championing that work but also troubleshooting larger institutional challenges to it. As one staffer explained, "One thing that [Clark] did well that I didn't realize that she did . . . I knew that it was raining, but [Clark] was like an umbrella."[25] They went on to explain that part of Clark's role had been to shield the newsroom from the micromanagement of station executives and the CEO in particular. Others echoed this sentiment. When Clark's successor, Sarah Glover, was announced,[26] several shared that they were optimistic that she would continue pushing DEIB and community engagement work at WHYY and that she "understands the importance of diversity in the newsroom." But at the same time, they were concerned that without "change in the executive culture" it might not matter who was in that role. As a staffer explained, Glover, who identifies as Black, may do valuable work and institute changes, but they are unlikely to be sustained without institutional shifts: "I think it starts from the top. If it were a priority for everybody, it wouldn't be such a heavy lift from certain people. . . . I think that she was the best pick, but hiring somebody Black but not empowering Black people is a dangerous thing, and it's an unfair thing."

I spoke with CEO Marrazzo about resources, salary, and the challenge of sustaining DEIB and community engagement work after Clark had announced her departure from WHYY. He maintained this work remained a priority but offered a perspective on the newsroom that differed markedly from those that I had heard and would continue to hear from current and former newsroom staffers: "From my perspective resources have been plentiful. The newsroom has been growing quarter over quarter for years. And it's more diverse now than it ever has been."[27] He noted that wages and benefits at WHYY were determined by "internal equity and external competitiveness considerations" and that they drew on "data provided by third-party consultants." This went both for newsroom salaries as well as his own: "The CEO compensation is set by our board of directors using outside advisors. And while I am very well compensated, it's against a very specific set of objectives, performance measures, and is competitive with other CEO positions in like-sized public media and not-for-profit entities." When asked about the issue of retaining newsroom staff, he explained that "the dynamics of the free-market economy" meant it was impossible to prevent people from being "poached" and that "organizations own jobs, people own their careers."

At the time of writing, the new VP of news and civic dialogue was just starting in her new position, and it was too soon to know how she would grapple with the narrative of a newsroom struggling to retain staff, with the challenge of reinvigorating the DEIB work that had been on hold, and with supporting the community engagement work that had been making progress but was not always synchronized with the newsroom as a whole. But as noted by many within and outside the station walls, the situation highlights the challenges of having a public media culture that, while giving latitude to individual initiative, generally offers little in the way of institutional accountability infrastructure. Based on my own observations within public media and conversations with other current and former staffers, this situation is not unique to WHYY. The question remains, however, what other approaches news organizations might try to build more robust accountability infrastructure with a greater potential for sustainability.

INQUIRER: AN INTERNAL ACCOUNTABILITY INFRASTRUCTURE

We're all having these conversations and we're putting in so much work. But at the end of the day, what are we dishing out?

—*INQUIRER* STAFFER ON THE *INQUIRER* FOR ALL PROCESS

The *Inquirer* has undertaken a considerable quantity of work in its push toward the goal of antiracist culture change. Multiple *Inquirer* for All committees had been organized. Over time these had involved as many as eighty staff members, including veteran white editors. As one manager explained, "There's so much structure, so many people, that it keeps going. It's not dependent on the resilience of a single individual." The structure also sought to ensure that work toward antiracism would be prioritized and that the labor of DEIB would not disproportionately fall on journalists of color. This said, as numerous staff members shared with me early in the process, this was not the *Inquirer*'s first DEIB initiative. Many were uncertain that these efforts would yield different results, particularly given what they saw as a lack of trust within the newsroom and because they noted many of the same managers "who have been steering the ship all this time, that have steered us off course" were still in key roles.

One of the most frequent concerns raised was the pace of change and whether the *Inquirer* for All processes that had been established were sustainable. As one staff member shared, "I think that I don't know if it's taking a long time or if this is how long it should be taking to do certain things." Staffers who participated in the various *Inquirer* for All working groups explained that change was slow because of processes that were cautious and deliberate. Participants explained how implementing an intervention such as the Content Consult Slack channel, for example, could have been pushed through faster. But doing so, they believed, would have risked "more instances where people felt personally attacked or objected to the process." Some noted that the work at times felt very bureaucratic in how it went about drafting and building consensus around potential policy shifts: "It's been so frustrating that it's moving slow, but I keep on thinking, well, it's actually trying to be a real policy. . . . I almost feel like this is something where at least maybe even if it's this excess of bureaucracy, it's trying to be a serious part of the core documents for the company, as opposed to just a PR moment."

For some BIPOC journalists, however, this emphasis on policy was a reminder that while they "thought we were a little further along" in the push toward an inclusive newsroom, remedial work was needed:

Corporate America needs structure, right? So we hand you a document, 20,000 documents, about how to treat people. But really it's about humanity, right? It's about seeing Black. It's like every document I put together opens another document that I need to point out that Black people are human too just like you.

You have to put in a policy, or you have to put in a structure for everything that you want changed. That is my biggest frustration, because I'm like, "You know, this has been solved, and why am I working at a place that's still like, 'Oh my God, we need to tell people to ask people how they identify.'" That's so like 1997, to me.

One manager explained, "The pace of change and the expectations around the pace of change is going to be a pain point for the foreseeable future": "You got 190 years versus eight months or six months of serious work. And it's been long and hard and exhausting work in the short amount of time we've been doing it, but you also are accounting for a lot of baggage that comes with the institution."

The "daunting" challenge, the manager suggested, was to get "people to accept that this is just going to be the way that we have to operate for the foreseeable future." As a consultant working with the *Inquirer* for All project explained, *Inquirer* staff need to "recognize that it is a journey, not a destination. It's not something they will necessarily reach, and that's not a failure." They suggested the *Inquirer*'s work toward antiracism was not something that could get "a *Good Housekeeping* seal." And the work would not prevent racism from manifesting in the future: "We'll only know how good it is until we spring a leak in the boat. . . . It's not a matter of if it happens, it's when it's going to happen. And when that happens, what then will be the manifestation of the work?"

As the *Inquirer* sought to transition its *Inquirer* for All DEIB work from a project in response to a crisis to an ongoing part of its operational structure, they began to question what a sustainable structure would look like. Managers conceded that under their initial structure of working groups, "We've asked a lot of people to give a lot." Staff did not receive additional compensation for the many meetings and initiatives they worked on. They were instructed to complete work within their working hours, but many attested this was unrealistic and reported feeling burned out. While some staffers cycled off their working groups, others felt conflicted about doing so, worrying that turnover would further slow the pace of change or that BIPOC staff would be underrepresented.

The *Inquirer*'s effort to create a structure where white journalists took responsibility for doing DEIB labor raises some critical questions. Managers recognized the need for white journalists to do more work to challenge structures that had bolstered whiteness. They also recognized the need for BIPOC journalists to be given the opportunity to step away from this work if they wanted, particularly given it could be intense and potentially retraumatizing. However, a number of staffers raised concerns about having DEI working groups that ended up being all white, given the small percentage of BIPOC newsroom staff. One manager suggested there were workarounds to this challenge: "More white people should be involved in this work anyway, as long as we have avenues in which we're pulling in that feedback from [BIPOC] individuals on a more ad hoc basis without making them draft up policies and putting comments on documents and all those things. I think we can get the feedback from the people of color within our organization without forcing them to be the ones really leading the charge for it." Another BIPOC staffer observed they had actually noticed some white colleagues leaving the working groups "just when people are starting to feel uncomfortable": "People are like, 'Oh, I got to go. Too hard for me. I'm busy.' Well, shit. We're all busy. . . . You don't want to prioritize the needs of half the city you cover. . . . You can't take an hour out of your week to come and help us figure this out and actually be a better person because that's not a priority?"

These reflections highlight the challenge of trying to ensure that the labor of DEIB is equitable in a system where it is voluntary and uncompensated. It required a complex balance of encouraging white journalists to undertake the labor of DEIB work while also working to decenter whiteness and to ensure that these journalists are held accountable to the needs and interests of BIPOC colleagues. All of this was further complicated by a lack of a concrete accountability infrastructure. As discussed in chapter 2, the *Inquirer* had work to do to solidify a process for integrating DEIB goals into performance reviews and goal setting for staffers. As a manager underlined, "It's hard to hold someone accountable if they don't even have a goal plan, right?"

These concerns underline the difficulty of creating shared expectations among staff about the ongoing labor needed to build an antiracist newsroom. When I circled back to managers nearly two years on from their initial *Inquirer* for All set up, they had made some changes to its structure and operations. They had shifted to a "project-based model" where each working group focused on one goal per trimester. This meant if they finished their task in under four months, they would take a break. If not, it would get rolled over to the following trimester. They told me they did this to address concerns that committees had felt overwhelmed trying to do everything at once with no sense of closure. They said the trimester strategy was helping, and while they still had a lot of staff involved (in the range of sixty staffers), they said they saw less turnover in participation than they had previously.

INQUIRER: TRANSITION AND UNFINISHED BUSINESS

Like WHYY, the *Inquirer* also saw turnover within key roles in its *Inquirer* for All work. Notably in June 2022, their vice president for diversity, equity, and inclusion, Jameel Rush, left to take a DEI position with Google. Whereas WHYY's VP Sandra Clark was situated over the newsroom, Rush's leadership on DEIB work was positioned on the business side as a company-wide role steering *Inquirer* for All and other company-wide DEI initiatives. Rush joined the *Inquirer* in December 2020, just as we were completing our initial diversity and inclusion audit. He was there for just a year and a half, but it was a very intense eighteen months in terms of DEIB activity.

I asked Rush what progress he did or did not see during the time he was at the *Inquirer*. He acknowledged a lot remained "unfinished" but that there were "some things that we were starting to get right." He noted that they had made progress around "representation" and "general leadership focus and attention toward DEI." At the same time, "the culture change, that takes a long time, especially with a heavily tenured organization, you just don't get to that in a year and a half." Rush identified some key areas where work was needed including supporting middle management in building their "cultural competency—to understand integrating DEI into everything from editing to just the way they manage people on a day-to-day basis."

Rush acknowledged that more work was needed around pay equity and "codifying the pay structure." This observation explains perceptions recounted by other staffers that more work was needed to establish pay equity across the board, leading to a trickle of NewsGuild discrimination grievances, as well as some who were upset but had not taken formal action. Rush estimated that this and many of the projects they were working on would probably take another year or year and a half "before we could even talk about, okay, 'what's the systemic culture change?'" But Rush was heartened that there did seem to be a shared vision for this work: "Everyone, collectively I think agreed that those things needed to get done. It was just a matter of bandwidth, of when we could get to it."

Rush also noted areas where work had yet to be done but was needed. This included the need to rethink their approach to "the new talent landscape": "We talk often about attrition, but the reality is, I don't know that we've done the work to understand what does 'good' look like for retaining a journalist? . . . What is the ideal number that we say like, all right, we've got the best out of this person and we've given them everything we can give them to set them up for the next stage in their career?" Rush suggested they needed to come to an understanding of what "healthy turnover" looked like—and that it was more likely to be closer to two or four years than fifteen years or more. Indeed, this was a question that many journalism organizations I have spoken with have been grappling with. While journalists decried a lack of retention, there was also muddiness about what goals for employment tenure would be realistic and mutually beneficial. With some at WHYY complaining about the *Inquirer* poaching staff and some at the *Inquirer* complaining about national outlets poaching staff, the question remained: What does a healthy circulation of talent look like? Were there ways to support the circulation of talent to encourage greater equity and opportunity?

Looking at Rush's departure in the larger context of the *Inquirer*'s push toward antiracism, I could not help but compare it to Sandra Clark's departure at WHYY. Both vice presidents played influential roles in their respective institutions' DEIB work. As with Clark, Rush's absence would mean some areas would be on hold until his replacement was brought on board—for example the future of any sort of community advisory council. But the *Inquirer* had built a substantial internal infrastructure and recently hired someone to manage operations of *Inquirer* for All work—would it be enough for the work to continue with limited interruption?[28] As work on community engagement and DEIB efforts evolved at both organizations, I reflected on my initial assumption that reactive, crisis-driven efforts to pursue antiracism would be less fruitful than proactive efforts. My thinking on this would continue to evolve, as I explore in chapter 6, but these developments were nudging me toward the conclusion that the motivations behind DEIB initiatives may be less of a determinant to an initiative's sustainability than how they were structured and the resources invested.

WHYY AND THE *INQUIRER*: DIFFERENT STRUCTURES, SOME SHARED CHALLENGES

WHYY and the *Inquirer* are two very different news organizations. They are different in medium, size, and business structure. Because of these differences, I cannot and do not want to attempt apples-to-apples comparisons between them as institutions. However, the variance in how each approached the issue of establishing accountability infrastructure for antiracism offers insights to consider for organizations interested in institutional transformation. Further, both organizations make significant contributions to Philadelphia's news and information built environment, and as such, it is also valuable to consider how their work contributes to larger efforts to make the system as a whole more equitable and antiracist. In what follows,

I attempt to offer some partial takeaways from my observations of these organizations, both in areas where they have made progress as well as areas of continued struggle.   .

BUILD AND MAINTAIN INFRASTRUCTURE, NOT PROJECTS

Moving journalism toward antiracism is not a goal that can be achieved by a project with a fixed end date. Particularly in institutions that remain majority white, the pursuit of antiracism will always be a work in progress that requires ongoing maintenance. Because of this, there are limits to what can be achieved by a one- or two-year grant-funded project, particularly when said project is focused on the production of deliverables versus the establishment of infrastructure.

The areas where each organizations made the most progress and had the most hope of sustainability were the ones where they were able to develop infrastructure—for example, WHYY's establishment of a source tracking system and performance review goals and the *Inquirer*'s establishment of *Inquirer* for All committees and working groups that also developed processes and tools for internal accountability. But this infrastructure requires maintenance—and maintenance requires sustained resources and support. For this reason, the *Inquirer*, with its sustained support from its owner, the Lenfest Institute, has had some advantages over WHYY, which has relied on short-term grants from a variety of funders.

Additionally, infrastructure comprises human resources, and the sheer number of *Inquirer* staffers participating in *Inquirer* for All (some eighty people since its inception) dwarfed the handful of WHYY staffers who explicitly focused on cultural competency or community engagement efforts. This difference in approach suggests a greater prioritization by the leaders of the *Inquirer* to mandating that management and staff dedicate time to the labor of DEI. Of course, this was bolstered by the support of Lenfest, which allowed the *Inquirer* to hire people with roles specifically devoted to *Inquirer* for All–related work, such as the management of the steering committee and its working groups and the formation of a communities and engagement desk. But even before those roles were in place, compared with WHYY, a considerable investment had been made involving a substantial number of staffers in an ongoing infrastructure with no end date. Critically, the *Inquirer* also deliberately recruited veteran white editors to participate to ensure that labor was not disproportionately shouldered by BIPOC employees, and overall it did more to challenge colorblind ideology by at least setting goals for increasing representation of BIPOC journalists. Of course, the maintenance of infrastructure also requires ongoing political commitment to accountability by leadership—continued progress is neither guaranteed nor necessarily linear (as I will discuss more when discussing developments at the *Inquirer* in chapter 6). Both of these cases underline the importance of organizational leadership and governance structures that incentivize a pursuit of antiracist work.

SHARING POWER REQUIRES IMAGINATION

One of the stickiest challenges both organizations have and continue to grapple with is how to incentivize the sharing of power, let alone the relinquishing of power within their organizations. While the *Inquirer*'s Rush noted there was a lack of shared understanding of what "healthy turnover" looked like, there was even less vision for what healthy power succession could mean. This conversation was conspicuously absent from official discussions within both institutions. This is not to say it was not on the minds of many of the staffers I spoke with. Questions and concerns around how to encourage veteran managers and staff with power to share it, or to step aside, were frequently raised by journalists at both institutions. Staffers I interviewed pondered how this could work for colleagues, be they middle managers or the heads of institutions.

A frequent conundrum raised was whether organizations could create off-ramps to encourage staffers not aligned with visions for more equitable and antiracist organizations to adapt or leave. As one *Inquirer* employee lamented, they did not know what could be done about "people who probably should opt out, and I'm not sure why they don't opt out, because they're not aligned with where the organization is going and are very unhappy like in every way, shape or form. . . . I don't understand why you would be miserable and just sit in it." This sentiment echoed that shared by WHYY staffers who noted the problem of people who opted to spread "misery around" instead of leaving. Similar frustrations were shared within the context of trying to improve accountability infrastructure such as performance reviews and a sense of being flummoxed that overall participation in efforts to make these organizations and their journalism more antiracist was voluntary. Little in the way of "carrot" incentives existed and even fewer punitive "sticks." Staffers' observations reinforced my conclusion that relying on voluntary goodwill efforts is not enough to push toward accountability and meaningful power sharing.

Some conversations did unearth interesting brainstorming around what it might look like to offer off-ramps or alternative pathways to encourage power sharing. We pondered, for example, whether there could be things like rotations of positions—for example, where editors rotated out of their role after a certain term. We even contemplated ideas around term limits for upper management. None of these ideas were explored seriously, given the many barriers they would face—including union regulations and the obvious problem of political will. Similarly, we also had conversations around the need for succession planning within the ranks of top executives. Here both organizations faced different structural realities. As discussed earlier, within public radio the CEO was accountable to a board, but in its present form, staffers suggested that many board members were seen as "friends" with longstanding relationships with the CEO. The *Inquirer* also had a board (as did its noncontrolling owner, the Lenfest Institute), though the *Inquirer* had a relatively new publisher.

Notably, within both organizations, the boards that had formal governance power were distinct from their respective community advisory bodies. Each organization had somewhat different approaches. Like most public radio stations, WHYY had a community advisory board, though the process for which community members could join this board and the backgrounds of its members in terms of race/ethnicity and class were relatively opaque. The *Inquirer*, as mentioned, was considering establishing a community advisory council (though its future was uncertain). Their noncontrolling owners, the Lenfest Institute, had a "Visioning Table" that consisted primarily of BIPOC journalists and media makers in the area. None of these groups had the formal ability to influence questions of accountability or succession. It also was not clear what pathways there were for community members to join such bodies or the extent to which either included or would include perspectives from community members who were not leaders of industry or NGOs. As will be discussed more in chapter 6, neither institution came close to proposals for community-led boards where members are elected by some combination of communities and/or nonmanagement staff. Their lack of accountability infrastructure at the executive level and their lack of succession planning are not uncommon for media organizations but point to a critical barrier to sustaining work that is antiracist and accountable to communities.

"ANTIRACISM" REQUIRES QUESTIONING MARKET-DRIVEN ASSUMPTIONS

While WHYY and the *Inquirer* had different business models, a persistent theme when discussing barriers to antiracist practice and culture change at both places was how each organization conceptualized their "audience." Journalists at both institutions spoke of a perceived dependency to a disproportionately white and wealthier audience as either print subscribers or public radio members. This introduced a hesitance to reform editorial practices that framed stories as *for* white audiences, with coverage of BIPOC issues and communities explained in a way that was *about* them but not for them. At WHYY, staff argued that fears about potentially alienating a white audience were based on assumptions about the white audience and did a disservice to existing and potential BIPOC audiences. At the *Inquirer*, managers and staff also noted a need to clarify goals related to audience, particularly given print versus digital tensions: "Until they get to a place of clarity around audience, all this other stuff is going to just feel like you're constantly tugged in multiple directions no matter where you sit in the organization, and that's CEO on down. . . . The tough thing is that's not going to be decided anytime soon, as long as the money is still so deeply tied to print. They're still another three to five years before they have the flexibility to go in another direction."

Despite their existence within mission-oriented organizational structures, both news organizations were steeped in definitions of "growth" and success tied to a neoliberal market structure. Given that racial inequity has been intertwined with capitalism in the United States since its earliest days, this created an inherent tension for efforts with the stated aim of antiracism. This is not to say that more circumscribed efforts to pursue racial justice and greater equity are not possible within a capitalist framework, but doing so will require the business sides of news organizations to have conversations about what an antiracism business model would mean alongside conversations taking place on the newsroom side of organizations.

To date, at both organizations, these conversations have primarily been piecemeal, centered on particular projects and carving out exceptions for them to allow them to stay consistent to their mission. For example, *Inquirer* editors worked in close consultation with the business side to enable the communities and engagement desk to develop new products such as a free newsletter and SMS service. Likewise, a WHYY staffer monitoring audience traffic to *The 47: Historias Along a Bus Route*, the bilingual Spanish-English series created by a NICE partner, positioned the series as a "loss leader"—having value for their relationships with the Latinx/e community despite having a high resource expenditure and a small audience. But there were also stories at both organizations where staffers saw their newsrooms' goals clashing with the business side. At the *Inquirer*, staffers noted with frustration that the *More Perfect Union* series on racial justice was metered behind a paywall. At WHYY, BIPOC staffers in particular complained about marketing events they saw as tailored to elite and white audiences and about initiatives aiming to support diverse vendors but where they were being asked to do additional labor to nominate potential businesses. Staffers at both organizations spoke of a lack of clarity around how the overall business models of their organizations were synchronized with plans to become antiracist news organizations.

CHANGE REQUIRES COLLABORATION THAT CHALLENGES NORMS

Progress for any one news organization was important, but its impact on antiracist work in the larger news and information built environment of Philadelphia would be limited if in isolation. In communication infrastructure theory (CIT) terms, the narratives coming from an outlet as one node in the storytelling network would be unlikely to reach community members who had either severed ties with the outlet or never tuned in, given their perceptions that the outlet was not "for" them. In addition, some community members avoided local news in the storytelling network in general because of its overall association with negativity. As one employee noted, "People don't necessarily form perspectives about just individual institutions unless they're deeply immersed in the work. So, when I speak to broader community members, they say, 'news media covers Black people this way.'" They went on to describe how the practices of other news outlets, such as using headshots of people accused of crimes, made residents cast all news media in a negative light: "It's an ecosystem of news coverage that does harm to communities, and fixing just one of them isn't going to fix the issue. It does need to be a collective work."

Both WHYY and the *Inquirer* participated in some collaborations with other news outlets, such as via the *Broke in Philly* series run by Resolve Philly, discussed more in chapter 4. But from conversations with staffers as well as external community and media actors, I learned that the organizations had varied approaches to working with community stakeholders and with other local media in the region. WHYY had a history of collaborating with community groups and other local media, and their NICE project centered on collaborating with and supporting community journalists and content creators. As discussed, despite this substantial track record they still faced challenges getting newsroom staffers and station management invested in this work, and some resisted questioning journalism norms and practices such as maintaining an "objective" distance from communities. But conversations suggested that these norms may have been more intractable among *Inquirer* staffers, several of whom shared reservations about working with nonprofessional journalists or collaborating with groups like Resolve Philly, whom they associated with "advocacy." Likewise, I sometimes heard complaints from external community and media actors who said they had faced challenges in trying to partner with the *Inquirer*. An *Inquirer* employee acknowledged that while they had seen some progress in efforts to listen to community stakeholders, they were not sure the *Inquirer* "sees itself in having a role in partnering with other media institutions." While they saw the value and mutual benefit in this, they had been surprised that "there's a level of resistance here that is very strong." Looking at these cases with a CIT lens, when it came to the local storytelling network, there seemed to be more work on strengthening links between the network actors (local media, community organizations, and residents) taking place at WHYY.

BEYOND TWO NEWSROOMS

As I write this, WHYY and the *Inquirer* are both facing critical junctures as they seek to weather moments of transition and to push beyond a series of projects, be they proactive or reactive. Each has attempted to varying degrees, with varying amounts of institutional investment, to build accountability infrastructure to push toward antiracism. But DEIB infrastructure has primarily been internally focused and often not synced with outward-facing community engagement or collaboration efforts. These newsrooms may have made some advances that lessened the influence of colorblind racism on the narratives that they circulated in the local storytelling network, but without strengthening links within the network, they were unlikely to reach the public they sought to connect with. Without these links, these institutions were also not accountable beyond their internal leadership structures—leaving them vulnerable to changes in personnel or internal political winds.

In the chapters that follow, I will look at whether and how external actors in the local community as well as the larger U.S. DEIB space may have the potential to supplement the work of individual newsrooms with broader accountability infrastructure that might help strengthen local storytelling networks. But first I turn to another Philadelphia initiative, Resolve Philly's community newswire service, as it attempts to create an infrastructure within local storytelling networks for collaborative community-centered journalism to circulate between communities and news organizations. I'll explore how this effort may or may not intersect with the efforts of these individual newsrooms and its potential to contribute to more antiracist coverage circulating within the region.

4

IMAGINING A COMMUNITY-CENTERED WIRE SERVICE

Hi. How you doing?"

"Good. What're you guys doing?"

"These are free resource guides. They're part of our Germantown Info Hub project . . ."

On a chilly March afternoon in 2022, the foot traffic on Germantown Avenue was relatively sparse. Maleka Fruean, a community organizer, and Rasheed Ajamu, a community reporter, had set up a table with their project's name, "Germantown Info Hub," emblazoned on a burgundy tablecloth. While passersby were not plentiful, most were curious. As I lingered by the table, I noted how the team members interacted with them with a friendly greeting and a light touch. The table was neatly arranged with a line of community resource guides, which had been compiled and then updated since the start of the pandemic with information on a range of areas such as food, housing, COVID testing, mental health, and unemployment benefits. There was also a place to sign up for the Germantown Info Hub's email newsletter and to respond to their query about what community issues and stories people would like to see reporting on.

While Fruean and Ajamu were working for a community journalism project, their approach drew more heavily from community-organizing strategies than anything taught in a journalism school. Indeed, this was a point frequently remarked on when I took journalism students out to observe them "tabling" and to participate in their outreach efforts. Their interactions were very different from what they'd known of journalists talking to community members while reporting a story. They weren't looking for quotes but instead were focused on building a sense of trust and shared investment in the community. Unlike reporters coming in from outside, they were community members themselves trying to get a better sense of what issues were on people's minds. And they always made a point to offer something first before asking people for anything—in this case offering a printed version of their community resource guide. Students participating in this process often remarked that it felt very different and less extractive than a more transactional approach to reporting and that they were surprised by residents' willingness to share openly about community challenges and possibilities—from negligent landlords and gentrification concerns to ideas for community farming initiatives. They also noted the informality and comfort with which Fruean and Ajamu interacted with residents and how some residents whom they had met before made a point of stopping by to check in.

My reflections on the Info Hub are heavily influenced by my own history, having cofounded the project following a research study on the information needs and assets of the Germantown neighborhood of Philadelphia. As noted in the introduction, this was a majority-Black and mixed-income community where many residents felt mainstream news media had a history of disproportionately negative and racist coverage. Working with a community advisory group and later bringing on a core staff of a community organizer and community reporter, we had started the project with the goal of circulating information relevant to the community inside Germantown, as well as sharing more representative narratives about the community through solutions-oriented stories and collaborations with metro news outlets to help improve relationships between residents and local media.

Since its founding in 2018, the project has gone through a number of shifts and changes, experienced staff turnover, navigated the challenges of building trust with residents with a deep mistrust of media, and grappled with how to evolve when the pandemic forced the team to shift away from the face-to-face discussions and events that had been a mainstay of their work. My own involvement with the project has shifted as well. While I initially was actively involved as a manager of the initiative, I stepped away from day-to-day operations first to act as an advisor helping with funding and fiscal sponsorship operations. Then, at the start of 2022, the Germantown Info Hub project officially became part of Resolve Philly. While I helped navigate this transition, my own involvement since early 2022 has been as an outside researcher with no formal operational responsibilities.

It is from this vantage that I have been following the process of the Germantown Info Hub becoming the first pilot "bureau" in Resolve Philly's developing community newswire service (CNS) project.[1] The project seeks to establish "a network of hyperlocal bureaus that serve neighborhood information needs and also functions as a mechanism for more authentic and accurate community-level coverage." The goal is for each bureau to support nontraditional community journalists and "info captains" in crafting and distributing stories about their communities. Stories would be circulated within the community, but some would also be adapted and fed into a metro-level wire service. The hope is for other bureaus and citywide news organizations to draw from the wire so that they circulate narratives coming from community members—perspectives that they may not be able to access otherwise. Participating news organizations may include some that Resolve already has relationships with. Resolve built a collaborative network of more than twenty local news partners (including the *Philadelphia Inquirer* and WHYY) through its "Broke in Philly" solutions-oriented reporting project, which focused on economic mobility from 2018 to 2023 (the collaborative network continues but was shifting to a new topical focus at the time of writing). Resolve plans for the CNS to focus on communities that have felt excluded from mainstream local news coverage and newsrooms, particularly BIPOC communities. Through this, CNS hopes to address the problems explored in earlier chapters: newsrooms producing coverage *about* but not *for* communities of color, with narratives framed by editors far removed from said communities.

In this chapter, I follow Resolve and the Germantown Info Hub team as they begin to develop this new initiative because it attempts to pursue a vision for a more equitable news and information built environment in the Philadelphia region. I look at how Resolve's goals relate to communication infrastructure theory's (CIT) local storytelling network[2]—particularly relationships between local media, community groups, and residents. I focus on how this intervention might affect the larger news and information built environment by circulating narratives in the storytelling network that are more community centered and seeking to push toward antiracism. To do this, I draw on observations of the Germantown Info Hub and Resolve over the past four years, as well as interviews with project team members. I note how the emerging CNS network may connect between local storytelling networks and what that could mean for residents' sense of multicommunity belonging. I also look at how this work is shaped and made possible by the collaborative infrastructure created by Resolve and collaborative projects that preceded it in Philadelphia and at how the prospects for this work may be affected by relationships with media partners including the *Inquirer* and WHYY, who have a range of expectations regarding journalism norms and collaborative practices. I assess how plans for the CNS address goals for circulating antiracist narratives, how they are informed by Resolve's internal culture, and how they may establish infrastructure to hold local journalism accountable to communities.

AN ANTIRACIST WIRE SERVICE?

While the Germantown Info Hub had been focusing on the information needs of their neighborhood since 2018, the idea for a community newswire service emerged from conversations at Resolve in 2021. The team was reviewing a request for proposals by the Kellogg Foundation for ambitious ten-year projects focused on addressing racial inequality. Resolve's team was brainstorming with other possible collaborators, including the Community College of Philadelphia (CCP) and the New School's Journalism + Design program. As Resolve's cofounder Jean Friedman-Rudovsky explained, they were exploring "what are some really big and bold dreams that we have when it comes to the ease and flow and access to news and information—and how does that really anchor any pursuits of, or any efforts towards racial equity at large?"[3] As they brainstormed, a number of ideas emerged, including what it might look like to have hubs around the city. As Friedman-Rudovsky recalled, "I don't even remember who was like, 'Oh, it's like a wire service, but at the community level.'"

Through their "Equally Informed" initiative, Resolve had already been developing what they called an "Info Hub Captains" network—"a cohort of community leaders that will work with us to identify information needs in the city that we can answer through our text line or through reporting from our Broke in Philly partners." The term "info captain" itself referenced a sense of place, as it connected with a Philadelphia tradition of having "block captains" who organize fellow residents to do things like block cleanups. According to their blog post describing the program, the goal of the Info Hub Captains network was to "provide a sense of community among folks who are already naturally well connected, which will empower Philly residents to tell their stories and provide support for organizations with resources trying to expand their reach."[4] Community leaders who joined as captains were paid a stipend and participated in a range of activities including regular meetings, a workshop series focused on media run in collaboration with CCP and Journalism + Design, and contributing to a community newsletter.

As director of community news and information access, Kristine Villanueva was at the heart of the Info Hub Captains initiative and helped think through how this effort could connect with a community newswire service. As Villanueva explained, their goal was to support existing informal information systems that included everyone from neighborhood organizations, to "aunties and uncles on the block," to young civically engaged people. In many ways, Villanueva's description of these information systems resonates with what communication infrastructure theory would call the local "storytelling network"—which includes both formal community organizations, informal networks of residents, and local media. Talking about the people they sought to support, Villanueva explained: "These are people that people in the neighborhood go to for solid advice or verification or resources for a thing. And it's just like, how do we streamline that and utilize that for more representative storytelling, and addressing other information needs that newsrooms may not be aware of on a very granular level."[5] The community newswire service, then, would complement the work of Info Hub captains. Villanueva explained that the captains could also participate in the CNS by contributing to the bureaus in various ways.

When I first heard about the plan to launch a network of Info Hub captains, I was intrigued. Not only did "Info Hub" resonate with our own Germantown Info Hub project, but the concept of this initiative instantly made me think of how it had potential as an intervention in local storytelling networks. The captains themselves were storytellers in their neighborhood's network—circulating information and narratives about their community and its issues both among networks of residents and community organizations. By supporting these community leaders and supporting their work circulating community information and stories, the project was potentially intervening to help strengthen this network. In addition, when I later learned about Resolve's intention to integrate them into their plans for a community newswire service, I likewise noted how this design followed the logic of communication infrastructure theory by potentially strengthening the links between info captains and local media. Communication infrastructure theory research elsewhere suggests that when residents, community groups, and local media are connected, they tend to circulate shared stories about a community. Where local storytelling networks are more integrated, researchers have found that residents tended to have a stronger sense of belonging and a shared understanding of community issues.[6] Furthermore, because the CNS would look to share stories between its different bureaus, it had the potential to create an infrastructure to bridge between storytelling networks that may have otherwise been bounded by geographic or identity-based divides (see figure 4.1). In this way it bore some resemblance to WHYY's NICE project's work to encourage sharing between partners (as discussed in chapter 1)—though with the potential to simultaneously reach metro-level outlets.

The grant from Kellogg did not come through for Resolve. But the seed of the CNS idea had been planted. Around the same time Resolve was developing their idea, I was working with the Germantown Info Hub team to think about possible next steps as they needed to apply for additional funding and wanted to find a new fiscal sponsor. The Germantown Info Hub was already a partner in the Broke in Philly reporting collaboration and overall had a sense of alignment with Resolve's mission of making journalism more equitable and engaged with communities. Talking with Resolve, we explored possible scenarios to join forces and came to a consensus that we had an opportunity to combine visions—to continue to pursue the mission of the Germantown Info Hub while also beginning to grow roots for what could be the CNS's first pilot bureau. We put together a plan for transition and collaborated on a grant proposal for the Germantown Info Hub to join Resolve and begin to pilot the CNS concept. With

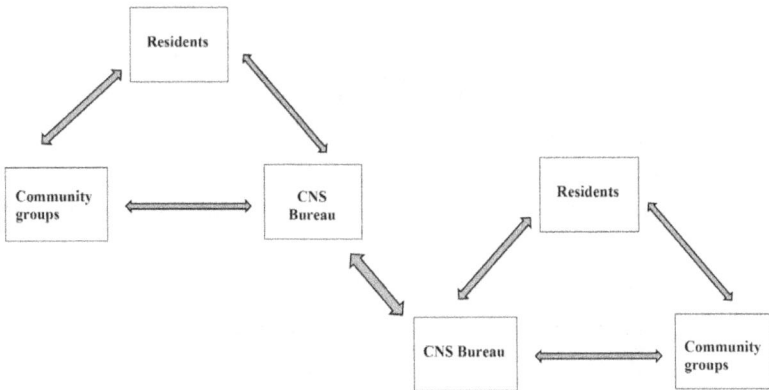

FIGURE 4.1. Bridging between communication infrastructure theory's "storytelling networks."

support from the Independence Public Media Foundation, which had previously supported both the Germantown Info Hub and Resolve, the Germantown team became Resolve staffers at the start of 2022 and began to explore what this new initiative would be.

COLLABORATION THAT CHALLENGES NORMS

As discussed in chapter 3, getting journalists to collaborate with one another or with communities often requires them to set aside some of the dominant norms and practices of the field—particularly ones that prioritized competition and a belief in "objectivity" rooted in a distanced remove from communities.[7] Of course, as Friedman-Rudovsky pointed out, collaboration, particularly in the form of wire services, does have an established history in journalism going back to 1846: "What I like about this model is that in some ways, it is using tried and true methods. The AP [Associated Press] was one of the first experiments in collaborative journalism. So it's like, how do we turn that on its head? How do we use some of those fundamentals that journalists inherently respect and understand and also weave in some of these new philosophies and approaches and the challenges?"[8]

As Resolve sought to weave in new approaches to journalism, Villanueva also spoke of "democratizing journalism" or "demystifying the process of journalism" through the CNS and Info Hub Captains effort. She offered the example of how the Germantown Info Hub as their pilot bureau was beginning to work with an Info Hub captain. They saw it as a way to listen to more sectors of the neighborhood and to expand "the definition of what journalism could be."

Like WHYY's NICE project locally or national initiatives like City Bureau's Documenters program, the CNS and Info Hub Captains work was attempting to expand who gets to participate in acts of journalism.[9] This was a variation of the "citizen journalism" approach disparaged by the veteran journalist I spoke with at the *Philadelphia Inquirer*. In many ways this approach posed a direct challenge to the dominant norm of "objectivity."

Freidman-Rudovsky explained that their work was premised on the idea that "those closest to the neighborhood or communities or issue being covered inherently have a better perspective rather than a worse one." The Germantown Info Hub's community organizer and reporter were "rooted in those communities and therefore are going to do better coverage—rather than the exact opposite, which is what the myth of objectivity and some teachings in journalism school would have you think."

When I spoke with the Germantown Info Hub's reporter and community organizer about how stories from their or other possible CNS bureaus would add to the larger metro news and information built environment, both discussed their positionality, coming from Germantown and identifying as BIPOC, and its relationship to dominant journalism norms. Fruean, the community organizer, immediately honed in on what was added by the proximity of community storytellers: "If you're getting stories in these communities from people who actually live there, their perspective is already going to be different . . . because that person already has a different investment in that community."[10]

Ajamu, the community reporter, noted that in addition to geographic proximity, their intersectional identity shaped the perspective they brought to their work serving a majority-Black and historically marginalized neighborhood: "People say that you're not supposed to bring bias into journalism, but I myself am a Black person. . . . Being the reporter for the Germantown Info Hub adds already a certain layer of antiracism because I am constantly trying to uplift the underdogs in general." Fruean also acknowledged that her investment in the community at times left her with a sense of tension and uncertainty about how to navigate her work as part of the world of "journalism" that "wants to distance itself and be a distant observer."[11] Counter to that dominant interpretation of objectivity, she approached her work as "part of the community," where "this is a story that might affect me and my neighbors." She says in the process of working with Resolve she has been learning how to balance "journalistic ethics" with digging into issues with "deep empathy, deep listening, active listening . . . coming from a place of heart." Notably neither Fruean nor Ajamu came from traditional journalism backgrounds—neither had been employed as journalists for a news organization before their work with the Germantown Info Hub and Resolve.

I was curious how the push and pull between personal investment and journalistic practice that they referenced might play out on the pages of stories produced from CNS bureaus. And I was curious what Resolve's editor Gene Sonn thought about the Germantown Info Hub stories he had begun editing. Sonn came from a background in more traditional newsrooms, including WHYY. But interestingly, when reflecting on Info Hub content, he concluded, "I don't think the underlying reporting is all that different."[12] Sonn noted he had set the ideal of "objectivity" to the side in favor of the goals of "accuracy" and completeness: "I feel much more comfortable striving for 'complete' and 'accurate' than I do 'objective.' Because I think I can come a lot more close to 'fully accurate' and 'fully complete' than I can to fully 'objective.'"

COMMUNITY NEWSWIRE SERVICE
DESIGN AND WORKFLOWS

In a team retreat in early 2022, the staff of Resolve was given an exercise to help think through how the community newswire service would work. Staffers were divided into four groups, each with their own persona—a community member living in Germantown, a listener of WHYY who lives in the Philadelphia suburbs, an editor at a citywide general interest publication, and a reporter in Germantown or another hypothetical bureau. The goal was for each group to consider "what problem could the CNS be solving for": "For example, a problem for a community member in Germantown is that other folks throughout the city may think of them as a stereotype through the lens of the crime coverage. . . . Or the editor at the citywide general interest publication wants to be covering neighborhoods more but is working with a shoestring budget and doesn't have the reporters."[13] The Resolve team was aided in doing this exercise by the fact that they had staffers in the room who aligned with these personas—for example, who were residents of Germantown or from other historically marginalized communities—as well as staffers who had worked as editors for metro-wide outlets. But the structure of the exercise called on staffers to empathize beyond their own identity categories and to think through both challenges and possible solutions. The hope was that this would put a check on the tendency to "go quickly into let's do this and this and this," with "everyone bringing their own conception of how the thing could be."[14]

As the Resolve team worked on the design of the CNS, they emphasized the need for "taking a step back" to think through whom their project would serve and how it could address problems. Through exercises like the one they did at this retreat, they began to identify their focus: "We want to solve the problem of a lack of authentic coverage about communities around Philadelphia. Not just the lack of coverage, but the lack of ease of accessibility of that coverage and of news information." While they emphasized the value in not trying to go "full force" too quickly, they also noted that they intended to try out elements of the initiative even if they were still solidifying the larger plan. As Friedman-Rudovsky explained, "I think a lot of organization's tendency is to feel like they have to get a perfect system in place and then launch everything at once." While she said she also had this tendency, exchanging lessons learned with other heads of organizations led Resolve to an alternate approach: "This model is more like, just test it out. . . . Let's have [Germantown Info Hub's] Rasheed or Maleka write a couple of articles, for a more citywide audience. And let's offer them to a couple of partners and see what we come up against, right? . . . We test things out and then we actually know in real life what are the complications."

Because of their experience working in collaborative journalism, Resolve emphasized the importance of figuring out workflows—what Villanueva called "one of the very unsexy things about journalism."[15] In the case of piloting CNS activities, this might mean figuring out how a story written by a staffer of a bureau would be edited—would the citywide outlet want to edit a story that had already been edited by Resolve editors? How would this work be done—would it be on Google Docs, or would there be complications with that? They knew from past experience that seemingly minor pragmatic challenges could derail an initiative—hence their desire to try out elements and troubleshoot as they refined what the process would look like.

As they had already begun working with the Germantown Info Hub, they were beginning to feel some of this out. As Resolve's editor Sonn explained, as he edited stories he tried to assess "which ones do I think would have legs outside Germantown?" Doing this, and occasionally working with the reporter, Ajamu, to broaden stories to expand who would be interested, left Sonn feeling "more hopeful that there is going to be a lot of opportunity for that" and that "the premise of the community newswire services is actually quite strong." Ajamu similarly was positive about the experience of considering how some stories could connect to residents of other neighborhoods. Several of their examples related to hyperlocal efforts to hold various authorities accountable to the community—including the local postal services and the police. They also mentioned stories exploring questions related to land use and development and how the stories connected with cases in other parts of the city.[16]

Sonn explained that he could draw on a "parallel thought process" from his previous work in public media, where reporters would occasionally produce stories for both local stations and a national network. He suggested that when they expand the wire service in future, they may create a checklist to use during the assignment and story development process to determine whether "going in, do we think this has legs in that way? . . . What do we need to make sure that it'll work?" At the same time, he was clear that CNS had a dual mission and that they were "not envisioning that every single story that they write would go out city-wide." People writing for the bureaus would also need to meet "their neighborhood's needs" and be able to highlight stories that "nobody else [outside the neighborhood] might care about but could be the equivalent of viral in your neighborhood." He didn't want reporters to feel that "I have to write a citywide story, so I'm gonna be a bad journalist in my neighborhood in order to meet that goal." Sonn acknowledged there were inherent "opportunity costs" but hoped to figure out some percentage of stories that could go out citywide: "There isn't a perfect world where we get to do everything. But hopefully, we can find a balance that feels right, that there's a consistent enough flow of stories to the citywide service . . . so that everyone can kind of count on it. But we don't feel like every story has to be done in that mold."[17]

Sonn noted that even though they had not formally launched the CNS, other citywide outlets had already republished some Germantown Info Hub stories. He also noted times the Info Hub had put things "on the agenda" and seen other outlets follow up by reporting stories on the same topic. While the latter may be a "form of flattery," he suggested: "I think what our vision is is that we would get the kind of more traditional outlets familiar enough with the various neighborhood outlets that they wouldn't just parachute in and do their own version of that local story. . . . We could envision [the larger outlets] using [the neighborhood bureau's] story or doing one in partnership together." In this way, the CNS sought to expand the collaborative infrastructure available not only via new bureaus but also for existing news outlets in Philadelphia.

BUILDING ON A
COLLABORATIVE INFRASTRUCTURE

Sitting in Resolve's Broke in Philly collaborative meetings, I was often struck by how some of the smallest details sent powerful messages.[18] The collaborative had more than twenty media partners, ranging from large established outlets to smaller community and ethnic media outlets, all committed to collaboratively reporting on economic mobility. The size and finances of these partners varied greatly, but Resolve as conveners and editors took care to structure the collaborative mindful of power dynamics. For example, during the project's first year, at a partners' meeting around a crowded table at the *Philadelphia Inquirer*, Friedman-Rudovsky started out the meeting by inviting the representative of one of the smallest outlets, a Spanish-language internet radio outlet called Philatinos, to share what they had been working on.[19] This outlet, largely run by one journalist, had the same number of votes in the collaborative as the *Inquirer* or the television station NBC10. And decisions about how to spend the funds available to the collaborative were done by vote—at designated times, a partner or group of partners could suggest an idea and budget for something they wanted to do, and each of us would go around and say "yes" or "no"—or ask questions to clarify what was being proposed. Resolve organizers also emphasized equity over equality in that at times they gave more funds to partners who lacked the resources of larger partners and recognized that participation and what was needed to make it possible would look different for different partners.

The approach to collaboration taken by Resolve builds upon a rich tradition of collaboration successes and failures in Philadelphia. Most directly, Resolve and their Broke in Philly collaborative built upon an earlier initiative they had done called the Reentry Project, which ran from November 2016 to November 2017 and focused on issues facing formerly incarcerated citizens as they reintegrated into society following release from prison.[20] The journalism scholar Magda Konieczna recounted this earlier project, noting how it involved a "stepladder" of collaborative practices including "simple sharing, collaboration on stories, collaborating on method, organizing events, allocating money, and working to resolve a problem in the community."[21] As discussed in the introduction, the Reentry initiative itself took root in a news and information built environment that had seen a number of previous collaborations, some responding to the challenges of digital disruption, as chronicled by C. W. Anderson, as well as a regular series of collaborations connected to mayoral campaigns (a tradition that is continuing ahead of Philadelphia's 2023 mayoral race).[22]

As noted by observers of all of these past collaborations, bringing together media organizations in a field that had traditionally prioritized competition required ongoing relationship building, navigation of power dynamics, and troubleshooting. A significant part of this was the negotiation of workflows, as noted earlier. Different outlets often had their own individual processes and bureaucracies. As discussed in previous chapters, they also adhered to varying degrees to journalism norms and practices such as objectivity—with some remaining skeptical of Resolve's emphasis on connection to communities or their framing of issues in ways that some more traditional journalists perceived to be associated with "advocacy."

As Broke in Philly's editor Gene Sonn explained, even with their existing collaboration among professional news organizations, sharing stories could be complicated. He explained that a lot of content was produced by different partners on the collaboration's theme of economic mobility, but while stories were posted on the project's Broke in Philly homepage, they were only rarely shared directly between partners' outlets. Resolve and its partners were considering whether in the future they may aim for a smaller flow of stories but have those stories be more collectively planned and coordinated.

In some ways, the community newswire service would offer more options for direct sharing of content between the different bureaus, which would potentially bridge hyperlocal storytelling networks. But as noted earlier, the hope was also to share neighborhood-level stories with citywide outlets. Sonn said in some ways this may not be that much harder than content-sharing relationships among existing partners: "Editing stories for the Info Hub has actually made me think that there's less of an obstacle than I imagined." He noted it was primarily a difference of "tone and style"—something that always had to be navigated between outlets. Critically, Sonn was optimistic that there were some positive developments in the Philadelphia news and information built environment—including work planned by the new editor of the *Inquirer*'s communities and engagement desk (discussed in chapter 2)—that could make collaboration efforts "a little bit more fertile." He suggested, "I think timing can be everything . . . having people with open minds in the right positions." As has been noted in earlier chapters, collaborative and community-engaged work for many newsrooms depended on "having the right people." Without those people, collaborative efforts would likely be "grinding it out and having to celebrate very small victories." Reflecting on this, Sonn noted that in some ways this reality presented a bigger challenge for their Broke in Philly collaborative than for the CNS, as the former was more sensitive to "the ups and downs of having people who are believers and people who are just kind of going through the motions. But my hope is that in the community newswire service, the structure will be different. So that that will be less of a factor."

Despite the challenges of managing the expectations and commitments of media partners, members of the Resolve team emphasized that even their imperfect history of collaboration was hugely significant in how it positioned the possibility of tackling something as ambitious as a metro-wide community newswire service. Friedman-Rudovsky, the co–editorial director, called a history of collaboration in an area "a necessary precondition" for tacking a CNS: "It's just going to require the communication flows and trusted relationships that have built up over the last many years. . . . I would have a hard time seeing something like this take shape in a place where there isn't some sort of collaborative process that's been going on for a while."[23]

"GOING AT THE COMMUNITY'S PACE"

Checking in with Resolve's Equally Informed team members in the spring of 2022, one of the events that several mentioned as an example of how CNS bureaus might contribute to larger citywide discussions was a community discussion event being planned in Germantown. In late May, the team organized an in-person community discussion about affordable housing as a collaboration between the Germantown Info Hub, Philly Rent Control Coalition, and Germantown Residents for Economic Alternatives Together. The goal was to bring together Germantown organizers with others working on the issue at a citywide level and to experiment with how a conversation centered in Germantown might explore issues of interest to a broader audience.

I asked the community organizer, Maleka Fruean, what she thought of the event after it took place. She explained that they were largely happy with the discussion but that it was small—with only about ten people. Because of the pandemic, this was their first indoor in-person event as part of Resolve. For context, in the early years of the Germantown Info Hub project, community discussions tended to draw more in the range of thirty to forty people. Fruean acknowledged, "We had to shake the rust off." That meant not only thinking about getting people there on the day but also about how to facilitate a discussion about a complex issue with both citywide and Germantown organizers who didn't know one another. She explained: "I was trying to figure out how to have everyone feel seen and feel heard, but at the same time, I'm realizing, there needs to be micro conversations about very specific topics, laser focused."[24] Fruean shared that while this initial conversation may have been rough around the edges, it was valuable in bringing up a broad range of issues so they could chart out what follow-up would be helpful. She said she was working on organizing follow-up conversations, including one to talk through whether and how they might adapt a project used by organizers on the West Coast that maps eviction data. She explained that as a team they would likely also produce service journalism and other stories exploring elements such as how the zoning process worked and issues related to deeds, deed fraud, and the Fair Housing Act.

Notably, when we spoke, more than a month after the event, these stories were still in development. There had been a number of external factors contributing to this, including COVID cases and holidays, but the timeline did highlight how, unlike some conventional news organizations, the Info Hub was able to allow a longer timeline for stories when needed. As Resolve's Villanueva explained when reflecting on how they worked with community members and community initiatives more broadly, there was a need to go "at the community's pace."[25] Their editor, Sonn, suggested that overall they had not found this to be a problem. Sonn and Ajamu explained that for the Germantown Info Hub they had been aiming for between one and three stories a week and had generally attained that. There were challenges, however, working out priorities and expectations for editing timelines, for example. As Sonn noted, "How far in advance does a story need to be out there for it to have that ability for the neighborhood to be prepared for an event happening at a certain date in a certain time?"[26] There was a sense that the benchmark needed to be rooted in what would be valuable for residents rather than routines and expectations of journalistic productivity. And overall, as had always been the case with the project, the emphasis continued to be less on producing journalistic content than it was on building relationships and facilitating connections between community members.

Over the course of their transition to working with Resolve, I checked in periodically with the Germantown Info Hub team to see how they felt their work was going. About three months into their time with Resolve, I stopped by a tabling event outside a local park, and Ajamu and Fruean were both very positive about their new organizational home. Both noted the value of drawing on more team members and resources. As Fruean noted, "Our small team was good. But this is good because there are people coming from a lot of different journalism backgrounds, and also a lot of different organizing backgrounds. . . . I've been gaining a lot of knowledge from the different people's perspectives." Ajamu agreed and added that one reason this worked so well was because "we're not adapting to them, they're more so adapting to us."

This was not to say there were not challenges. Talking with Fruean six months in, she acknowledged "there's definitely growing pains." The Germantown Info Hub had started as a small community-led project, and they were still trying to figure out how to best integrate it into the larger city-wide work in a way "that makes sense and is conscientious and is able to be organically grown through community engagement." This was compounded by Resolve as an organization experiencing rapid growth. Resolve started out four years prior with a staff of two, then between 2019 and 2022 it grew to a staff of twenty, raising 7 million dollars along the way. Villanueva, who explained that she alone had gone from managing two staffers to managing six over the course of a year, said she had learned a "big lesson" as the Germantown project joined Resolve: "It's hard to do it all at once."[27] She noted that they had really needed the first six months to establish a rhythm of working. The next steps will include establishing how they support the Germantown project within the frame of the larger community newswire service goals—and synthesizing "how does it all fit together" within the larger framework of Equally Informed and Resolve. In the case of the Germantown Info Hub and the CNS, both the pacing required to build and maintain community trust and the pacing required to operate within a growing and increasingly complex organization would take time. Viewed through a communication infrastructure theory lens, this experience underlines how even when an intervention is proceeding with consistent dedication to strengthening ties between storytelling network actors, the process can require patience and ongoing support.

COMMUNITY ACCOUNTABILITY
INFRASTRUCTURE

When I talk with people about how the Germantown Info Hub got started, one of the first things I always mention is how the project was cofounded with a community advisory group. The initial group included residents who had participated in a workshop where we brainstormed how to respond to what we learned from our research study about Germantown's news and information needs and assets. The concept of a "hub" came from ideas raised at the workshop by one of the founding advisory group members, and the shape and form of the project grew from a series of follow-up conversations with group members. As project activities started, we began having first monthly, then bimonthly, meetings. The composition of the group changed. Two of the most active members left after having a falling out with each other related to a local political issue. At the same time, we worked to recruit new members who were connected to parts of the neighborhood beyond the central commercial corridor—particularly in the more marginalized East Germantown.

As a co-organizer of this project, I was aware that I was accurately seen to be an outsider—a white academic not from Philly, let alone Germantown. Adding to that, our project was also associated with two not universally trusted institutions—news media and a major university in the city that some associated with forces of gentrification. Critically, we did have some neighborhood connections through our collaboration with my colleague Professor Marc Lamont Hill and the community space adjacent to his Uncle Bobbie's bookstore and café. And as the project grew, the Info Hub's two full-time staffers came from the neighborhood. Nevertheless, from the start, I was eager for the project to have a mechanism to ensure that it was responding to an agenda set by residents who represented a range of intersectional identities in the neighborhood, particularly regarding race and class, and who were connected to community issues and assets. I was hopeful that an advisory group could be this accountability mechanism, in conjunction with regular face-to-face outreach and sharing information and soliciting input via an SMS texting service. In its early days, the advisory group did shape the direction of project activities—for example, it would never have occurred to me to organize a community event about trash and sanitation, but the advisory group knew this issue touched on critical dynamics related to disinvestment, gentrification and development, and local politics. The result was a vibrant and packed community discussion.

Because of the early role of the advisory group, I was a bit saddened when Fruean, the community organizer, updated me on their activity: "It just wasn't working."[28] This is not to say I was entirely surprised to learn they were not currently active. Despite our ambitions to move toward shared governance of the project, keeping momentum with the group had always been challenging. Some group members had heavy workloads running community organizations or local businesses. The pandemic brought new stresses and the need to shift to virtual meetings. Fruean explained that in the past several months when they would put a call out for input from advisory group members, they had only heard back from "a couple people here and there." She even thought some may have moved away from Germantown. "The people themselves are working in their own capacity," she explained, but as an advisory group, "it just wasn't clicking." Fruean noted that advisory group members were busy and also needed more regular pay. While in the past the Germantown Info Hub had paid modest honorariums to advisory group members whenever grant funds allowed, our process was somewhat irregular and insufficient given the demands on their time. Because of this combination of factors, Fruean and Ajamu decided they needed a new approach. Instead of inviting advisory group members for regular meetings, they would instead organize open monthly check-ins, which could be in-person outdoors or virtual and might be either informal conversations or more structured community discussions. This would be open not only to advisory group members but others who might be interested as well. Fruean suggested this would allow them to have "as many voices as possible to try to add to the conversation." And Ajamu observed that their first attempt at doing this virtually had yielded good insights into what people were working on, "how they're showing up in the community," and what reporting they wanted to see. They particularly appreciated that it did not feel extractive, as people who would have otherwise connected were doing so through the Zoom call.

Despite the team's current shift in approach, they and their Resolve colleagues are still interested in exploring how a community advisory group or equivalent structure could be more successful.[29] In addition to more regular pay, we discussed the importance of establishing clearer expectations up front, both about what participation entails and how a journalism project worked. Ajamu noted that in the past they had encountered difficulties not necessarily with advisory group members but more generally from people with "agendas" who want to be involved but had mismatched expectations: "I don't think an agenda is wrong. I just think that people have to realize that I can't report on, you know, your store having a sale or something of that sort." A revitalized advisory group could include an opportunity for residents to learn about the journalistic process in a way that was "mutually beneficial." Villanueva shared that they had also begun thinking about how advisory groups could represent a wider spectrum of community experiences, "particular lived experiences that are not really reflected well in media" such as "people experiencing homelessness, people who are trying to overcome addiction, things like that." When I reached out to some advisory group members, they echoed the importance of continuing to expand group membership to include of a broader swath of the neighborhood—including key demographic groups such as youth, who were likely to be affected by violence. They also underlined the need for more consistent outreach and for paying participants when possible. One member noted that while the group was focused on information, it had the potential to go beyond amplifying "talk." As they explained, "We need some action." They suggested the Info Hub could assist by offering a space for organizing and coming up with new ideas for addressing key concerns such as gun violence and gentrification-related displacement.

COMMUNITY-CENTERED
COVERAGE AS ANTIRACISM

Whatever form of accountability infrastructure Resolve's CNS pursues, the Germantown Info Hub team and their Resolve colleagues are clear that accountability to the community must guide their work. Resolve is not only making an intervention in communication infrastructure theory's local storytelling network by connecting local media and community stakeholders. It is also working to potentially strengthen these ties by establishing accountability infrastructure to hold the network actors with comparative power (itself and other local media) responsible for addressing the needs and concerns of those with less (historically marginalized community members). Notably, Fruean conceives of this work of accountability through a lens of antiracism: "Germantown is a predominantly Black neighborhood; if we have more Black voices at the table, saying, 'this is what stories we want to hear. These are the stories we want to connect on.' That in itself is a good start. . . . But then to continue on that path, you need to listen to the voices."[30]

Fruean explicitly challenged journalism norms that conceptualized audiences through race-neutral colorblind framings. In addition, being responsive to community needs and interests meant appreciating the complexity of the majority-Black neighborhood, which was not monolithic. For example, she explained, some residents wanted to learn more about gun violence, but others were tired of hearing about gun violence and wanted to hear about "what kids are doing." Fruean's challenge was to find ways to acknowledge and respect both perspectives. "Direct community engagement" for her was more meaningful than putting out a statement about being antiracist as a news outlet: "I don't want journalism to turn it into some performative act. I need it to be something real."

Ajamu also saw the project as contributing to antiracism by providing narratives that offered a fuller range of intersectional representations. They had empathy for the residents that Fruean noted wanted an alternative to gun violence coverage: "I don't like to report on gun violence. . . . And that's not me running away from it. It's just that I have to deal with it on my own everyday anyway."[31] Ajamu said they sought to offer a wide range of stories featuring Black, Brown, and queer people and countering fatphobia, transphobia, and homophobia, which they noted were "all derived from white supremacy as well—so whenever you do work around any of those things, I think you're doing antiracist work without necessarily knowing it." They argued that covering positive and solutions-oriented stories from the community—be it about community fridges or urban farming—offered an important counter to what residents found in "mainstream reporting" and was actually more accurate. "Taking time to understand that everything that bleeds doesn't necessarily have to lead is like antiracism work in itself," Ajamu argued.

When making editorial decisions, Ajamu and others at Resolve's Equally Informed team centered BIPOC residents, their needs, and interests. This affected what stories got covered and prioritized and what narratives they in turn circulated in the local storytelling network. Ajamu offered the example of a story about decriminalization and clinics set up to expunge the records of people with marijuana charges. They noted how for that story they wanted to make sure it went out both in print online and on their radio program—"specifically things that are going to affect Black and Brown folks more, we need to make sure the reach is as far as it can be." Villanueva, the project editor, contrasted Resolve's approach with that of other news organizations. She offered the example of how a news outlet chose not to cover the presence of a white nationalist extremist group at a rally in Philadelphia because, as a staffer at the outlet told her, it did not get violent. She explained that she had been hearing concerns about the group from fellow Filipinos who felt threatened by their presence. She noted that had the outlet centered the concerns of BIPOC residents who faced a greater risk from the group, they may have made different choices: "Once you start centering their specific needs and experiences, then you actually look at it much differently."[32] While she understood a rationale of not covering the group to avoid amplifying their voices, she explained that it could have been framed in a way that centered the concerns of people of color, letting them know, "Hey, this is potentially dangerous for you, maybe you should consider not being here." Helping more vulnerable residents make choices that affected their safety imposed a fundamentally different frame, she argued—one that could include violence prevention. She offered another example of how newsrooms covered events that had a high risk of gun violence, suggesting journalists should "help people make more informed decisions about what they're participating in" and potentially "hold city officials accountable for the way that they set up these very public, very big events."

For Villanueva, the work Equally Informed was doing was "inherently antiracist" because it was advocating for equity and access and working for "people of color being able to better advocate for themselves or make more informed choices." This shaped the information and stories the Germantown Info Hub and others within Resolve's Equally Informed project chose to cover, as well as how they worked to make sure residents could access information and participate in discussions about it. Equally Informed did not have to navigate the challenges shared by journalists at the *Inquirer* or WHYY, who felt fiscally beholden to disproportionately white audiences and, as discussed in earlier chapters, made assumptions about what those audiences wanted. With financial support coming from foundations committed to BIPOC information needs, Resolve's Equally Informed could adhere to its mission and produce content *for* BIPOC communities, not only about them. This allows the project to challenge colorblind ideology and better meet those communities' information needs. Once the community newswire service is underway, it also has the potential to amplify content that is responsive to BIPOC communities to wider audiences in local storytelling networks via media partners.

AN ANTIRACIST WORKPLACE CULTURE?

As earlier chapters explored, many news organizations have struggled to match their intentions to make more equitable and antiracist journalism with the internal cultures of their workplaces. At the *Inquirer* and WHYY, staffers, especially BIPOC journalists, shared experiences where their desire to meet the needs of communities ran up against editorial and management decisions that centered white perspectives and audiences. Workplace culture and practices, which were often infused with colorblind ideology, limited the organizations' work to circulate more antiracist narratives or strengthen links within the local storytelling network. I was curious how this may be similar or different within Resolve, as a relatively new organization that was explicitly founded to pursue issues of equity.

As noted, Resolve has experienced considerable growth. At the time of writing, its staff included people with a range of lived experiences and identities: "queer, non-binary, former incarceration, former houselessness, first-generation immigrant, second-generation immigrant, Black, Latinx/e, AAPI, English as a second language, growing up with extreme financial insecurity, and people at the senior leadership level who have not completed college."[33] The organization followed a co-leadership model, led by cofounders and co–executive directors Jean Friedman-Rudovsky and Cassie Haynes. As co-EDs, Friedman-Rudovsky and Haynes have worked to build what they call an "equitable structure" that attempts to infuse DEIB not only in how they think about representation in their content or staffing numbers but also by focusing on the "policies, people practices, and workflow that enable *real* equity in a newsroom."[34] They have spoken and written publicly about how they have developed policies around things like unlimited paid time off, paid medical leave, and a workplace culture where people were encouraged to do things like book therapy appointments or other wellness practices during work hours.

When I spoke with staffers, many mentioned how the work culture had a sense of intentionality about how people were treated. While there were managers and teams, a relatively new staffer noted that it did not feel hierarchical: "We see everybody kind of on the same level." Another noted that Resolve had an ethos of paying attention to *how* people worked: "The way that we do stuff at Resolve requires more time and attention. . . . So it's like, 'This person works best in this way. How can I shift the way that I work with them so that we can work more symbiotically together?'" Many mentioned how the culture was influenced by having personnel coming from a range of professional backgrounds. While some were seasoned journalists who had previously worked for more traditional newsrooms, others came from community organizing backgrounds or local government. For many, Resolve was their first experience working in the world of journalism, meaning they did not need to unlearn dominant journalism norms and practices that acted as barriers to antiracism work in some newsrooms. One staffer remarked that "even the traditional journalists are saying, 'We know there's something that is not exactly right about [traditional journalism practices].'"

The pairing of Resolve's editor Gene Sonn and Germantown Info Hub's reporter Rasheed Ajamu was an example of the organization's juxtaposition of personnel with established newsroom experience and personnel with varied professional and lived experience outside journalism. Ajamu had never worked as a journalist before the Germantown Info Hub, while Sonn was a veteran editor. But Ajamu noted that "the same way that [Sonn] challenges me, I challenged [Sonn]." They explained that there were times where they used language or drew on contexts based on their identity that were unfamiliar to Sonn: "He's easily teachable the same way I'm easily teachable, and we can have those conversations." Ajamu said they valued Sonn's perspective and gave an example of how they sought out his input when working on a sensitive story: "I can trust him with my work, and I can trust him with guiding me the right way."

All of this is not to say that there were no challenging issues within Resolve's workplace culture or that issues of cultural competency did not arise. In one of the virtual meetings I sat in on for Info Hub captains and Resolve staff, there was a conversation that illustrated both how easily potential microaggressions can arise but also what it means to create a culture where they can be neutralized. Before the business of the meeting got underway, there was a lighthearted conversation about food. Afterward, Ajamu noted how African American Vernacular English terms had been used in the conversation: "I don't necessarily always feel comfortable with non-Black people saying stuff like that. But it was also brought to the group by a Black man, right. And so then [the non-Black staffers] also shared their experiences about how they heard it." Ajamu noted that there was a

subtext to one of the terms the group discussed associated with homophobia, "but I didn't bring that into the space, because that wasn't their understanding. And sometimes you also have to know when to just let people
enjoy things and when to actually speak up. . . . Sometimes people can just
learn things on their own." Ajamu said when the conversation began, they
felt uncomfortable about it, but by the end of it they felt better, largely
because of their sense that this was a group of Resolve staffers and community members who had cultivated a deep rapport and mutual respect across
lines of difference: "That is the relationship that they built with each
other. And you can't tell people how to have relationships with one another.
You can't tell people what their level of comfort should be with other folks,
so you have to sometimes know when to step back and when to step up.
And nobody in that conversation felt microaggressed, so there was no reason for me to have to say anything."[35] This anecdote highlights the complexity of having diverse groups of staffers and community members
building relationships. Staffers and other stakeholders have to navigate
expectations and thresholds for what is considered appropriate and comfortable as new configurations of people are brought into a circle of trust.

For Ajamu, what really mattered was that they felt that if this had been
a situation where they had wanted to speak up, they would have felt
comfortable doing so to Resolve colleagues. They noted they had seen an
example of a colleague who spoke out about a more substantive concern
related to decision making. The organization's leadership responded by
addressing it openly. After watching the co-EDs respond, Ajamu noted that
"the fact that [they] took the time to actually explain, and to listen, not to
just speak, but to listen to their actual concerns. Like it just spoke miles to
me, because a lot of people wouldn't do that."

Because I have focused primarily on the team involved with the community newswire service, I cannot draw conclusions about the totality of
the Resolve organization. I also have to note that staffers may have hesitated sharing particularly critical feedback with me about the co-EDs
because I am seen to be a collaborator and friend to them. This said, based
on observations and unsolicited feedback shared by staffers, my understanding is that while the organization does grapple with growing pains, overall

they have managed to integrate their stated commitment to equity into their workplace culture. Any heterogeneous workplace where staffers hold intersectional identities will always require a dynamic negotiation of difference as colleagues with varied backgrounds and cultural competencies come and go. But at least in my limited observations, people created a climate that valued this work and showed a commitment to syncing goals for equity within the larger system with equitable workplace practices and culture.

PLACE-BASED INFRASTRUCTURE FOR EQUITY

The pursuit of equity and a commitment to communities was a cross-cutting value across both Resolve's internal and external work. As a start-up journalism support organization, unlike the established news organizations discussed in earlier chapters, Resolve had the opportunity to design infrastructure from scratch to support their mission across their various projects. But because most of Resolve's projects are place-based, with a Philadelphia focus, these infrastructures for collaboration and accountability have begun to become layered and intertwined—presenting both opportunities and challenges.

Given their focus on the Philadelphia region, many of Resolve's projects have involved building relationships with some of the same media and community stakeholders. This can offer advantages. For example, trust built between a community organization and Resolve during Equally Informed's work on COVID-19 information could potentially transfer to their work with Info Hub captains or the community newswire service. Similarly, trust built between Resolve and media outlets partnering on the Broke in Philly collaborative could in future offer a jumping-off point to build relationships between community newswire service bureaus and these citywide outlets. Of course, this also means that trust gaps and points of friction in these relationships also have the potential to spill over across projects. So, for example, *Inquirer* staffers who told me they were skeptical about working with Resolve given perceptions of advocacy around Broke in Philly and other projects would potentially need to be won over to secure their investment in the community newswire service.

At the same time, Resolve can capitalize on new infrastructure it may build via the community newswire service to potentially fortify multiple projects. For example, their plans to develop community advisory groups to support CNS bureaus could provide an accountability function for other projects, such as its reporting collaborative (formerly Broke in Philly) and its media partners. As an illustration of one possible function of such groups, in the early days of the Germantown Info Hub project, the project hosted a series of "accountability conversations" where community members were invited to discuss a community issue using an article or series of articles from local media outlets as discussion starters. Community advisory group members facilitated small group conversations that included both residents and journalists who were involved in writing and editing the stories. Residents offered feedback on the stories and brainstormed questions and angles they wanted to see explored more, while also getting a glimpse into the reporting process. The forums provided opportunities for residents working on community issues to build relationships with one another and with local journalists. This is just one example of how community advisory groups can both hold local media accountable and start to build more constructive relationships.

At the start of 2023, the community newswire service remained in a nascent phase. Its first bureau, the Germantown Info Hub, had developed a workflow as part of Resolve's Equally Informed project and had begun to look ahead for how to share content about the neighborhood beyond the neighborhood. Many questions remained that would still need to be tackled to fully launch the CNS. The big one, noted Resolve's editor, Sonn, was how to develop other bureaus: "You don't want it to be a franchise model." The bureaus needed to be developed "with the needs of that neighborhood in mind" but also to do so in a way that it can be integrated into a larger network: "Not seeing it as 'Okay, we're just going to copy Germantown Info Hub in lots of different neighborhoods' but like "What are the strengths of Germantown Info Hub? . . . What are the unique and nonunique things about Germantown that led to that?' And then hopefully, we can figure out . . . how to do that same kind of building from the ground up."[36]

Friedman-Rudovsky also noted the need to be open to "different kinds of structures and models" for different bureaus. She suggested they could potentially collaborate with other community-centered journalism organizations to act as future bureaus without those organizations becoming part of Resolve. She noted the example of *Kensington Voice*, which has been a collaborator and partner with Resolve as well as with WHYY and the *Inquirer*. Likewise, she noted that there could also be bureaus where there is no "standing news operation" but where the collaboration is anchored on Info Hub captains and/or relationships with other community organizations.

This openness to building upon both neighborhood needs and assets resonates with the process model used to develop the Germantown Info Hub, which I detailed in my previous book, *Community-Centered Journalism*. The basic concept was to start with some sort of formative research about the community's needs and assets, then to collaboratively co-design interventions with community and media stakeholders in response. Such a model invites different actors in communication infrastructure theory's storytelling network to participate in a process that may allow them to develop a shared understanding of community issues and greater agency in addressing them. By challenging colorblind ideology and centering equity and antiracism in their application of this model, organizations such as Resolve have the potential to help local storytelling networks integrate BIPOC community stakeholders and circulate antiracist narratives.

COMMUNITY PACING AND
ORGANIZATIONAL CAPACITY

About six months into the Germantown Info Hub's time with Resolve as the pilot bureau in the planned community newswire service, the leadership of Resolve made a decision to adjust the CNS project's timeline. The cumulative effect of the pandemic and delays in filling critical management positions was taking a toll, combined with the weight of several time-sensitive projects with deliverables promised to community and newsroom partners. Resolve decided that rather than pushing toward their original goal of opening a new CNS bureau at the end of 2022, they would slow down their process. While the Germantown Info Hub's work would continue, Resolve decided to put strategic planning on where the next bureaus would go on hold. "We are all 100 percent dedicated to and excited to make this happen in Philly. But we realized we can't do it on our original timeline."

While this adjustment illustrates the challenges that can come from undertaking this work as part of a burgeoning start-up, the new timeframe had some advantages as well. Resolve's citywide reporting collaborative Broke in Philly was in the process of transitioning from its current project, focused on economic mobility, into its next iteration. To do this, project partners and Resolve staff were undertaking a planning process to brainstorm what came next. By slowing the CNS's timeline, they could synchronize planning for Broke in Philly with planning for the CNS—allowing them to potentially get more input and investment from external project partners. The delayed timeline may also allow them to incorporate community input via additional collaborative research I am coordinating to explore and pilot models for community accountability infrastructure with several local partners.[37]

Beyond Resolve's internal organizational timeline, there is also the timeline noted previously as moving at the "community's pace." While the only community currently engaged in the work of CNS is Germantown, it will be critical that adjustments to plans continue to be responsive to the needs and expectations of community stakeholders. Ajamu noted that so far Resolve has demonstrated a commitment to this: "Resolve has 100 percent been putting their time and effort into making sure that people understand that they're not just in their communities for like a photo op." They emphasized that the organization did seem dedicated to long-term relationship building and focusing on "how can we show up for you? . . . They're not coming in and assuming anything, they're asking them, how can we help?"[38]

Fruean noted that this sort of long-term showing up was going to be critical given the deep distrust she encountered in her work. For many residents she met at meetings, cynicism was entrenched for valid reasons: "It's like, 'Oh, the council persons here, because there's a primary coming up.' 'Oh, the journalist is here, because they want to get a quick story on this.' . . . There's never a follow-up. There's never organic, actual connection to what people are actually doing."[39] Countering this and building trust, Fruean argued, would not be a quick fix: "Sorry, foundations [who fund this work], it's not going to be broken down in a year, it's not going to be broken down in two years. It is something that's going to have to be worked on over and over and over again." For the Germantown Info Hub team, a slow pace was not necessarily a bad thing so long as it was sustained. Of course, as Fruean's reference to philanthropic foundation timelines hints, this sort of time can be a luxury not all projects can afford. The Germantown Info Hub was given a two-year on-ramp through support from the Independence Public Media Foundation. But longer-term sustainability will depend on Resolve's ongoing commitment to and success in seeking financing for this work, which at present hinges entirely on philanthropy.

* * *

It is too soon to know the scope of Resolve's vision for a community newswire service and the extent to which the stories coming from its bureaus will circulate in local storytelling networks. But just listening to Ajamu talk about the stories they were working on, for example, thinking about parallels in how West Philly and Germantown grappled with vacant lots at the neighborhood level, it was clear that seeds were being planted that might in future further a sense of multicommunity belonging and bridging between hyperlocal storytelling networks. With some parallels with the NICE project, the CNS initiative was setting out to create coverage both *for* and *about* communities in a way fundamentally different from traditional metro coverage models. Yes, there was a possibility that audiences at majority-white general interest outlets could in the future access these stories, and those audiences could potentially include traditional power holders in the city, who are often imagined as having the agency needed to make change. But CNS bureaus would also be imagining audiences connected with other CNS bureaus, who may be similarly marginalized. In this case there was the potential for a horizontal exchange of solutions-oriented narratives and perhaps the beginning of bridges between storytelling networks, a first step in the direction of shared belonging or alliance building.

In the chapter that follows, I will turn to another possible future CNS bureau, the community journalism organization *Kensington Voice*. I will explore how their experience raises questions around the interconnectivity of the local news and information built environment, how it is funded, and what community advisory and accountability infrastructure with teeth might look like.

5

IMAGINING COMMUNITY-GOVERNED SERVICE JOURNALISM

This is a space that's like extremely in progress." On a hot July day in 2022, Jillian Bauer-Reese was giving me a tour of *Kensington Voice*'s new office space, located in an old carpet mill. Entering through a bright pink door emblazoned with their pink and orange bullhorn logo, I was a little shocked by its size. Bauer-Reese explained that it was roughly 1,800 square feet, but the high ceilings made it feel even bigger. Pointing to the factory windows, she noted, "We're very slowly working on cleaning them and trimming them in white paint so that the place feels clean and safe. And . . . more inspiring or whatever, so people are inspired to make change."

Even as a work in progress, the space, shaped like a U, had clearly been thought through with attention to detail and a vision for the work *Kensington Voice* was planning beyond publishing community journalism online and in print. The lounge area had inviting upholstered chairs, and its purple walls featured portraits a Kensington artist had made of Ida B. Wells and Frederick Douglass. They were waiting on a donation of books that community members could read or take home. Past the lounge, in the center of the space, was the "newsroom," essentially three desks, occupied that morning by the communities editor, the editor-in-chief, and a new high school student worker receiving their first-day orientation. Past that, the U-shape opened up into a bright open space for community organizations to host classes, workshops, and meetings, now cluttered with worktables and lined with stacks of chairs. Tucked away on the other side of the U was what was going to be a community media lab with five desks and computers and a ceiling decorated with string lights.

This space had been a long time coming. *Kensington Voice* was founded by Bauer-Reese, a Temple University professor, around the same time as the Germantown Info Hub. Rather than growing from an academic study, *Kensington Voice* grew out of one of Bauer-Reese's classes, where students informally surveyed Kensington residents about what they wanted from local journalism. Residents told students they felt their neighborhood was stigmatized by news coverage of the open-air drug market that had grown there in recent years. Responding to these concerns, *Kensington Voice* took a solutions-oriented approach, producing monthly online magazines exploring themes suggested by residents, as well as workshops and other opportunities for face-to-face interaction and participation. The project, managed by Bauer-Reese, was staffed initially by journalism students and recent graduates and institutionally housed at Temple University. But because of Temple's risk management regulations, the project's affiliation with the university meant *Kensington Voice*'s efforts to establish a physical presence in the community were first restricted by bureaucracy and then upended all together by the pandemic. This is why, when I met Bauer-Reese in their neighborhood space four years after their founding, they were still painting and unpacking.

Kensington Voice was not only deepening their physical connection to the neighborhood, but, now independent of the university and under a new fiscal sponsor, they also had a new governance structure. The project had a new board with governance powers—and it was composed completely of Kensington community members. Unlike the other Philadelphia-area media organizations I have profiled so far in this book, for *Kensington Voice*, community members were not only in "advisory" roles. They had the power to weigh in and reject budgets or even to change the leadership of the project. In this chapter, I explore what *Kensington Voice*'s experience illustrates regarding what happens when a media organization attempts to share governance with community members. I'll look at how they attempt to enact a vision for community-governed service journalism and explore how their work and organizational structure departs from traditional approaches to journalism. I'll also examine the potential pitfalls of launching a community board with accountability power, or "teeth," in a system not built for this approach and the challenges of collaborating and finding a sustainable "lane" within Philadelphia's local news and information built environment. Through this I will explore how *Kensington Voice* is using accountability infrastructure to center equity and antiracism and show how this shapes the narratives it circulates in communication infrastructure theory's (CIT) storytelling network. But I will also look at how the challenges it encounters illustrate larger dynamics influencing local storytelling networks.

"DIRECT SERVICE" JOURNALISM

When the *Kensington Voice* project started, I and others in my department associated the project with excellent student journalism. Bauer-Reese had a reputation of working with students to produce award-winning and beautifully designed long-form digital reporting using a solutions journalism framework. The project did produce this content initially. As the project matured, though, it became less reliant on student journalists. They were able to pay staff and community contributors for content through grants from local journalism foundations[1] (though many staff were recent graduates). More critically, *Kensington Voice* began to develop additional streams of work that centered the suggestions of their ever-growing circle of partner organizations and community contacts. This is why the "newsroom" part of the *Kensington Voice* physically occupies a central but relatively small footprint in the larger organizational space.

Outlining how their organizational structure has evolved, Bauer-Reese explained that they currently had two overall branches of work—the newsroom and "direct service." The latter included activities connected with workforce development and creative expression, for example, training in internet literacy, creative writing, or software like Adobe Illustrator. This "creative workforce development" not only offered residents valuable skills but also potentially could address "some of the underlying problems that we've heard expressed to us in the neighborhood." Bauer-Reese explained that generations of oppression and marginalization had taken a toll on residents' mental and emotional health: "One of our goals is to provide a space that decreases that emotional pain through creative expression."[2] She noted that they hoped that in the future they would be able to have someone with social work experience leading their direct service operations and staffing the media lab to facilitate trainings that respond to residents' needs.

Bauer-Reese gave some concrete examples of how the space and such an infrastructure could offer residents practical benefits. By spending time in the neighborhood in their new space, she had encountered residents who might benefit from a variety of programs. For example, she recalled how a person who helped them with renovation work in their space nearly gave her an incorrect receipt because they didn't know where to put a comma in a number. Once they were fully staffed with an operational space, they could invite a financial literacy organization to come to do a training. Because *Kensington Voice* had been working in the community for several years, they had built up partnerships with several such organizations, including one that advertised in their publication. She explained that if something like that happened, and if it was an issue that was affecting many in the neighborhood, *Kensington Voice* might write a story about it that included a resource list with information on other trainings. Those resources could then be shared with the person staffing the media lab, who could share information with residents who came in and partners: "So, instead of creating a transaction between a journalist and a community member . . . the space itself, people who work there are providing something, so it doesn't feel like we're extracting from them."[3]

This emphasis on training programs follows *Kensington Voice*'s work running storytelling workshops for community members and youth since early in their operations. While some of these activities led to participants who contributed content to the publication (and were paid for doing so), they were largely focused on giving residents avenues for expression separate from any expectation of publishing journalistic content. Bauer-Reese explained how she thought about the value of this work and its connection with their larger mission: "I think of journalism as really targeting this policy-level change. A lot of the time I'm writing stories that are supposed to make an impact on policy and kind of trickle down and benefit all these other layers of the system. But that takes a really long time. And people who are just people, who don't have any experience with journalism, like they don't feel that change, right. And I think that decreases trust for journalists." Because of this, Bauer-Reese wanted residents to feel like "they got something from us" and also to connect "community members with each other, through these storytelling tools." This was not to say these community-centered objectives would not contribute to *Kensington Voice*'s reporting: "that relationship that we then build can inform things that we're writing about that are actually important to the community."

BUILDING RELATIONSHIPS THROUGH PARTNERSHIPS AND OUTREACH

Visiting the *Kensington Voice* office, the team gestured to one of the desks, where several pieces of artwork were laid out. These were submissions from local residents to their all-ages art contest. The contest was sponsored by a group focused on public health and vaccine hesitancy. As the web page later set up for the public to vote for their favorite submissions explained, "*Kensington Voice* saw this project as an opportunity to encourage community connections, conversation, and creative expression about a health issue that continues to disproportionately affect the communities we serve: COVID-19."[4] Art submitted ranged from paintings to poems and connected in some way to themes related to the pandemic. The winners stood to be rewarded between $250 and $750 based on age category.

Bauer-Reese explained that the contest would never have existed had it not been for one of the members of their community board. Back when *Kensington Voice* was first starting, before the board even existed, one of its now members had reached out to Bauer-Reese to suggest they do more with arts in the community. The team listened, with this art contest being only the latest attempt to implement the advice. Bauer-Reese noted that all those who were now board members had shared key input over the years, and "We've taken everything that they've told us seriously, and we've done all of it."[5]

Developing relationships and listening to community stakeholders have been key practices for *Kensington Voice* even before they had a board. Since their inception they have had numerous partners, including social service providers, libraries, community organizations, local businesses, and media organizations. In terms of CIT's local storytelling network,[6] they have actively worked to build relationships between all three categories of storytelling network actors (community organizations, networks of residents, and local media). The nature of what partnership entails varies, from sharing venue space for events to sharing media content. Many partnerships are related to outreach activities—for example, they partnered with Mural Arts to hire local artists to decorate newspaper boxes. These boxes and some other shelves were then shared with twenty different partner organizations where residents can get copies of *Kensington Voice*. These partners ranged from churches to senior centers to a pharmacy. Bauer-Reese explained that they also do a lot of "street-level engagement" such as "pop-up newsrooms," where *Kensington Voice* staffers set up in public spaces (also known as "tabling") to interact with residents and hand out newspapers that include an updated guide with information on COVID-19 resources—always offering materials in both English and Spanish.

COMMUNITY BOARDS WITH TEETH

When it came time to transition from working as part of a university to working with a fiscal sponsor, the team knew they needed to set up a board for *Kensington Voice*. For most organizations, establishing a board with governance powers meant considering criteria like potential board members' fundraising capacity, their capacity to be donors themselves, and competencies like legal skills. *Kensington Voice*'s approach was different. As one of the staffers explained, "it was kind of all hands on deck" as staff members suggested community members: "Our mindset was thinking of people who are very active in the neighborhood that have interacted with *Kensington Voice* pretty frequently. So at least they're aware of who we are and what we do pretty well."[7] All eight of the board members they came up with were community leaders in the neighborhoods that make up the greater Kensington area they served. Many wore multiple hats as block captains, artists, social service providers, and civic association representatives, among other things. And rather than expecting the board members to contribute financially themselves, these board members were paid a stipend for their time participating in bimonthly meetings ($500 for one year).

Bauer-Reese reflected on how *Kensington Voice*'s experience varied from what she knew of other nonprofit boards. While she said she had limited board experience, in the conversations about recruitment she recalled that "they're always like, we need a lawyer. We need somebody who does this."[8] Her experience resonated with my own limited experience serving on or working with boards, where it was more common for boards to have members chosen based on profession or for the depth of their pockets rather than lived experience as community residents. *Kensington Voice*'s approach looked distinctively different, according to Bauer-Reese: "We just have residents that care about making positive changes in the neighborhood. Frankly, I don't know what some of them do for a living because that wasn't relevant when we were organizing." *Kensington Voice*'s only criteria was lived experience and an understanding of neighborhood issues. As a staffer explained, the board played the role of a "compass": "These are the people who know the pulse of the community; they are the community."[9]

The team explained that the board worked with them to offer both input and oversight: "What are stories that you'd like to see in this paper? What are we missing? . . . What worked? What didn't work?" They explained that they asked them about everything from big-picture issue areas to small design questions: "It can easily become a thing where you think you know what's best for the community, when it's like, no, the community knows what's best. So having that input to know if we're on the right track has been really important."[10] As the team explained it, the board functioned both to "keep us in check" and as a source of valuable ideas both for issue areas to explore and for activities to pursue. Bauer-Reese noted, "If you go down the list [of board members], every single one of them has given us something that shapes what we're doing as an organization, which is what . . . in my opinion a board should be." *Kensington Voice*'s board was designed to function as accountability infrastructure—and in doing so it was creating a sort of interlocking two-way connection between community residents and local media in CIT's local storytelling network. By giving the board governance powers, *Kensington Voice* was trying to take some of the power it had in the local media storytelling network node and shift it to the node of residents.

This is not to say the operation of the board was without challenges. As the team member coordinating board meetings noted, they sometimes felt like they were "winging it"—"it's something really new for me."[11] Given their limited experience with nonprofit boards, they noted they had to feel their way through things like how to structure the leadership of the meetings. They didn't yet have formal officer positions; the rules and processes were still being worked out. Choosing community leaders from the neighborhood also meant everyone was "super busy." As Bauer-Reese explained, "The neighborhood has so few resources that the people who have found a way to provide resources creatively . . . they're just constantly running around and doing all these programs for people."[12] As a result, scheduling meeting times could be challenging. And while Bauer-Reese expressed gratitude for the board members they had, she conceded that there was potentially value in seeking out members who had expertise in areas like fundraising or legal matters. While the *Kensington Voice* board was strong in terms of authentically representing community assets, there were tradeoffs in not pursuing the kinds of social and financial capital prioritized by conventional boards.

Of course, many of the organizations introduced in this book have had bodies designed to elicit input from the community, including community advisory boards. But from WHYY to the *Philadelphia Inquirer* to the Germantown Info Hub, each of these bodies had limits to the extent they could hold organizations accountable, given their structure. Prioritizing listening or even advising was not the same as having decision-making power. *Kensington Voice*'s board was different in that it did have governance power. They would be presenting them their budget for approval this year, and the board could terminate and replace the project's leadership. As Bauer-Reese noted, "The community should be able to hold us accountable." The money *Kensington Voice* received from funders, she added, was intended to go to "things that are important to the community"—so the community should have oversight on what those are. For Bauer-Reese, "accountability is, basically, that we're doing what we said we would do. And the things that we said we would do are connected to things that you told us to do."[13]

Kensington Voice's board is still finding its feet, and it is too soon to know the extent to which it will opt to exercise its accountability powers. But its existence as accountability infrastructure has already guided the project in a direction that prioritizes direct benefit to the community over the pursuit of journalistic awards. Bauer-Reese explained, "When we ask people, 'What do you want in community news?' Normally, they want a space where they can build skills and also tools and training, so that they can build their own power." Sharing governance power with community leaders pushed *Kensington Voice* to prioritize how they could meet the information and expression needs of residents rather than centering an idea of what prestige journalism needed to look like: "Yes, we do journalism, but our actual focus is individual-level impact. Like, if we can provide you a place to come where you can express your emotions creatively and you feel a little bit better when you leave."[14] Staying true to their mission meant the spectrum of initiatives the *Kensington Voice* team might work on could range from election coverage that involved asking mayoral candidates questions submitted by residents while simultaneously planning a poetry slam for a local soccer club's girl's empowerment group.

REPRESENTATION AND ANTIRACIST
WORKPLACE PRACTICES

As with all the other media organizations discussed in this book, conversations about representing "the community" and pursuing antiracism applied not only to the coverage and programming *Kensington Voice* planned but also to workplace practices. As a start-up media organization, *Kensington Voice*, like Resolve Philly, has had a free hand to reimagine what an equitable workplace can look like. Because they are a comparatively small organization with a geographically specific remit, in some ways they have been able to adopt more radical transparency in their work practices, though many of their practices have yet to be systematically formalized.

Since the project was initially formed, Bauer-Reese has worked to make the staffing of the project more reflective of the majority Latinx/e community the project sought to cover. Bauer-Reese identifies as a non-Hispanic white cisgender woman who is not a resident of Kensington. The project was initially staffed by a mix of Temple students and recent alums, including others who identified as non-Hispanic white, and nonresidents. But over time, as they gained additional funding to fully staff the project, Bauer-Reese worked to recruit multiple staffers who identified as Latinx/e, including the editor-in-chief. She also worked to bring on staffers who were connected to Kensington and adjacent neighborhoods—having either grown up there or lived there. This included residents who were not college educated but whom they had connected with through their project activities. She explained that in recruiting, they have tried to consider "employing people who directly reflect the people who live there. Ideally, have the same lived experiences as the people who live there."[15] Presently, all of the eleven project staffers (three full-time) other than Bauer-Reese identified as Latinx/e and/or Black. Bauer-Reese also has attempted to model power sharing by divesting herself of managerial power, though she continues to act as a program manager, managing all fundraising and the space: "I am aware that I have a ton of power. And I'm identifying it and putting it into little buckets in some way. And then I'm trying to do a warm handoff to other people. . . . I totally want to be super involved in this. But I don't want to be *the* person. You know what I mean? The person who makes the final call for this or that."

Bauer-Reese, whose work on the project is almost entirely pro bono,[16] explained that as she has tried to take steps to account for her own power, she also has tried to think about how to create organizational practices that encourage equity: "I think it's about shared power within our newsroom and between our newsroom and other people in our environments, which requires transparency on all levels." This transparency extends to the critical issue of pay equity—an issue that when not addressed, as the experiences of the *Inquirer* and WHYY have shown, has potential to undermine trust and staff morale. Bauer-Reese explained that *Kensington Voice* had a somewhat unusual participatory budgeting process: "Everyone has to know what every single person at this organization is making. And they all have to agree on it. And last year, when we did this, we had an in-person conversation. It was like a salary negotiation, I suppose, but with ourselves. I made it very clear that I'm going and getting this funding, and I can weigh in and give advice, but whatever you all decide on, that's what we're going to do for salaries." Bauer-Reese noted that they followed the process with a form for staffers to provide anonymous feedback. She explained that the first time they tried this process there were some disagreements, but she believed overall the transparency and dialogue was productive. She said they've also tried to address systemic inequities she and others had observed at other workplaces—such as the issue of bilingual staff being expected to do uncompensated labor to translate work. *Kensington Voice* has a "bilingual pay rate": "If you're using a second language for more than 10% of your job, you get more money. There's a stipend that goes on top of that." She said she was still trying to determine best practices in some other areas. At present, staffers with different education levels performing the same role were paid the same, but "one of the things that's now nagging me is . . . if you went to college, you're now in student loan debt. . . . then people are being oppressed by the student loan system."

An awareness and attention to oppressive structures and ways to counter them was a running theme not only in thinking about who was in the newsroom and the languages spoken but also in how they approached their coverage. As a staffer noted, they tried to ask of themselves, "How diverse are the sources that we are going to? How many of them are experts within their own community?" They gave an example of doing coverage related to COVID-19 and trying to find medical personnel who were from the community or clinics in the community and who "look like the community and understand the community."[17] They also noted that they had put a lot of deliberation into the development of a style and ethics guide and had included a lot of input from a variety of organizations and affinity groups. Another staffer noted that part of their efforts to create more equitable and antiracist coverage involved including more historical context in their coverage and connecting to the lived experiences of staffers in the newsroom when relevant.[18]

When I spoke with staff members in July 2022, they had yet to codify their DEIB practices. As Bauer-Reese noted, when it came to antiracism efforts, they were just "doing stuff quietly." She said she preferred this approach to public-facing declarations and initiatives that could often be "performative." Their approach may also relate to the reality that they were not engaged in the work of repair but rather in visioning from scratch and working with staff who were not unlearning harmful practices and dominant journalism norms. It was notable that for most of the staffers, *Kensington Voice* was their first newsroom job. As one staffer explained, "I haven't really dealt with a lot of legacy media and the microaggressions that you can experience. . . . So far, it's only been something I'm hearing about. But it also made me more grateful to be here." They noted that they hoped to continue to add practices to encourage greater equity and acknowledged that there were likely things "we haven't thought about, since we're just starting up." They were aware that it would be critical to ensure that as they hoped to grow as an organization they would have to develop internal infrastructure to encourage new people to feel welcomed and to ensure that they continued to work with community members who were most affected. Based on Resolve Philly's experience of rapid growth and the potential pitfalls of bringing new people in with varied expectations and levels of trust, there would seem to be value in seeking out ways to develop guidelines or

other infrastructure to help ensure that growth and succession stay faith-
ful to the project's commitment to diversity and equity goals.

PROMISE AND PERILS OF
A COLLABORATIVE SYSTEM

The first week of August 2022, I noted with interest a story in the *Inquirer*
exploring the city's and community groups' approach to summer play
resources for children in Kensington, after some programs and even pools
were closed because of concerns related to violence and narcotics use. The
story seemed to be one of the first to come out from the *Inquirer*'s new communities and engagement desk. Out of curiosity I checked *Kensington
Voice*'s page to see whether they had covered the same story. On their page
they had posted an earlier story done by a WHYY reporter. Both stories
included scenes from an event on August 2, and it made me curious what
it meant to have this mixture of metro news organizations and hyperlocal
outlets covering the same communities, the same "turf." What did this illustrate about how resources are distributed and how outlets navigate their
lane?

When I asked *Kensington Voice* about the story, multiple team members
expressed frustration about how this particular chapter unfolded. Before
the *Inquirer* or WHYY came out with their stories, *Kensington Voice* had
released a service journalism guide to "Keeping Cool in Kensington."[19]
When they found out an area pool was to be closed after an altercation
where pool staff were reportedly assaulted, they updated their guide and
began working on a larger story about public recreation spaces and how their
closing affected the community. In addition to the pool, a local library had
been closed, and other summer recreation programs had been limited. They
were working on a story about the city's pop-up "PlayPark" program for
kids, when they saw that WHYY's Billy Penn had published a story about
one of these play parks. A *Kensington Voice* staffer explained that when they
saw that, they decided, "Okay, I'm gonna have to pivot this entire thing."[20]

Because they prioritized getting information out to their audience, they reached out to Billy Penn, whom they had worked with before, and asked to republish the story on the *Kensington Voice* site. Billy Penn agreed, and *Kensington Voice*, who publishes work in both English and Spanish, also translated the story and shared the Spanish-language version with Billy Penn. About a week later, as *Kensington Voice* was still working on their now pivoted larger story about access to community resources, a WHYY news reporter ran a story about the closure of recreation programs on certain streets because of security concerns. *Kensington Voice* had planned to include that in their story, but when they saw the WHYY piece, they reached out again and asked to share the story on their site and to share the Spanish-language version: "I think that was a good example of how to work together when we're overlapping reporting in these communities. Because it's necessary reporting at the end of the day. And it is very important for other Philadelphia news outlets to put their eyes on Kensington."[21]

The *Kensington Voice* staffer explained that these exchanges with metro-level outlets were constructive. They had, however, had less constructive interactions with other metro outlets. They shared an example of a journalist at another metro outlet who reached out and asked them for sources without acknowledging that they as an outlet might already be working on a related story. They noted that the journalist could have framed their outreach in a more constructive way: "Like, 'Hey, are you guys working on this right now? How can we make this a possible collaboration between our news outlets,' versus being, 'Hey, can you tell me about all the orgs that you know about in Kensington?'"[22]

While they were welcoming of collaboration, such requests gave them pause: "If it comes to a point where you're asking for my knowledge, should I be compensated for that?" The staffer worried that there was the potential for requests from larger news outlets parachuting into the neighborhood to be extractive: "If larger outlets are going to utilize the knowledge of hyperlocal neighborhood news outlets to better inform their own stories, the labor of those smaller outlets should also be acknowledged and treated (or compensated) fairly because this is part of their job."[23] They noted a concern that some larger outlets had the potential to be extractive both to them as a news outlet and to the community. They had spent four years building up trusted relationships in the community. They did not want to risk losing this or continue a previous "toxic cycle" by connecting sources to journalists whose practices they were uncertain about. They were happy for more news organizations to focus on Kensington, but they hoped there could be more care and collaboration: "It's good to have as many resources as possible in the community; it's just a matter of coordinating them."

When Bauer-Reese and her students founded *Kensington Voice*, the only other media in the area was a long-running community newspaper serving the adjacent neighborhood of Juniata (which closed in 2021).[24] At that time, national outlets and metro Philadelphia outlets had been producing high-profile reporting on Kensington's open-air drug market. Criticism of how that coverage represented the community was one of the reasons Bauer-Reese and students pushed to start an outlet that was community centered and avoided sensational parachute reporting. But four years into their project, numerous newer media initiatives purported to share community-centered stories from the neighborhood or to otherwise address the information needs of Kensington residents. In addition to coverage by WHYY and the *Inquirer*'s communities and engagement desk, Resolve Philly had an Info Hub captain from Kensington (a community leader who was also involved with *Kensington Voice*), and Temple University's Logan Center for Investigative Reporting had a podcast project in development featuring a Kensington community leader.

Having a greater number of more heavily resourced and textured narratives about the neighborhood offers a potential if limited counter to decades of stigmatizing coverage and distrust of news media. But in addition to these projects, staffers noted others that never came to fruition. They shared the example of the Lenfest Local Lab, which had become part of the *Inquirer*,[25] and their efforts to build a community newsletter. They reached out to *Kensington Voice* to be a partner. The Lenfest Local Lab explained they were working to make the partnership a paid collaboration, but *Kensington Voice* received no funding from the initial partnership.[26] As a partner, *Kensington Voice* was asked to share information and input. This included sharing contacts they had developed over their years of working

in the neighborhood—expending their social capital by asking those contacts to trust this new project associated with the *Inquirer*: "And then all of
a sudden, they got laid off, and the whole thing went away. And it's like,
okay, that looks bad for us."[27] The *Inquirer* decided to stop their support for
the Local Lab—laying off four full-time staffers and closing out projects.
For *Kensington Voice*, this experience reinforced a narrative that news media
could not be relied upon to follow up on commitments to the community.
As one staffer noted, "You have to be very careful. When you're starting
projects, I feel, because you could also mess it up for the next person coming around."[28] In the *Inquirer*'s case, this meant not only did their false start
potentially leave a bad mark to overcome for other journalists reaching out
to Kensington community stakeholders—but also for their own *Inquirer*
projects that would follow, including their communities and engagement
desk.

Beyond the risk of being tarred by association with ill-fated media ventures, more journalism projects connected to the neighborhood potentially
meant more competition for funding. Bauer-Reese explained that aside from
the Independence Public Media Foundation, they no longer had "eggs in
the journalism funding basket." Observing other grant-funded projects
focusing on Kensington, like the *Inquirer*'s Local Lab work, she found the
strategy of funders to be frustrating: "We're already doing this. So why don't
you put somebody here [at *Kensington Voice*]? And we'll just do it." She worried that journalism funders saw *Kensington Voice*'s work as too aligned
with advocacy and had all but given up approaching them for funding. By
supporting larger news outlets instead of projects close to the community,
she cautioned, philanthropy was "propping up legacy news organizations."

Even when other media projects had more positive experiences in the
neighborhood, *Kensington Voice* had to navigate how additional media
activity in the community had the potential to affect their relationships and
the availability of funding. They gave the example of Resolve Philly. *Kensington Voice* had long been a partner in Resolve's Broke in Philly collaboration. Bauer-Reese explained that her initial understanding of Resolve's
partnership model involved partner news organizations, who were closest to community members, interacting with community members—and

Resolve "supporting that collaboration." But now, Resolve was developing multiple additional initiatives, including Info Hub Captains and the community newswire service. They were building their own relationships and conducting their own outreach in Kensington, apart from their collaborating with *Kensington Voice*. Bauer-Reese worried this had the potential to be confusing to community members, who may lump all the media efforts together without context about who all the players are. In addition, while *Kensington Voice* continued to collaborate with Resolve and respected them as an organization, because of how Resolve Philly had grown and developed an extensive network of funders, Bauer-Reese had concerns that Resolve was now in some ways competing for funds to do something that *Kensington Voice* may have been able to do in a more "community-oriented" way. *Kensington Voice* did not feel it had the capacity to compete for such funding dollars and, more than that, was concerned that there was potential for duplication or waste from having "multiple organizations that are in the same space."[29]

Beyond the question of funding, Bauer-Reese lamented that projects by other organizations who were relative newcomers not based in the neighborhood risked amplifying the same narratives and voices already in circulation ("the same six stories"), rather than supporting a group like theirs that was familiar with the neighborhood's history and context and could expand on whose voices got amplified. Bauer-Reese shared the example of a new project another organization (not partnering with *Kensington Voice*) was developing that featured a Kensington community leader they had profiled. While that community leader had a valuable story, Bauer-Reese suggested it was a waste to just "redo the same story." It would be "more strategic" and "less harmful" to use a snowball approach—to contact that person and ask them to suggest contacts with interesting stories: "Let's build on each other. . . . Then we're not wasting as many resources. And we're being more inclusive and nuanced."

Another staffer shared a similar concern: "If I'm seeing people we may have approached a couple of times and seeing their names also come out more in other news outlets, it's like, OK, it's time to talk to someone new because it is not the same three people that live in Kensington."[30] They wanted to improve the fabric of collaboration in Philadelphia so that metro-level and hyperlocal outlets could complement one another: "trying to fill those gaps and making sure we're not doing the exact same thing in the exact same place to the exact same people." They noted that outlets should take care not to "jump on the labor of others" and think about "at what point for which stories do we reach out to collaborate? . . . How do we work together with people who have established relationships in the community to make as accurate journalism as possible?"

* * *

Kensington Voice's experiences underline the potential value in collaboration. Being in conversation with *Kensington Voice* projects could ensure that efforts are additive and not duplicative. But their experiences also demonstrate the importance of centering equity in any attempt at collaboration in the local news and information built environment. Reflecting on their many collaborative partnerships, *Kensington Voice* team members noted experiences that ran the gamut from productive to extractive. There were, for example, the positive experiences with WHYY's Billy Penn outlet, who always took care to direct traffic to their site. However, they also recalled challenges with other partners, including working with the *Inquirer* via the Broke in Philly collaboration, where they suggested that the *Inquirer* did not adequately appreciate the resources required to produce bilingual content.

Reflecting on how collaboration structures had and could work, Bauer-Reese shared how the ideal of the collective power of collaboratives was often to "uplift" the coverage and people closest to the communities: "The collaboration just keeps handing people up and up and up to build power. And that's great, right? Like when you start to have people building power. But then, at certain levels, you have people who are now coming in that might be harmful in a way. So you've just handed somebody over to somebody who is going to be using an oppressive approach." This experience made *Kensington Voice* approach collaborations with larger media institutions and media personalities with caution. Their relationships with community members were foundational to their project's success. So while they had engaged in collaborations since their inception, they had to be mindful of how they could protect their relationships and sources while doing so. Their experience highlights how progress strengthening local storytelling networks is not always linear. *Kensington Voice* could build trust and share power with community stakeholders, strengthening storytelling network links. But allowing extractive actors to connect to this network could potentially damage network ties and contribute to distrust between residents and local media more broadly.

A VISION FOR SUSTAINABLE
DIRECT-SERVICE JOURNALISM

When I met Bauer-Reese after a university faculty meeting in August 2022, unlike some colleagues, she did not have the look of someone who had gone on a summer holiday and was now refreshed and ready to face a new semester. (Admittedly, neither did I.) She explained, with enthusiasm tempered by frustration and exhaustion, that in addition to setting up a new community space, she had spent the summer working on a new strategy with *Kensington Voice*—complete with a theory of change and a business plan. They began by trying to more clearly set out their vision, she explained, referring to her notes: "We fight for system-wide change by prioritizing the needs of individuals; we provide a place and programs where all people can exercise their voice to positively impact their attitudes and emotions, their relationships, their communities, and society. Sometimes that results in publishing their voices, and sometimes it doesn't. . . . Journalism is one of the many things that we can do here."[31]

Their conclusion that journalism was more a means to an end than an end in itself grew out of frustration with what she called "muscle-memory interventions that are not meeting anybody's needs." Bauer-Reese wanted questions to shift away from "how many stories have we published? How many viewers do we get? Blah blah." Her logic reminded me of Sarah

Alvarez's initial reason for starting the on-demand service journalism organization Outlier Media in Detroit.[32] Bauer-Reese suggested: "Why don't we just go to the beginning of this and figure out what people's needs are and figure out how to fulfill them and advance them?"

In their attempt to do that, through conversations with community members and the guidance of their community-led board, they came up with four primary goals: (1) providing a creative outlet or opportunities to help people decrease emotional pain, (2) decreasing social isolation, (3) increasing community cohesion, and (4) increasing social power. By doing this, they hoped that people "can build up a community voice and find solutions that work for a large number of people."[33] Whereas traditional watchdog reporting focuses primarily on impact at the policy level, for *Kensington Voice*, "policy change that results from something we published is nice to have, but when we make a positive impact on the quality of one individual's life, we consider our mission accomplished."

To pay for this, Bauer-Reese explained that they were focusing on five categories of revenue. They continued to use advertising because they had advertisers approaching them. They also had contracts focused on community engagement and circulating public health information, including government contracts. *Kensington Voice* would continue to do gifts and grants, as well as memberships. But an area Bauer-Reese was particularly excited about was sponsorships—for example, sponsoring opportunities such as their art contest, which could be accessible ways to engage people who may not be as interested in news stories. They also were developing a "story topic sponsorship model" to offer story topics based on needs, such as housing: "you don't get editorial control, but it helps us get people to pay for us promoting some kind of conversation and information about something that they care about."[34] Of course, the idea of sponsorships is not unheard of within media. Funding for issue areas has long been a common practice, for example, in public radio. And in some ways their approach reminded me of practices undertaken within the sector of international media for social change and media development—where organizations such as BBC Media Action or Internews would seek funds from a range of donors on priority issue areas, while setting guidelines to ensure some independence within their editorial practices.[35]

Bauer-Reese explained that the *Kensington Voice* team was excited about their new strategy, and she was optimistic it could work. But she had two main reservations. They needed a runway to get started—some bridge funding while they established themselves. The other concern that worried her, however, was something of an indictment of the lack of trust within Philadelphia's supposedly collaborative news and information built environment. She was worried that people with more connections would appropriate *Kensington Voice*'s ideas and undercut their ability to get funding: "It's not going to work if I put my shit online and people all of a sudden start snatching different aspects of it." She didn't like feeling that *Kensington Voice* had to be "sneaky about it."[36] Bauer-Reese emphasized that "we want to share our ideas, our model—what works, what doesn't work." At the same time, they had experiences where others with more organizational heft had adapted practices *Kensington Voice* was doing and leveraged them for funding. They wanted to make sure they were able to establish themselves before the marketplace for potential funders was saturated.

VISIONING COMMUNICATION HEALTH WITHIN A SICK SYSTEM

The experiences of *Kensington Voice* offer insights not only for those concerned about the communication health of this one neighborhood but for what its successes and challenges indicate about Philadelphia's larger news and information built environment. Like Resolve Philly's community newswire service, *Kensington Voice* had a vision for amplifying the narratives of historically marginalized communities and centering their information needs. *Kensington Voice* went even further by giving a community-led board governance powers to keep the project accountable to residents. But their experiences with collaboration were mixed. While they appreciated working with the fellow start-up Resolve and were open to exploring additional collaboration as part of a community newswire service, they were also cautious to ensure that collaboration with larger actors did not undercut the relationships they had cultivated or their ability to seek funding for their work. Their collaborative experiences also intersected with established news organizations, including WHYY and the *Inquirer,* and illustrated how missteps by an organization in the past can cast a shadow over newer good-faith efforts. For example, the *Kensington Voice* team now viewed the *Inquirer* with hesitancy after less-than-positive previous experiences and projects that were abruptly shuttered. Just as journalists must grapple with the historical reputations of their institutions when interfacing with community members, they must also navigate accumulated mistrust when collaborating with other media actors within the system, particularly those with less power and fewer resources.

Kensington Voice's financial challenges also illustrate the constraints imposed by trying to do local journalism, even a reimagined direct-service journalism, when the business model for local journalism is broken. While creative, some of *Kensington Voice*'s business strategy amounts to tinkering at the edges of market failure. There may be little other option, of course, until more system-level changes, such as the public funding Victor Pickard and others have advocated for, come to pass.[37] In the interim, the experience of *Kensington Voice* suggests there is room for an intervention within systems like Philadelphia for larger journalism organizations and funders with comparatively more power to seek more equitable approaches to distributing funding and resources. For example, funders may understandably prefer the bureaucratic simplicity of funding larger organizations with the capacity to subgrant to smaller groups to do community-level projects or to do them themselves. But this process can divert funds away from community-level media organizations—not only *Kensington Voice* but also other neighborhood newspapers, as well as smaller outlets owned by and/ or serving BIPOC and other marginalized identity-based groups. Philadelphia has the valuable bones of collaboration already via Resolve Philly and a history of past collaborations. There is an opportunity to rethink how to more equitably value the relationships cultivated and the knowledge gained by community-centered and, particularly, community-governed media. Assigning a dollar sign to care and the relationships it nurtures is both difficult and potentially problematic. However, if outlets like *Kensington Voice* or others are to meet the needs of their communities, there must be a way to better circulate opportunities and funding.

In addition, *Kensington Voice*'s experiences illustrate how the promises made to communities by various media actors often become intertwined. For a resident, it could be hard to keep track of what media organization was responsible for any outreach they may encounter. And when an initiative from one organization falls through or doesn't go well, it could reflect badly on a group like *Kensington Voice*, which might have acted as a connector between a community stakeholder, or "source," and another media outlet. For this reason, while *Kensington Voice*'s own internal accountability infrastructure via a community board had great value in strengthening local storytelling network links, there is also a need for accountability infrastructures for other media actors that come into the community. In the chapter that follows, I will explore the idea of external accountability infrastructures and initiatives working to connect and encourage collaboration between media outlets to address DEIB and community engagement across local journalism systems.

Finally, there may be a benefit to syncing up the work of reimagining more equitable and antiracist journalism across multiple levels—from national (or even international, though that is beyond the scope of this book), to metro-wide, to hyperlocal. The expansion of City Bureau's Documenters to Philadelphia via Resolve holds promise with regards to its potential to build infrastructure and draw on lessons learned across the United States. But it is notable that before their coming to Philly was announced, *Kensington Voice* staffers had begun exploring how to do their own grassroots variation of Documenters. They had reached out to various civic agencies to see if they could pay people who go to meetings to record them on their phones and post transcripts on their website. While Resolve has a national and international reputation and is regularly invited to elite events featuring journalism innovation leaders, *Kensington Voice* staffers were not as linked up to national engaged journalism conversations and conferences, what some have called the "meta-level organizations" that play an influential role in how innovation in local news is conceived (and which I will focus on more in the chapter that follows).[38] *Kensington Voice* hadn't heard about City Bureau's large grant or expansion, though even if they had, it would be unlikely they would have been identified as a partner for a metro-wide project the way Resolve was. The question remains how *Kensington Voice* might, as part of the community newswire service or not, sync with and add to the infrastructure afforded to these larger initiatives in a way that continues to strengthen local storytelling networks. Their staff have energy, creativity, and relationships to push the reimagining work to potentially more radical spaces. Doing so, however, will require rethinking how trust and resources circulate within often intertwined and overlapping media "lanes."

6

EXTERNAL SUPPORT FOR EQUITABLE LOCAL JOURNALISM

Entering the Philadelphia Free Library on a hot August day, I followed the sound of drumming and spoken word to a large event space, where I was happy to find an open chair. It was WURD Radio's Founder's Day event. The annual event celebrated the legacy of Walter P. Lomax Jr., a Philadelphia physician and philanthropist who in 2003 established WURD radio, one of only a few Black-owned radio stations in the United States.[1] The event was being broadcast live, and as the poem celebrating Nina Simone concluded, WURD staff set up for their final panel of the day, focusing on "the role of Black press in perilous times."

As the panel featuring WURD radio on-air hosts began, each panelist offered their thoughts on the role of Black media. Some spoke of the unique "obligations" of Black-owned media, while others spoke of possibilities to "articulate the vision for . . . the kind of society we actually want to live in."[2] One host noted that from the Nation of Islam's *Final Call* to the NAACP's *The Crisis*, Black-owned media had historically "never stood separate" from social movements.[3] But while hosts offered positive constructs of what Black media contributed, several also underlined how they were distinguished from "mainstream" media. Solomon Jones, one of the WURD hosts, noted that he'd seen mainstream media "from the inside" as a columnist. While he said some outlets did "allow" him to share his "authentic voice," he noted that in general, "You have people who know nothing about our community, not necessarily trying to tell our stories, but trying to tell *their* stories *about* us." Andrea Lawful Sanders, another host, likewise observed that "often when quote-unquote mainstream media comes into our communities, they do the surface stuff about our schools, about our lives. We live the experiences. We understand the nuances around our lived experiences. And so we're able to articulate and speak to the subject matters that would often be ignored." Sanders continued, making a pitch for the audience to consider donating to WURD by becoming annual members, noting, "We don't get the funding that other people get."

Representatives of one of the biggest funders for local journalism in Philadelphia were sitting directly in front of the hosts at that moment. In fact, Jim Friedlich, the CEO of the Lenfest Institute for Journalism, sent out a tweet underlining several points made by panelists about the value of Black media, though this last one was omitted.[4] The Lenfest Institute had awarded WURD with multiple grants in the past, and they continued to support URL Media, a national network supporting Black and Brown media organizations of which WURD was a member.[5] But Sanders's point underlined a larger question vexing Philadelphia's news and information built environment: if the larger goal was to create a local system that served Philadelphians more equitably, how should resources be prioritized between funding and supporting outlets by and for BIPOC audiences versus established majority-white news outlets? What should the balance be between repairing outlets that tell stories *about* communities and bolstering outlets that tell stories *for* and *with* communities? What should institutions that support journalism be doing to make sure resources get distributed more equitably in local systems?

So far in this book I've looked at efforts to repair two long-established majority-white institutions, and I have also examined two more community-centered start-ups (where at least half the staff identified as BIPOC) working to reimagine what journalism in Philadelphia could look like. In this chapter, I will explore questions about the external institutions and structures that both support and complicate the work of pushing these and other organizations toward greater equity and community engagement. I'll pay particular attention to actors who influence journalism not as practicing reporters or editors but as representatives of groups that support various aspects of journalism. A considerable amount of journalism studies research has been dedicated to exploring the relationship between journalism practice and "outside institutions" or "metaorganizations" like nonprofit journalism support organizations, training centers, and foundations.[6] As many have noted, these actors have been "modifying the logics of news production."[7] They can determine what is and is not funded and how innovation is theorized and translated—often through the lens of their own interests in self-preservation.[8]

In the sections that follow, I focus on external actors that intervene in local journalism with an emphasis on community engagement and equity—especially those that brush up against Philadelphia's system. I will begin by turning to the world of philanthropic foundations and their role in pushing local journalism to either repair or imagine anew. I will then look at how philanthropic support is often intertwined with the work of DEIB actors, including journalism support organizations and consultants. Finally, I'll look at attempts to create external accountability bodies locally and nationally and at how national efforts by metaorganizations to create community-centered infrastructure for news and information may both support and compete with local initiatives. Through these explorations the chapter will grapple with a larger question—if the goal is to make local journalism more equitable, does it make more sense strategically to focus on shifting existing infrastructures and institutions or building new counter-infrastructure? And if a both/and answer is needed, given larger structural dynamics in the United States, what does that look like? As I explore the role of metaorganizations in addressing these strategies and in influencing local storytelling networks, this chapter will also raise additional questions for future research.[9]

FUNDING REPAIR?

"Reimagining" was the theme of Lenfest's 2022 "summit," held at a hotel in Philadelphia's Center City.[10] The space had the energy of reunion, with many of us seeing one another for the first time outside the confines of a Zoom screen after years of pandemic. (I even saw some people I had only known via Zoom.) There were journalists and representatives from the journalism support world from around the United States as well as Philly locals—including representatives of all of the organizations I've profiled in earlier chapters. There were also familiar faces from the WURD radio event, including the WURD host Andrea Lawful Sanders, who was the summit's emcee. Over the course of the summit's two days, participants raised many of the same questions I was agonizing about as I attempted to write this chapter. As is often the case at conferences, some of the most substantive discussions took place not on the plenary panels but in the informal conversations over meals and in hallways. In these spaces, the formal narratives and rehearsed talking points were chewed, processed, and translated—often vacillating between admiration, inspiration, and disgruntled frustration.

In one such conversation with a group of participants who had attended numerous journalism conferences, we noted the contrast between the national and local panels focused on reimagining journalism. The first panel had featured representatives of leading local and regional journalism initiatives from around the United States, all BIPOC-led, including Documented, Outlier Media, and Scalawag. Leaders of these organizations shared examples of how their community-centered and engaged approaches challenged longstanding journalism norms and practices and how they saw their work contributing to big-picture visions for redistributing power and wealth. Reflecting on news outlets' target audiences, Outlier's Sarah Alvarez emphasized, "I want to see us center more marginalized people. And I also want to see us decenter people who already have more than they need in terms of information and access to power."[11] But when the substantial seven-person panel that followed took the stage, the scope of reimagining seemed to have constricted. While the first panel had shared innovative practices for ensuring that community members determined the focus of their journalism, most of the Philadelphia media organizations took more traditional approaches to reporting. While some mentioned collaboration, many of the long-running Black press outlets expressed frustration with mainstream outlets poaching both their stories and their workforce—underlining how reimagining can be constrained if questions of repair of majority-white systems are not addressed. Several panelists noted challenges of financial sustainability and difficulty accessing philanthropic support. Overall, their discussion painted an image of a local system where questions of basic survival were at least as salient as questions of transformation.

As we debriefed on these sessions and the gaps between them, we wondered what the goal of these conversations was. The difference of tone between the first panel's focus on innovative practices and the second one's emphasis on basic subsistence needs seemed to parallel a gap researchers such as Patrick Ferrucci and Jacob Nelson have observed between journalism funders and individual newsrooms:

Because foundations within the U.S. tend to focus more on solving problems facing the news industry as a whole rather than on those facing individual news organizations, they want to both fund journalistic experimentation with uncertain outcomes, and to share those outcomes with the broader news media environment. The result is a situation where news nonprofits and foundations increasingly work together, yet are motivated by distinct, sometimes conflicting goals. The former often want to survive from one year to the next, while the latter often want to figure out what journalistic techniques can help all news organizations reach sustainability.[12]

Similar to the journalists Ferrucci and Nelson spoke with, some of the summit participants I talked with shared a sense of ambivalence about mixed or muddy goals. Who were these discussions for? Who needed to hear both the visionary ideas and the pain points the panelists were sharing? Who had the power to advance visions and work to repair harms? Several noted that there were some noticeable absences among attendees. Where were senior representatives of the larger mainstream news outlets, who had been invited and who had the potential to change policy and practice? The *Philadelphia Inquirer*, for example, was only represented by one sports editor, and the editor of their new communities and engagement desk was supposed to be on a panel but had pulled out.[13]

While I was pondering these questions, I bumped into a relative new-comer to the Philadelphia journalism scene. They were working with a start-up and exclaimed how delighted they were with the discussion—and how it had given them a sense of solidarity to hear from other BIPOC journalists centering BIPOC communities. The contrast between their appreciative perspective and that of the more cynical conference veterans underlined the challenge of creating a space that could be valuable for such a wide range of stakeholders. Despite this complexity, when I spoke with Lenfest's program director Shawn Mooring after the summit, he was pleased with how it had unfolded. He noted that the panels were not intended to "solve all of our problems" but rather to catalyze conversations.[14] Critically, he said, they were key to informing how Lenfest would develop and roll out programming. In this way, the goal had as much to do with informing Lenfest as a funder as with what particular participant constituencies may have gained.

Helping shape how Lenfest understands the Philadelphia news system was not an insubstantial goal, given the role it played in Philadelphia's news and information built environment. As other researchers have argued, foundations and other external organizations supporting journalism have largely tended to reflect "an upper middle class, pro-corporate orientation," with mixed records on DEIB in their own institutions.[15] While foundations could support efforts encouraging diversity and pluralism, they tended to emphasize "market-based solutions" and "an entrepreneurial logic" that could undercut "more radical critiques of journalism."[16] For this reason, it was notable that the summit's first plenary panel included radical systemic critiques, such as when Cierra Hinton, the executive director of Scalawag, explained that they were "an abolitionist media organization" that is trying to help their readers imagine something beyond "racial capitalism" and that "this system that we're existing in right now does not have to be the way that we continue to exist." At the same time, over the course of the two days, I lost count of the number of favorable references to "entrepreneurs" reinventing and reimagining journalism.

This tension between challenging and reinforcing systems may also reflect Lenfest's institutional structure and dual mission. Established in 2016 through a donation by the cable entrepreneur H. F. (Gerry) Lenfest, the Lenfest Institute is the noncontrolling owner of the *Philadelphia Inquirer.* This was a "pioneering experiment in nonprofit ownership," explained Lenfest Institute's CEO, Jim Friedlich.[17] As he noted, Gerry Lenfest wanted to ensure the *Inquirer* was financially stable, independent, and "above reproach"—and that no donor could "push the *Inquirer* around." For this reason, Friedlich explained, "We have a deep dedication to the transformation of the *Philadelphia Inquirer* but don't control it on a day-to-day basis." Alongside their support for the *Inquirer,* which included work on digital transformation and DEIB, the Lenfest Institute's board also decided that their broader mission of "saving local journalism" called on them to support the broader "Philadelphia news ecosystem."[18]

I spoke with several philanthropic workers connected in various ways to Philadelphia-area media funders, including current and former staffers of area foundations, to better understand the relationship between philanthropy and local journalism.[19] Philadelphia has been one of the most heavily resourced local news and information built environments in the United States, with investments of more than $50 per capita.[20] Almost everyone I spoke with noted the challenges that came from the structure of Lenfest and the fact that it raised funds that were restricted to the *Inquirer.* "It's hard to be a neutral ecosystem convener, when you also have financial and other incentives for the *Inquirer* to do well, to be seen in a favorable light," explained one philanthropic worker. "I think a lot of the pushback that Lenfest gets in the ecosystem is because of that very tension."[21]

To their credit, in addition to raising funds for and supporting the *Inquirer,* Lenfest also funded the local "ecosystem" through multiple initiatives, including funds to support BIPOC media founders, capacity building for BIPOC journalists, and support for DEIB work at other organizations, including WHYY. Nevertheless, stepping back to look at the overall allocation of their funds, the *Inquirer* did indeed get the lion's share—roughly $4.5 million in 2021 as compared with $1.2 million for all other Philadelphia "ecosystem" projects.[22] Lenfest's leadership pointed out that in addition to supporting investigative journalism and "digital transformation and acceleration," the funds going toward the *Inquirer* were intended to help this "anchor" news outlet address DEIB issues and strengthen its connections with BIPOC communities.[23] This included everything from paying for some job search costs to ensure a diverse recruitment pool, to funding the communities and engagement desk and the More Perfect Union project, to paying the costs of the *Inquirer*'s diversity and inclusion audit.

But while some critics lamented the substantial amounts Lenfest directed to the *Inquirer*, others noted that the amounts probably were not enough to incentivize change. They questioned the utility of philanthropic support for large legacy newsrooms "to convince them to try something" like community engagement or DEIB practices.[24] The *Inquirer* had a budget of $110 million—Lenfest's $4.5 million contribution to that amounted to a comparatively small drop and was not "setting the agenda."[25] Meanwhile, even smaller amounts to other smaller organizations, particularly BIPOC-led ones, could be transformative.

This calculus was leading others within the local news philanthropic sphere to different conclusions regarding the balance between supporting legacy organizations in the work of repair and supporting BIPOC-centered efforts. "I have to wonder what kind of leverage funders actually have in each of these scenarios," reflected Molly de Aguiar, Independence Public Media Foundation's (IPMF) president: "What would it take for IPMF, for example, to incentivize 6ABC or the *Inquirer* to truly, meaningfully share their power with communities, who are, by the way, continually and deeply harmed by their coverage, and what would it take for funders to help maintain those organizations' commitment to being held accountable long-term, regardless of leadership changes and other factors?"[26] Grappling with such questions led de Aguiar and IPMF to invest the bulk of their funds toward "supporting those who are creating new systems," including BIPOC-led, -centered, and, ideally, -owned outlets.

This approach positions IPMF as an outlier within the larger media and journalism funding field. Citing Foundation Center data analyzed by the Democracy Fund, the Borealis Center noted that between 2009 and 2015, of $1.2 billion on grants for journalism, only 6 percent went to "efforts serving specific racial and ethnic groups."[27] While these numbers have likely grown in recent years, numerous philanthropic workers I spoke with noted the ongoing challenge of philanthropy reproducing the inequities of media systems—suggesting that some of the same people responsible for inequities in corporate media had shifted over to the nonprofit sphere and were now "making decisions about funding."[28] This observation of similarities in who holds decision-making powers squares with what Rodney Benson found in a look at the boards of both corporate and nonprofit news organizations and foundations, concluding that "financial elites" dominate the oversight of all these organizations.[29]

Some funders, including Lenfest, were attempting to critically assess how their internal structures could better represent the diversity of the communities they served. At the Lenfest Summit, a panel discussion featuring Lenfest, the Knight-Lenfest Local News Transformation Fund, and IPMF funders discussed the importance of those making funding decisions having lived experiences as members of BIPOC or other marginalized communities and/or having experienced financial insecurity. Shawn Mooring, a Lenfest program director who identifies as a Black cisgender man, noted, "Lived experience brings a lot to the work and allows you to not only speak the same language but empathize, in a very different way."[30] While the Lenfest Institute benefited from Mooring's lived experience and that of the participants in its Visioning Table advisory group (which consisted primarily of local BIPOC journalists), these roles were positioned structurally under their CEO, who identified as a white cisgender man and reported to a separate governing board. And while Lenfest was funding a growing portfolio of BIPOC-centered initiatives, constraints within their design made it unlikely they would deviate from their pattern of allocating a majority of their funds to a majority-white newsroom (the *Inquirer*).

Scanning the journalism funding landscape, while there were local exceptions like IPMF or the Knight-Lenfest Local News Transformation Fund (which also centered a racial justice framework) and national funders like Borealis or the Pivot Fund that focused on BIPOC-led initiatives, funders channeled the bulk of large grants to majority-white newsrooms.[31] IPMF's de Aguiar acknowledged that despite concerns about the challenges of repair efforts, "you can't completely ignore the harmful actors in the ecosystem" and that "there is a case to be made to support opportunities that may arise within majority-white newsrooms, where you might have a strong BIPOC leader pushing for important changes, and you want to show your solidarity with them, and you're in a position to help improve the working conditions for BIPOC employees in the newsroom. Another scenario is supporting outside organizations that are applying pressure to newsrooms to change."[32]

These and other reflections shared by participants in the journalism philanthropic world offered insights into how they thought about their role as influencers in local journalism. They noted both the possibilities and limitations for funders to play a role in the work of reimagining in Philadelphia's news and information built environment or likely any local journalism system. But as de Aguiar's last point hints, another tactic funders can and to some extent have already taken is to support actors outside newsrooms, including other metaorganizations, working to push local journalism in the direction of greater equity and antiracism. I turn next to some of these repair workers attempting to develop and support greater accountability infrastructure.

REPAIR WORKERS AND
INFRASTRUCTURE BUILDERS

Growing up in a small town in central Pennsylvania, Letrell Crittenden learned early that news media did not represent people who looked like him fairly—if at all. Crittenden, who identifies as an African American/Black cisgender man, says communities of color in his hometown have largely been invisible in the local press, with the exception of crime coverage. It was one of the reasons he decided to become a journalist. And so in 2003, then in his early twenties, Crittenden found himself working as a crime reporter for the daily paper in Utica, New York. One day, leaving the court-house, a local Black pastor approached him. He told him he and his stories were "racist": "And I was like, you've got to be kidding me. I'm the only African American reporter there."

Crittenden admitted that at first he "kind of blew him off," but then he decided to take a closer look: "I looked at my stories, and I was using a lot of official sources. . . . I was really good at producing multiple stories a day—which means that I'm not providing any context for anything. I'm just covering crime, as it happens, using official sources."[33] That insight pushed Crittenden to take a step back. Neither his intentions nor his identity had insulated him from the dominant practices and norms of his training and the newsroom's productivity expectations. He weighed this critical assess-ment with challenges related to the internal culture of his workplace. He recalled how he felt he had no mentorship and had a hostile relationship with one of his managers.

This combination of factors propelled him to leave the world of report-ing and go to grad school. Crittenden then spent years researching and teaching journalism in academia—and I myself have been fortunate to col-laborate with him on research in the past.[34] But in 2021, an opportunity arose that drew him back into newsrooms in a different role. Now, as the director of inclusion and audience growth at the American Press Institute (API), Crittenden works with newsrooms on some of the very issues that first drew him to and then pushed him away from journalism. Central to his current work is an "inclusion index" he developed to assess newsrooms on seven main areas: newsroom diversity, inclusion/belonging of workers of color, representation of communities of color, engagement of communi-ties of color, trust of communities of color, understanding of assets to con-nect with communities, and infrastructure.[35] Drawing on his own experi-ences, he argued that it was critical to take a comprehensive approach to DEIB in newsrooms:

As I look at my journey, it wasn't just the coverage; it was my mistreatment in the newsroom. It was that I didn't do any type of engagement on a regular basis with the community. It was being reminded of trust issues. And also when we talked about community assets . . . not understanding anything about the neighborhoods we're covering, other than let's go to these churches and the NAACP and acting as if that is getting a good sense of the dynamics in the community. So it was based on all these different issues that I decided to move to this approach that was much more holistic.[36]

Crittenden is now one of many DEIB workers attempting to influence and help with the repair work of newsrooms and larger news and information built environments around the United States. Some, like Crittenden, do this work from within larger metaorganizations like the American Press Institute. Others work as individual consultants. While individual newsrooms sometimes commission this work, it is often supported by philanthropic funders. Over the course of my observation, both of the larger anchor newsrooms I followed in this study of Philadelphia's news and information built environment undertook some form of diversity, equity, inclusion, and belonging (DEIB) training. Usually, these trainings were conducted by national organizations, such as the Maynard Institute, and supported by foundations, such as the Lenfest Institute. These interventions were usually contracted with one specific newsroom, and what grew out of them was generally not shared publicly (with the exception of what I shared following WHYY's initial cultural competency trainings).

I only had the opportunity to sit in on a few of these trainings, but I spoke to more staffers after the fact. As noted in previous chapters, some common themes emerged from these experiences. Staffers, particularly BIPOC journalists, often noted that the trainings were opportunities to take the temperature of their workplace—revealing where their colleagues were at in terms of reflexivity and awareness of the influence of white supremacy in their newsroom and their lives. Some found the experience productive, others demoralizing. Some noted who was not in the room or who was checking their phone and not giving their full attention to the discussion. But even those who noted the significant value of the opportunity also were clear that this training alone was not a solution. Without follow-up, it was not enough.

NPR's Keith Woods's training at WHYY did have a follow-up component—and it did lead to some concrete changes in production practices, notably around source tracking. But reflecting on some of the numerous trainings and workshops he had organized and observed at National Public Radio and member stations around the United States, Woods noted, "I cannot make you attend, I can't make you learn." Opportunities for learning had value but needed to be structurally supported and reinforced within organizations: "The high functioning organization has people below me, and over to the side, advocating and pushing and promoting and expecting people on their team to be growing." Woods emphasized that DEIB work needed to go beyond training individuals or beyond creating entry-level fellowships for BIPOC journalists if institutions wanted to push toward structural transformation: "So much work in DEI is just coming in somewhere in the middle of that story and trying to change the whole thing based on a single intervention. . . . You have to be able to get up high enough and see that big picture to be able to know what to change."

A big-picture assessment of NPR had led Woods to push for institutional strategies such as baking DEIB requirements into hiring processes at every level—and critically examining policies that at first glance appeared race blind. He shared the example of how NPR shifted its practice of hiring temps because it had been biased in favor of those who could afford to do precarious labor: "And when you cut by class, you also cut by race in America. So without ever having made a single decision by race or ethnicity, the structure, the first door in, affected everything else." Woods noted points along the "pipeline" for journalistic talent at multiple levels of experience and how small alterations in requirements and recruitment approaches had allowed them to make improvements.

Incorporating DEIB into hiring was a way not only to increase the representation of BIPOC journalists; for Woods, it was also a way to screen for capacities among white job candidates:

If ability to do work in a diverse society and a diverse organization is a requirement of the job, then we are doing much less of the remediation work—that is the most dominant piece of the work that I do every day. And we are doing something else with our time and our energy. If I hire somebody who is white, who has thought about this issue before they came to my organization and demonstrated that they are in the game, I don't have to enlist them in anything, because they came in with a personal and professional commitment to the work. Now I can figure out a higher ask of them than I might otherwise.[37]

Woods argued that recruiting white people who were already doing "the work" could help alleviate the additional labor that gets imposed on BIPOC journalists and contribute to a more equitable workplace culture. He offered the example of white journalists asking BIPOC colleagues to take on uncompensated labor like sensitivity reads without investing adequate research on the front end: "Can you read this piece for me? Well, yes, and how much work have you done before I pick it up? Are you just vomiting out your thoughts on the page and then asking me to come behind you and clean it up?"[38] For Woods, integrating DEIB capacities into the hiring process and establishing expectations for journalists to be critically reflexive about the influence of whiteness on their work practices had the potential to create more equitable workplace cultures. Without these kinds of structural fixes, he acknowledged, the DEIB "remediation" work required to repair newsrooms could have a "groundhog day quality." For example, "The next time a new white person walks through this door there is going to be a chance that they're going to say, 'I don't see color.' And then you're going to have to go back all over that whole thing again."[39] For some BIPOC journalists, such remediation work was unsustainable and led them to step away. Woods's example suggested that for a DEIB intervention to work, even if it was initiated by an outside DEIB consultant or metaorganization, meaningful change required marrying this to internal organizational-level structural work.

* * *

For the American Press Institute's Crittenden, Wood's emphasis on making structural adjustments in HR and work practices connected directly with one of the core pillars of API's Inclusion Index—infrastructure. Crittenden was deeply skeptical of DEIB training efforts that did not recognize the need to build and/or repair infrastructure. He said he'd seen many instances where DEIB work was a performative "check a box" exercise that was "not really interrogating the causes of what's happening." He was particularly critical of internal initiatives led by staff or by independent consultants who were not able to share critical truths publicly: "If you're working from an internal standpoint, are you really going to be the one who tells your bosses that you're doing a bad job?"[40]

Crittenden's Inclusion Index was notable not only for its holistic approach but also for its attempt to work with cohorts of news organizations within a single local news coverage area. One of his first big initiatives in this new role led him to the city of Pittsburgh, Pennsylvania (a five-hour drive from Philadelphia). This was a city he knew well as a former resident and from research he had been doing there on the challenges facing BIPOC journalists. "The level of trust that community residents have for Pittsburgh newsrooms is in the toilet," Crittenden said. He explained that research with community members showed many residents, particularly from BIPOC communities, had a generalized distrust with "Pittsburgh media" as a whole; it was not limited to specific newsrooms. This led Crittenden to design a cohort program that could offer a collective and ideally collaborative intervention to repair relationships between communities and local journalism.

I had the opportunity to see the cohort in action briefly while participating in a Zoom session focused on DEIB and newsroom culture. This was part of a two-day intensive workshop with representatives from all of the five participating newsrooms. Newsrooms included the daily legacy newspaper, the competing legacy newsroom that was now digital-only, the alternative weekly newspaper, a nonprofit digital outlet, and a student news site.[41] Each newsroom had to send a team that included someone from senior management, someone responsible for audience/community engagement, and a "frontline" reporter or photographer. Over the course of the workshop, teams worked with Crittenden and other representatives of API and of Trusting News, a metaorganization founded by Joy Mayer that worked with newsrooms on a myriad of issues related to building trust. Newsrooms were also paired with a local consultant or mentor, a Pittsburgh-area journalist designated to help each newsroom establish goals and follow-up plan.

The workshop was preceded by formative research conducted by Crittenden and his team to assess the needs and assets of each newsroom as well as of the communities they purported to serve. Through interviews, focus groups, and newsroom surveys, Crittenden explained that they had gotten insights from more than one hundred people, including both Pittsburgh residents and newsroom employees. On the first day of the workshop, Crittenden shared what this research told them overall about Pittsburgh's "ecosystem" and shared with individual newsrooms their specific Inclusion Index scores, essentially their "grades," which were informed by this research. These scores were determined based on Crittenden's seven criteria, which looked at facets of the DEIB culture inside newsrooms, representation of and engagement with BIPOC communities, and, critically, how efforts were or were not institutionalized through infrastructure. This last point proved to be notable for a number of newsrooms and for some a source of surprise:

> Some newsrooms got grades that were lower because, yeah, you talk about these things, but you don't have infrastructure behind them. Some newsrooms probably got grades that they thought were higher, because there's a lot of work to do, but they've at least put in the effort to start building the infrastructure. For instance, one newsroom really isn't diverse, but they've actually, in the past few months or year, put in an infrastructure to really deal with that issue. They're better off than a newsroom that may be more diverse, but a lot of that their diversity may be by happenstance.[42]

Crittenden noted that one phenomena he had encountered repeatedly was newsrooms pointing to a particular DEIB initiative ("we do this one

thing really well"), expecting it to shoulder the weight of the entire organization's challenges. It wasn't good enough to hire and prominently show-
case a well-regarded BIPOC journalist, for example: "I think that a lot of
newsrooms take this approach. 'Well, we hired people.' Well, your newsroom's toxic. They're gonna leave. Or 'We've developed this section.' Did
you actually ask the community if this section is going to be relevant to
their information needs?"

The piecemeal approach he saw many newsrooms take led him to conclude that a holistic and research-based strategy was key: "If you can't deal
with everything, at the same time, you should at least have an assessment
of where you are. And then try and build a plan on how you're going to
deal with the most immediate needs." Following this approach with the
Pittsburgh cohort meant that recommendations varied from newsroom to
newsroom and were based on the particular strengths and weaknesses of
each. And at times the recommendations they shared focused on addressing a fundamental gap within the organization (for example, a lack of clarity regarding who should be doing what and the chain of command) before
progressing on what might be a more overtly DEIB goal: "It has to be a
functioning newsroom. And if you are lacking basic things that a newsroom should have, then you're not going to be able to do any DEI work."
Crittenden noted that following their workshop, newsrooms would have
three months to work with a mentor to develop their follow-up plans, getting community input along the way. They would then share these plans
publicly at an event, setting clear goals for action over the six months to
follow.

Listening to Crittenden recount assessments and recommendations, I
couldn't help but connect the issues he raised with concerns I'd heard nearly
verbatim from Philadelphia-area media workers over the course of researching this book. Regarding both WHYY and the *Inquirer* (cases I detailed
in chapters 1 through 3), I had variations on the same concerns about newsroom structures and disconnects between DEIB or community engagement interventions and institutional or community-based needs (as well as
concerns that particular projects were used to deflect critiques of larger
institutional deficiencies). I also appreciated the fact that the cohort model

was responsive to the way many residents I have spoken with in Philadelphia navigated news media, at times allowing their frustration with one outlet to taint their perception of all news or at least all "mainstream" (usually majority-white) news organizations. Crittenden noted that a cohort model like this could have value in a city like Philly—where he lives and which he knows well—and which is notable for its preexisting collaborative infrastructure.

Crittenden explained that the cohort model API was trying in Pittsburgh had two key potential advantages. It created an infrastructure that facilitated cohort members collaborating on recommendations like community engagement and recruitment. The other advantage was one he acknowledged was primarily based on anecdotal observation of news "ecosystems" across the United States rather than empirical research—the cohort model attempted to establish positive peer pressure: "It tends to have an influence on even those newsrooms that aren't involved, because at some point, they're gonna have to deal with the fact that, 'We're not doing this cool thing that the other newsrooms are doing and it's impacting our image.'" Crittenden hoped that this might start to encourage newsrooms who have not yet formally joined this work, including broadcasters, to begin to adopt DEIB and community engagement practices even if they did not formally join.

At the time of writing, API's Pittsburgh cohort was still working on their plans, and it would be premature to draw conclusions about whether they would translate into concrete progress, let alone institutional or system-wide transformation. Nevertheless, through its holistic, research-based, and collaborative design, API's inclusion index was notable for not only attempting to create accountability infrastructure but for encouraging the establishment of collaborative accountability infrastructure. Critically, by requiring participating newsrooms to publicly disclose their plans (if not their entire Inclusion Index scores), API's approach had a dimension of public transparency—which has been a key point of contention for several of the newsrooms featured in this book. While of course their advocacy for external accountability was also justifying their own existence as an external group, API's work did offer an illustration of how external metaorganizations can attempt to push local journalism systems to create infrastructure to encourage equity.[43]

PUBLIC ACCOUNTABILITY
INFRASTRUCTURES FOR REPAIR

Not for the first time over the course of researching this book, a Tweet from Ernest Owens, president of the Philadelphia Association of Black Journalists (PABJ), sparked a storm within the Philly media Twittersphere. In a thread that started, "Philly, we have a problem," Owens focused attention on the departure of the *Inquirer*'s only Black male reporter not attached to the sports desk: "To put this in perspective, outside of sports—there's not a Black male reporter at @PhillyInquirer covering politics, community, education, pop culture, food, and more in a city that has more folks who look like them than the majority white reporters who have jobs there. . . . For all of the talk of DEI efforts at @PhillyInquirer, they continue to drop the ball every time they pretend they are hitting a slam dunk."[44] Owens's thread then proceeded to detail how PAJB had formed a partnership with the *Inquirer* in March 2021 but that the *Inquirer* had not followed up with PABJ to update them on *Inquirer* for All efforts. And he noted, "Yes, we've informed them of these issues behind, in front, and side-to-side the scenes."

When Owen's tweet received no response from the *Inquirer*, it was followed by the first public statement by the Philly Journalism Accountability Watchdog Network (Philly JAWN), the external accountability group I introduced in chapter 2. The letter was addressed to the *Inquirer*'s publisher, top editor, and "Philadelphia Inquirer leadership" and was signed by the heads of PABJ (Owens), the Philadelphia chapters of the Asian American Journalists Association and the National Association of Hispanic Journalists, and Free Press' News Voices project manager.[45] The letter opened:

We're writing to you as the newly formed J.A.W.N (Journalism Accountability Watchdog Network) Coalition to further underscore our disappointment and displeasure at the ongoing failure of the *Inquirer*'s DEI initiatives. These failures have led to the loss of multiple journalists of color within the newsroom over the last year, and as a result there are now zero Black male reporters at the paper outside of the sports desk. This means we are missing out on important perspectives to cover critical topics like public safety, housing, education, the LGBTQIA+ community, food insecurity, poverty and Black culture within Philadelphia.[46]

The letter warned that the success of a "few journalists of color" should not be "weaponized" to gloss over retention problems or to "pit reporters of color against one another." This statement reflected experiences that affinity group leaders had heard from BIPOC employees who had quit in recent months, even as some new BIPOC journalists were hired or promoted. The letter noted the *Inquirer*'s lack of response to past efforts by affinity groups to reach out and quoted our audit report's findings about a lack of representation of Black people in coverage. Referring to the *Inquirer*'s DEIB work as "glacial," the letter ended with a series of demands:

> We demand that the powers that be at the *Inquirer* immediately initiate good-faith, consistent and transparent communications with J.A.W.N. We demand dedicated meetings with Lisa Hughes, Gabe Escobar, the paper's leadership and the board of directors. If the paper fails to fulfill this demand, J.A.W.N. will initiate a public campaign against the *Inquirer*. As part of this campaign, we will let the public know that the paper of record has continued to fail to live up to its antiracist PR mantra, and that its coverage continues to harm, divide and build distrust among the communities of color it so clearly needs if it plans to survive in Philadelphia. We are beyond just talking. We demand action, answers and accountability.

When I first saw this letter, I was a little surprised by JAWN's ultimatum that a failure to meet demands would result in a "public campaign against the *Inquirer*." I wondered if there was an opportunity for the *Inquirer* to be more transparent about the work they had been doing and to update the public on their plans for addressing the concerns JAWN noted. But days later, a friend in the world of journalism studies in another state reached out to me, asking what was going on with drama at the *Inquirer*. They knew I had been following their efforts and had seen a flurry of outrage circulating via U.S. journalism Twitter. I assumed the previous JAWN statement must have gotten the attention of media watchers, but when I finally got to look at my phone there was a new Ernest Owens tweet, this time sharing a screenshot of an internal email to staff from Lisa Hughes, the *Inquirer*'s publisher. In the letter, Hughes referred to JAWN's letter as an "unwarranted public attack" that "diminishes the important work we have done since 2020." It then outlined a number of the *Inquirer*'s DEIB-related initiatives, including the More Perfect Union series, the communities and engagement desk, a soon-to-be-launched internship program, and *Inquirer* for All efforts such as the antiracist workflow guide and content consult Slack channel (referencing it as "an internal forum to collaborate on sensitive content"). The letter framed JAWN authors as outsiders and expressed a defiant response: "Although there are voices outside of our organization looking to downplay and disregard the hard work that goes on each and every day at the *Inquirer*, we know better. We will not be discouraged, and we will not give in to their demands, threats, and belittlement."

Reading this letter, my hopes for the *Inquirer* working constructively with Philly JAWN as an external accountability body shrank. Debriefing with colleagues familiar with the *Inquirer*'s DEIB efforts, there was a general consensus that the letter's defensive tone and othering of the local BIPOC journalism affinity groups would likely pour gasoline on the fire that JAWN had lit. I was unclear about the strategic aim of Hughes's letter—whom was this letter for? While framed as an internal letter, it was drafted to be comprehended by people unfamiliar with newsroom initiatives like the Content Consult Slack, for example. The choice to characterize the concerns of JAWN as coming from outsiders was also notable. As Owens later noted: "All of our demands and concerns were informed to us by their Black & brown staff and community members." He expressed concern that the *Inquirer* was publicly saying it refused to meet with BIPOC journalism affinity groups: "Our members who work there now feel unsafe and concerned about how they can [be] supported."

One of the coauthors of the JAWN letter was Vanessa Maria Graber, the president of NAHJ Philly and director of Free Press' News Voices. Graber noted that they first wrote the letter only after multiple private meetings where there had been "no movement." They felt compelled to proceed with the letter after witnessing "a hemorrhage" of BIPOC journalists leaving the *Inquirer*—including some whose work was "loved by our community" and whose loss she believed meant they no longer had anyone "advocating and writing for us." The response to the letter worried Graber:

> If I was a journalist of color working at the *Inquirer*, I would be horrified. So the message was not to us. The message was to their staff. . . . They did not respond to us at all. . . . But an email was sent to their staff, letting them know that organizations that represent them, or the journalists of color, are outsiders and are misleading and causing trouble and attacking. I would not want to speak out or advocate for myself, in that type of situation. So it was a way to silence and intimidate staff. It was threatening in a way that if you collaborate with these organizations, this is how you will be seen.[47]

Beyond concerns about what Hughes's letter might indicate about the workplace culture around transparency and accountability, Graber shared concerns that the letter did not offer a concrete response to how the *Inquirer* planned to address problematic content (such as using anonymous police sources) or to improve retention of BIPOC staff. When I reached out to Hughes, asking several questions about accountability to community stakeholders, she did not answer any questions related to Philly JAWN.[48]

It is too early to say how effective Philly JAWN is going to be as a force for public accountability for the *Inquirer* or the larger Philadelphia news and information built environment. JAWN leaders have noted that they plan to expand their focus beyond the *Inquirer* to other newsrooms and to bring more stakeholders in to their work: "This movement has to be intersectional. We have to have community members, academics, journalists.

We have to have community leaders, we have to have people in local politics, all working together to change these narratives." They were starting with a coalition of journalists because they were close to the work and could understand what was needed to "dismantle the ways in which white supremacy shows up in the newsroom." In their first public exchange, they drew on the extensive social media networks of their core board—and while the discourse was primarily concentrated on the insular world of Twitter, it was certainly heard by power brokers within Philadelphia media. At the Lenfest summit mentioned earlier, the Philly JAWN exchange was not mentioned by name on stage, but it cast a shadow, coming up in hallway conversations, including when participants speculated on why the *Inquirer* was not more prominently in attendance. It will be worth following what direction Philly JAWN takes in the future and whether it can grow to become lasting accountability infrastructure for local journalism.[49] Notably, the external accountability group has already received at least indirect support from key metaorganizations: it is connected to the Shift the Narrative coalition funded by the Independence Public Media Foundation.[50] In addition, the BIPOC journalism affinity groups whose heads participate in Philly JAWN receive funding from the Lenfest Institute—though Lenfest, which is the noncontrolling owner of the *Inquirer*, has made clear that they are not directly funding Philly JAWN.

The *Inquirer*'s exchange with Philly JAWN also revealed possible challenges inside their internal DEIB infrastructure. Discussing the situation with a DEIB consultant familiar with the *Inquirer*'s efforts, they acknowledged that *Inquirer* management did not have an easy task: "It's like you try to canoe down-river and someone's not only shooting arrows your way, but whacking you on the back of the head with the oars." They noted that the *Inquirer* had no one in their top DEI role during the time that they lost multiple BIPOC journalists and the JAWN letter was sent. This was a reminder that "you've got to stay on it 24-7. There is no offseason." If a prominent Black journalist or series of BIPOC journalists leave and there is no action underway to recruit and support additional BIPOC journalists, "if the folks from JAWN are asking 'What's the plan?' and got no response, then they're going to be forced to go outside and say, 'Hey, look, we tried to do this, and you're not fulfilling your commitment." Whether JAWN's strategy proves to be tactically rewarding is unclear, as is where the *Inquirer* will go from here.[51]

NATIONAL ACCOUNTABILITY INFRASTRUCTURE FOR REPAIR AND THE CASE FOR LIMINAL LEADERSHIP

The Philly JAWN example illustrated the challenges of forging functional accountability relationships between external accountability bodies and journalism organizations. It also demonstrated how this local Philadelphia story connected with a network of people interested in more equitable local journalism around the United States and beyond. As noted, when it unfolded, I heard from multiple media watchers and people connected to metaorganizations from around the United States who were interested in what could be learned from these developments. I also observed both expressions of solidarity for BIPOC journalists and admonishments of shame for news organizations circulating in the national journalism Twittersphere. This made me think more about how learning from interventions flowed from the local up to the national level but also about the role national accountability infrastructure does or does not play in efforts to make local journalism more equitable and community centered.

As I mentioned in chapter 1, multiple national initiatives have been working to push U.S. public media in the direction of antiracism, including Public Media for All and the Public Radio Antiracist Partnership. Like Philly JAWN, some of these also attempted to use public channels to pressure local media organizations to address DEIB challenges—though the pressure was usually more diffuse, with open letters and associations targeting DEIB issues connected to staffing and coverage within the system as a whole. These groups did have some success in creating remote affinity groups and an infrastructure for discussing and tracking DEIB goals among their coalitions. But these voluntary initiatives faced limitations in part because of a lack of investment from across public media leadership and a lack of openness to visions for accountability and power-sharing/-ceding processes.

The journalist and DEI trainer Celeste Headlee, who convened the Public Radio Antiracist Partnership, underlined that her efforts attempted to go beyond traditional diversity training to focus on systems, policies, and structures that are antiracist. The challenge was that doing this required meaningful accountability, questioning traditions of how things have always been done and who is doing the work: "Look, some people are going to have to lose their jobs." She noted that public media had a history of not holding top leadership accountable: "Once they get up above a certain level, now the rest of us, peons below, we lose our jobs all the time. We get laid off. We get redundancied. Our grant funding runs out and the project just ends. . . . But for those who are in management, who are largely white and largely male, there is this real hesitation to have people feel any kind of consequences."[52] Headlee observed that in public media it was more likely to see entire programs cut than for management to lose their jobs. When I asked her what could change this, she responded, "We have to force them out of their positions because they're not leaving."

Public Media for All's cofounder Sachi Kobayashi similarly noted that public media spaces needed to have "tough conversations" to move toward an "accountability plan": "You need a carrot and a stick, and start with the carrot by all means. Lots of training, all that. But if you don't set some parameters in advance about, this is all the training, this is all the resources we're going to give you, but you have X amount of time to get your behavior changed."[53] Kobayashi suggested that the failure to hold people accountable, let alone let them go, came from "centering certain people's comfort at the expense of our audiences." She noted that there were many leaders in public media that thought of DEIB work as a "nice to have" that would "blow over." As audiences changed, she predicted that their failure to adapt would make such leaders irrelevant: "I wish them luck. It's going to be real rough. Sometimes you have to sink pretty far down before you can kick off the bottom of the pool and come back up.

There's definitely a lot of cases where we're waiting for people to retire, too. It's not all going to happen at once."

Another Public Media for All member, who was a manager of color, raised the issue of how leaders think of their role—and how governing boards and others could encourage managers to see themselves as "change agents." In their situation as someone who identified as BIPOC but not Black, given the context of anti-Black racism in the United States, they noted: "People may listen to me more or see me as the right fit more than they would see a Black candidate. And so I see my role as being to make it a safer space for someone who may not fit as easily into people's idea of what a GM or CEO should look like or be like or what their background should be." They explained that they tried to think about their own work at a station by asking the question: "Is there a potential to make this change?" They acknowledged that this approach was not shared by many white peers in the system, even among those with good intentions: "I've met some people who are great, and they're great white allies, but they don't plan on stepping aside. . . . They've told me specifically that they plan on going nowhere and that they will be at such-and-such station until the very end, and that's their dedication, and they've been there a very long time, so they should deserve this position."

This sentiment underlines the difficulty of pinning hopes of DEIB progress in any journalism system on the enlightened intentions of leadership. It also resurfaces the question, raised earlier in chapter 3, of what kinds of structures or processes could encourage or push leaders to share power or step aside. They noted the possible value of frameworks like term limits, as well as having hiring conversations, particularly in instances where a white manager is hired, about conceiving of the job as a transitional role, to work as a change agent to prepare the ground for leaders of color. They suggested that a variation of this same conversation could be had with "the GM who's been there twenty-five years, or we have some GMs in our system who are close to eighty years old."

These national coalitions of public media workers and stations have of course not solved the conundrum of how to incentivize shifting power. Nevertheless, they have surfaced structural challenges such as these questions of leadership—issues that might be sensitive and more difficult for local accountability infrastructure to do, given that it would involve calling out specific individuals who often hold considerable power at the local level. These national accountability groups also raised some specific visions to implement greater accountability for public radio leadership—such as the Public Radio Antiracist Partnership's idea for community-led boards where nonmanagement staff and members of the public could nominate and vote on board members.[54]

Talking with leaders of this work about patterns among top managers in journalism, I was particularly struck by the observation that (mostly white) leaders with progressive intentions associated their dedication to journalism with a commitment to staying on the job—associating commitment to the mission with a sense of permanence. In questioning this and in thinking about how leadership could instead reimagine itself as part of a transition to something else, something more equitable, I was reminded of a reflection by Outlier Media's Sarah Alvarez at the Lenfest summit. Alvarez spoke about how Outlier collaborated with the *Detroit Free Press*, a legacy newspaper, in terms that evoked a sort of liminal moment of transition: "They have none of the structures that are going to allow them to thrive. . . . It is a ticking time bomb. But I think that they know this, and we're very lucky that at the leadership level they're trying to create as much value as they possibly can in the time that they have left. And so I think that for legacy media that is not able to reimagine, or is constrained by structures, that creating value along the way, is what I look for."[55]

Could "creating value along the way" be a mantra not only for legacy outlets that may have a limited shelf life given business model challenges and other constraints but also for progressive white leaders in the local journalism sphere?[56] Could DEIB workers and the metaorganizations that provide an infrastructure for this work make a case for *liminal leadership*, for a kind of enlightened impermanence, and normalize frank conversations around transition and succession? Could metaorganizations map out systems to support efforts such as community-led boards, coleadership models, and term limits? These are questions I cannot answer in this book but hope to raise for future exploration.

NATIONAL INFRASTRUCTURE
FOR REIMAGINATION

One of the most lauded projects in local journalism innovation spaces in recent years is the rapid growth of the Chicago-based nonprofit City Bureau and particularly its Documenters Network, which trains and pays residents to document public meetings in service of "community-powered reporting"—and to build a "national network for grassroots, participatory media."[57] Shortly after launching as part of City Bureau[58] in Chicago in 2016, Documenters began expanding beyond Chicago by partnering with media organizations in other cities. Then in 2022, Documenters received a $10 million grant, accelerating its expansion.[59] At the time of writing, Resolve Philly was working with City Bureau to plan the launch of a Philadelphia Documenters project, which had yet to be formally announced. The Documenters project would fit within Resolve's Shake the Table initiatives, which focused on local government accountability. While the shape, form, and workflow of the project was still being developed, if it followed the network's overall model, it would be challenging traditional norms of who gets to be part of the making of local journalism, offering pathways for residents outside the journalism profession to be trained and paid to commit "acts of journalism" by documenting meetings. The project has been framed as a way to serve unmet civic information needs and to democratize and reimagine local journalism.

This project had the potential to significantly influence how Philly residents accessed information about City Hall and other areas of civic life. What did it mean that the model for it came from a Chicago-based nonprofit that has essentially become a metaorganization? Like Resolve Philly, City Bureau, as a start-up journalism organization, experienced massive growth since it started in 2015. The local context of Chicago that City Bureau grew out of had many parallels to issues in Philadelphia—both were (and are) highly segregated cities where large sections of the city had a history of stigmatizing or absent coverage by disproportionately white mainstream news outlets.[60] City Bureau has been mindful of the importance of local context and power dynamics and for this reason has expanded Documenters not by running all the projects themselves but by collaborating with local partners in the cities where Documenter programs work. Additional research would be needed to explore how the implementation of Documenters programs varies between cities—how much are they responsive to both local needs and assets? To what extent do the local iterations of the projects follow a community-centered process that involves community stakeholders in co-designing the shape of projects?[61] Community-centered journalism initiatives generally are not intended to be scalable because they seek to be responsive to local needs and assets— but are the Documenters Networks perhaps was finding ways to do this?

Another question the phenomena of Documenters raises is how such metaorganizations entering local journalism systems do so in a way that is mindful of equity challenges within local political and funding dynamics. *Kensington Voice*, for example, had been exploring an equivalent to Documenters before they knew Documenters was coming to Philadelphia. As the researchers Wilson Lowrey, Danielle Deaverson, and William Singleton have noted, metaorganizations tended to support a system's dominant actors or incumbents, whether intentionally or not.[62] In this case, Resolve Philly functioned as an incumbent within the realm of community-centered journalism actors, as the local rising-star start-up already attending the same invitation-only national funders' conferences and City Bureau's own thought leaders' convenings.[63] *Kensington Voice* as a hyperlocal outlet operated outside of these circles, although they also collaborated with Resolve and even had the possibility of doing so more deeply via Resolve's community newswire service. This leaves it as an open question whether they may still benefit from or collaborate with a new Documenters initiative or whether it will limit their own vision for a hyperlocal variation on this model.

The case of Documenters' expansion offers an example of a national-level infrastructure entering a locale where efforts to build more equitable local journalism infrastructure are already underway. It is worth following how this case unfolds to better understand whether and how these infrastructures for reimagining may connect. On the one hand, such an attempt offers a possibility of system-level transformation; on the other, it poses the risk of recreating the same inequitable power dynamics it was designed to challenge if the nexus between the national metaorganization's infrastructure and the local and hyperlocal infrastructures are not handled with care.

These questions are worth considering beyond this specific example. City Bureau is of course not the only metaorganization intervening in local journalism spaces (even within Philadelphia). Similar questions could be asked about journalism engagement initiatives such as the Listening Post Collective, Hearken, and others. They can be particularly challenging questions when the metaorganizations or even metro-level local organizations may not be aware of all the local and hyperlocal stakeholders already doing valuable work to serve the information needs and amplify the assets of their communities. In communication infrastructure theory terms, metaorganizations have the potential to support and strengthen the links between actors in local storytelling networks (residents, community organizations and local media), but their reach will likely vary based on the depth of their mapping communication assets in the communities they seek to support. Particularly when seeking to further goals of antiracism, metaorganizations would do well to challenge colorblind ideologies and invest in a critical analysis of local realities that works to ensure that smaller actors are included and that power and resources are distributed as equitably as possible.

* * *

Whether focusing on repair or reimagination efforts, a range of external organizations are actively working to push local journalism systems toward greater equity and community engagement, with varied degrees of impact. This chapter surfaced a number of questions, many of which require additional research to do justice, but the experiences shared here hint at the possible influence of organizations that often have the financial and human resources that local newsrooms lack. These metaorganizations, of course, are shaped by their own interests. For many, the extent they can engage in radical imagining is constrained by their own interdependencies within a market-based capitalist system. In addition, many grapple with some of the same DEIB and accountability challenges as news organizations.

Nevertheless, they do influence local news and information built environments, through direct capital for media organizations, capacity-building resources, and their ability to convene and circulate thought leadership. The leverage they have to push toward more equitable journalism varies depending on whether they are undertaking repair work with large established outlets or working with smaller journalism organizations, and their approach is often shaped by their internal reflexivity regarding color-blind ideology and the lingering influence of white supremacy on power structures.

In the concluding chapter, I will synthesize some takeaways from the cases I've followed within the Philadelphia news and information built environment. I will attempt to distill some lessons learned that may be of interest for stakeholders within local journalism beyond this region and offer some practical recommendations for journalists, newsroom management, metaorganizations including journalism support organizations and funders, and journalism educators.

CONCLUSION

Transforming Through Process and Infrastructure,
Not Projects and Destinations

I f you think it's bad in Philly . . ."

"You're so lucky to be in Philadelphia . . ."

"What's going on in Philly?"

Conversations I've had with colleagues working to make journalism more equitable have frequently begun with a variation on one of these phrases. Often, they are followed by observations about how journalists in many locales around the United States and in some other countries confront steep battles to nudge their organizations, let alone their larger news and information built environments, toward greater equity and antiracism. Or the person notes the many innovative media initiatives happening in Philadelphia and the philanthropic support they garner. Of course, they also occasionally note controversies plaguing newsrooms featured in this book, some of which have gained notoriety far beyond the Philly metro area.

Over the course of researching and writing this book, I've thought a lot about what makes Philadelphia unique as a news and information built environment and what lessons might be distilled from its experience to researchers and practitioners elsewhere. As I've mentioned, this is a city with a substantial history of attempts at local journalism collaboration and innovation. It is also a city with one of the highest levels of philanthropic spending on journalism, at more than $50 per capita.[1] But this legacy of investment can be a double-edged sword, creating opportunities for experimentation and laying foundations for collaborative initiatives but also potentially digging grooves that are difficult to redirect or bubbles that artificially insulate problematic organizational behaviors. This combination complicates the idea of Philadelphia as a sort of "test kitchen" for local journalism innovation. In some ways it does function as an ideal site for reimagining local journalism practices, but the attention and resources it gets from metaorganizations means things might work in Philadelphia that will be challenging elsewhere. At the same time, resources could protect some Philly news organizations in a way that shields them from needing to make transformative change.

Because of this place-based complexity and the need for any genuinely community-centered intervention to account for both local needs and assets, as I conclude this book, I will offer some takeaways that center questions of practices and power dynamics that could apply to a variety of local journalism organizations and systems. I will first review how interventions attempting to make Philadelphia's news and information built environment more equitable and antiracist may be affecting local storytelling networks, from a communication infrastructure (CIT) framework.[2] I'll then offer more practical lessons learned for journalists, newsroom management, metaorganizations including journalism support organizations and funders, and journalism educators seeking to create more equitable internal infrastructure that challenges whiteness norms and improves their chances of establishing more equitable relationships between local journalism and BIPOC communities.

CONNECTING LOCAL STORYTELLING NETWORKS?

The cases in this book focused on a range of actors in local storytelling networks at both the hyperlocal and metro level. CIT primarily focuses on the relationship among storytelling network actors that include local media, networks of residents, and community organizations. In this book I looked at interventions aimed at the dynamics within local media organizations, as well as how these interfaced with interventions focused on the network ties linking local media to other storytelling network actors. This included interventions of repair within the established metro news organizations WHYY and the *Philadelphia Inquirer*, as well as interventions of reimagination undertaken by the journalism nonprofit Resolve Philly and the hyperlocal news outlet *Kensington Voice*. I also looked at the role metaorganizations (foundations, DEIB training organizations, external accountability groups) played in these and other related interventions attempting to make the local news and information built environment more equitable.

The nuance of these cases defy the simplification of my diagrams. However, I've attempted a basic overview of a preintervention state (see figure 7.1), where metro news outlets were primarily focused on a one-way distribution of content to audiences. They had ties with community organization and hyperlocal outlets, but these were occasional one-way relationships to extract sources for stories (whether they acknowledged doing so or not), not collaborative relationships. In this preintervention state, support

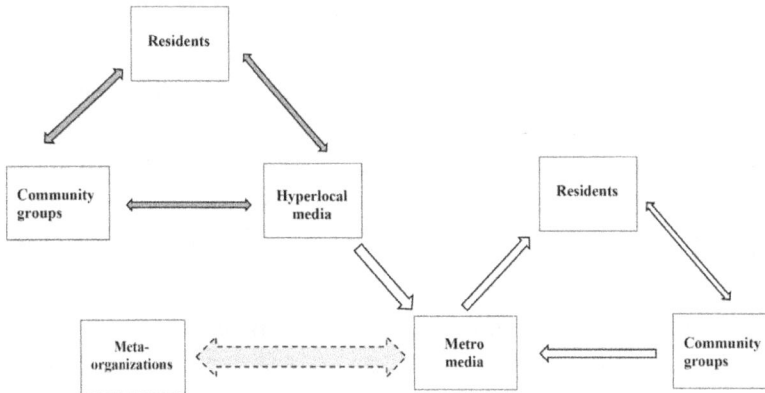

FIGURE 7.1 Communication infrastructure theory's "storytelling networks"—before interventions.

from metaorganizations (for example, funding or training) primarily went to metro outlets.

In figure 7.2, I attempt to show some, though not all, of the ways these relationships have shifted as a result of the various interventions explored in this book. These shifts are uneven, and for some organizations little has changed. But as a result of interventions seeking to pursue greater community engagement, which are often supported by metaorganizations, some links that had been one way became two way in this diagram. For example, metro organizations now conduct more community outreach, or they collaborate with hyperlocal media via projects like WHYY's NICE project or may do so in the future through Resolve's community newswire service. As noted, the extent to which these network ties have been strengthened varies depending on the organization. For example, while the *Inquirer* was beginning to develop two-way relationships directly with residents and community organizations through its communities and engagement desk, many had noted that it was less open to collaboration with other hyperlocal media outlets or external accountability bodies. Likewise, while some metaorganizations such as IPMF, Knight-Lenfest, and Resolve Philly (which had in some ways become a metaorganization in its own right) had begun to focus on smaller hyperlocal outlets and the network ties within the local storytelling network, because of the structure of their organization the Lenfest Institute continued to focus the largest portion of their funding on an established metro-level outlet, the *Inquirer*. (They supported a number of start-up and BIPOC-led initiatives as well, but the sums were smaller in comparison.) Other interventions not pictured in figure 7.2 include the efforts of local accountability groups such as the Philly Journalism Accountability Watchdog Group (Philly JAWN), which to date primarily focuses on metro news organizations (and, at the time of writing, had only established a one-way relationship with the *Inquirer*). In addition, other national metaorganizations and accountability infrastructure were brushing up against and influencing local networks. This included national antiracism coalitions within public media, as well as City Bureau's Documenters project. The latter, which at the time of writing was planning a launch of a Philadelphia Documenters project with Resolve Philly, had the

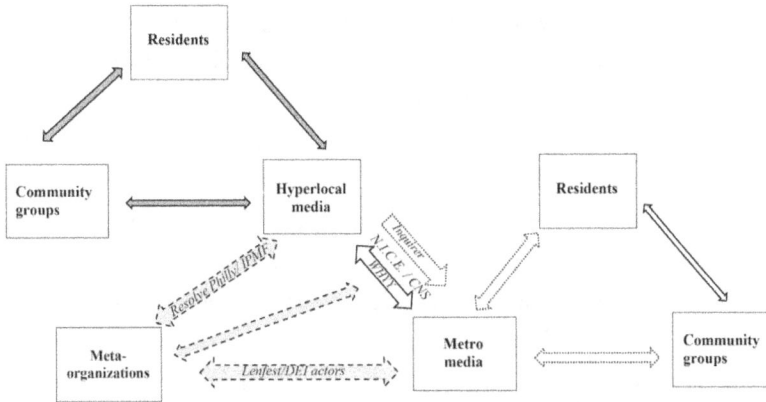

FIGURE 7.2. Communication infrastructure theory's "storytelling networks—after interventions.

potential in the future to support network ties between residents and community organizations and other civic actors. The work of those Documenters could then potentially be connected with hyperlocal and metro media actors but could also potentially disrupt some of these linkages.

This sketch of local storytelling networks only captures some of the contours and directionality of where these interventions may head. A fuller model would need additional dimensions to show, for example, connections between different hyperlocal media and influencers, as well as how some metro news outlets directly reach some of the same audiences as hyperlocal actors. Cumulatively, the interventions explored in this book do seem to be supporting more multidirectional ties between storytelling network actors. This is notable because strengthening such ties has been shown by other communication researchers to sometimes correlate with greater civic participation and a shared sense of community issues.[3] However, just as critical as the shape and intentions of these interventions is the extent to which efforts to push toward greater equity and antiracism are successful within the different nodes in the network. For example, efforts to strengthen connections between local media and residents, particularly residents from BIPOC communities, are unlikely to succeed if the internal structures of media organizations do not shift in the direction of greater equity. As discussed in previous chapters, when the internal culture of a newsroom is uncritically steeped in whiteness and colorblind ideology, the narratives it generates are likely to reflect this—replicating the white spatial imaginary discussed in the introduction and creating barriers to producing journalism *with* and *for* BIPOC communities.[4] Likewise, if the internal cultures of metaorganizations are not critically reflexive about equity issues, they are likely to unintentionally replicate inequitable power dynamics both internally and in their interventions. In the sections that follow, I will synthesize lessons learned from these case studies about the local media node in these networks. From these, I'll offer some recommendations for journalists, newsroom management, journalism support organizations, funders, and journalism educators invested in making local journalism more equitable and antiracist.

STANDARDIZE COMMUNITY-CENTERED
JOURNALISM PROCESSES

Many of the struggles Philadelphia newsrooms like the *Inquirer* and WHYY had over the course of my observation stemmed from a lack of infrastructure to integrate a community-centered and antiracist orientation throughout the cycle of reporting, editing, and circulating coverage. Community engagement was often siloed off as something special teams did, rather than integrated as a core reporting competency. If news organizations want to commit to equitable journalism, all reporters and editors will need to integrate skills such as community organizing and outreach into their reporting practices. Doing this will require adjusting production timeframes to allow time for reporters to build relationships when they are not on deadline seeking to extract a quote.

Some of the special projects discussed in earlier chapters may offer prototypes that could be adopted at a broader scale—for example, if reporters for the *Inquirer*'s communities and engagement desk are genuinely being allotted time to hold community office hours and/or attend community meetings (not for a story), this may be a practice all reporters could benefit from. Going further, the experiences of hyperlocal projects like *Kensington Voice* and the Germantown Info Hub offer insights into the relationship building required to do nonextractive community-centered work over time.

Reallocating time resources will require tradeoffs about what is and is not covered. But editors have always made such choices—with many historically prioritizing, even if unintentionally, the information needs and interests of whiter, wealthier constituencies.[5] If organizations are genuine about moving toward more equitable journalism, deepening their investment into relationship building with BIPOC and other marginalized communities offers an opportunity to recalibrate coverage priorities.

INTERNAL ACCOUNTABILITY INFRASTRUCTURE FOR EQUITABLE JOURNALISM

The cases explored in this book illustrate that equitable and antiracist journalism cannot hinge on good intentions. Particularly in majority-white news organizations, accountability infrastructure is critical to encouraging reflexivity among management and staff about the choices they make in the journalistic process.

My observations of efforts to implement accountability "tools" highlighted the complications that come from trying to quantitatively track the various ways white supremacy and anti-Black racism are imprinted on newsroom culture and practice. Yes, there was value in attempting to track who was and was not represented in coverage. But the value came primarily from actively engaging reporters and editors in the process (as WHYY did), as this encouraged them to be mindful of whose voices they were showcasing (for this reason, I am less interested in automated source tracking systems that don't directly involve the reporters/editors). The actual numbers tracked were interesting but incomplete. As the example in the introduction noted, source tracking might suggest quantitatively that a Black woman was represented by a Black reporter—but it will not reveal a racist framing used to construct a narrative. At the same time, while imperfect, quantification was valuable because it offered a way to create recognizable metrics to assess performance on DEIB goals.

Other examples of DEIB infrastructure offered potential to get at more nuanced issues, such as how whiteness influenced the framing and style of stories, but they came with additional limitations. The *Inquirer*'s Content Consult Slack channel offered a potential space for exploration and learning as reporters and editors discussed potentially sensitive stories before their publication. But the channel hinged on who opted in to participate, and many noted concerns that it felt like a fraught space or was seen as a "cover-your-ass" operation. The postpublication "retrospective" process offered additional promise to talk through both successes and areas that needed improvement, though the extent to which this process would meaningfully tackle issues around whiteness and antiracism was not clear at the time of writing. Finally, the antiracist reporting guide offered a more holistic intervention by offering questions to be asked of staffers in various roles at various points in the production cycle. However, many expressed dismay that there was no way to incentivize the guide's implementation. These examples suggest there may be value in creating performance metrics around participation in equitable journalism systems and processes. This of course is not so simple. For example, the *Inquirer* did try to note participation in *Inquirer* for All committees in performance reviews. But that committee work was optional. In addition, it is not asking the same thing to require a Black reporter, for whom participating in an intervention focused on antiracism could potentially be retraumatizing, and a white reporter, for whom participation could present a valuable opportunity for growth. Future performance metrics could be developed in a way that is not race blind but rather offers a variety of options depending on a staffer's intersectional positionality. For example, just as staffers may create personal development plans for craft or leadership skills in a performance review process, they could create a development plan to work on cultural fluency with marginalized communities they do not identify with (which may include identity categories such as a gender, disability, class, etc. in addition to race/ethnicity).

DEIB workers cannot offer a one-size-fits-all framework to implement internal accountability infrastructure. However, as the American Press Institute's Letrell Crittenden has recommended through his work with newsrooms, while it may not be possible to address every component in an institution at once, doing an initial assessment of needs and assets may aid a news organization in prioritizing infrastructure needs. When organizations accept that this work needs to be part of core operations and not a special project, they can begin to create supports for more equitably assessing information needs, developing sources, editing stories, and engaging communities in the content that is produced.

INTERNAL ACCOUNTABILITY INFRASTRUCTURE FOR EQUITABLE WORKPLACE CULTURES

There is overlap between the infrastructure needed to push journalism processes toward antiracism and that needed to create more equitable workplace cultures. It is unlikely that the former can be sustained without the latter. Because of this, it is critical that news organizations have investment not only within newsrooms but also across organizations. The shape and form this takes will likely vary depending on an institution's needs. For established institutions, the need for repair of historical harms complicates the work of building trust within workplaces. This may necessitate the establishment of ongoing infrastructures akin to *Inquirer* for All committees, taking care to ensure that participation does not fall disproportionately on BIPOC staff, but also holding white staffers accountable to BIPOC staffers as they set priorities and move toward goals. But as the *Inquirer*'s experience suggests, voluntary structures alone may not be enough to repair toxic cultures or create spaces that encourage retention if they are not paired with meaningful adjustments to who holds power and how people are compensated. While it may be challenging to fully adopt in a large, union-ized organization, some of the approaches of smaller start-ups like *Kensington Voice* offer compelling alternative practices, such as budget and pay transparency and participatory budgeting.

In addition to addressing issues such as pay equity, human resources systems also need to be synced across organizations to ensure more equitable recruitment, rethinking practices and channels, and questioning taken-for-granted criteria that may favor white and wealthier applicants. This may also mean adding in criteria for cultural competency to ensure that all applicants enter the workplace with an understanding of DEIB issues and anti-racism goals. Even when an organization is performing well, for example when it is under the leadership of a BIPOC manager attuned to issues of equity, putting infrastructure in place is critical to ensure that progress can be sustained and institutionalized even if managers change.

ORGANIZATIONAL GOVERNANCE AND TRANSITIONAL LEADERSHIP

As these Philadelphia cases illustrate, leadership and the organizational governance structures that do or do not hold it accountable can influence the scope of what progress is possible within an organization. For both WHYY and the *Inquirer*, as with many mainstream media organizations, top leaders reported to governing boards that had no accountability to the public or to staff. In the case of WHYY, the board had a more-than-twenty-five-year relationship with the CEO. The *Inquirers'* CEO was relatively new, but her response to Philly JAWN suggested she may not be open to dialogue with independent accountability groups. Given the structures in which they operated, it is not surprising if such leaders prioritize news outlets' financial bottom lines rather than goals around equity or community engagement.

The approaches of these leaders (who both identified as white) of established majority white news organizations stand in contrast with those of the smaller start-ups profiled that were comparatively less white. Resolve Philly's co–executive directors, one who identified as Black and one who identified as white, followed a coleadership model and worked to cultivate a work culture with a relatively flat hierarchy where staff with a diverse range of intersectional identities and lived experiences could directly engage them in accountability conversations. *Kensington Voice* had been led by a founder who identified as white, but she transitioned to a support role, hired and promoted editors who identified as Latinx/e to lead the outlet, and created a governing board consisting entirely of Black and Latinx/e community members.

I recognize that the organizational complexity of large established news organizations means what works for *Kensington Voice* may not work for the *Inquirer.* At the same time, leaders of larger organizations may adapt transferable elements from these start-ups—such as the idea that being a good leader may not hinge on the duration of leadership but on the transformative change that can be made while under one's care. This idea of transitional leadership[6] to transform organizations and systems is something that could be adopted at larger organizations, though doing so is unlikely without normalizing and incentivizing conversations about it. This points to a potential opportunity for metaorganizations (including funders) and external accountability bodies to encourage more expansive visioning that reframes giving up power as a positive accomplishment of transformation. Such conversations could similarly encourage discussion around related infrastructure to support transformation, such as community-led boards and term limits for executives.

EXTERNAL ACCOUNTABILITY INFRASTRUCTURES

Over the course of my observations, the journalism organizations in this book interfaced with a number of bodies that offered critical external accountability. These included the long-established infrastructure of trade unions—which were key to highlighting issues around pay equity at both WHYY and the *Inquirer*. BIPOC journalist affinity groups including the Philadelphia Association of Black Journalists and the Philadelphia chapters of the Asian American Journalists Association and the National Association of Hispanic Journalists played a critical role, both in directly organizing and publicly calling out news organizations through social media and other forums but also by collaborating on the Philly JAWN initiative. In addition, the national metaorganization Free Press supported both Philly JAWN and additional accountability work in concert with the Shift the Narrative Coalition, which focused on narratives around violence and policing.

While the relationships between these external bodies and established news organizations were tense at times, news organizations have an opportunity to approach such external actors with a spirit of shared goals. These actors may essentially be acting as "loyal opposition," prioritizing different interests and seeking change, but doing so with a shared sense of care for the news organizations and their missions. At a time when many communities were not engaged with these news organizations because of a lack of trust or interest, caring enough to express concern should not be taken lightly. Newsrooms and external accountability bodies potentially have a shared investment in sustaining news organizations that serve local communities. If these parties could establish a constructive working dialogue, there may be a valuable opportunity for learning and development, whereas an antagonistic relationship that primarily plays out on social media is likely to further erode trust in the news organization.

Newsrooms can also take more agency in supporting and collaborating with external accountability groups in a range of forms. While not every news organization will be willing to create a community-led governing board, there are numerous models for advisory bodies. What is crucial is for such infrastructure to incorporate a way for the news organization to share power with the external community group and not simply be performative or extractive by "listening" but not sharing any power in return. This is an area that will benefit from additional research, and I am currently collaborating with news organizations including Resolve Philly and Temple University's Philadelphia Neighborhoods to explore possible models by seeking community input and inviting residents to co-design infrastructure for equitable journalism.[7] It's also an area that is unlikely to be sustained without funders and other metaorganizations incentivizing the work—be it by funding BIPOC journalists' affinity groups, initiatives like Shift the Narrative or other yet-to-be-conceived efforts, and supporting news organizations like *Kensington Voice*, who are taking steps to meaningfully share power with community-led boards.

COLLABORATIVE PARTNERSHIPS

While collaborative journalism has a history in Philadelphia, as the cases explored here suggest, collaborations are not inherently equitable and can at times have unintended consequences. A lot depends upon the orientation individual news organizations and their staff bring to collaborations. Newsrooms in this book (and individual managers and staffers within them) varied greatly in terms of their openness to collaboration, their reflexivity about the power dynamics involved, and their commitment to equitable and nonextractive collaboration.

Many of the cases here highlight positive examples of what is possible in a system where collaborative groundwork is in place, but these cases also point to the complexity involved. Organizations like Resolve Philly have done considerable work building infrastructure for equitable collaboration through Broke in Philly and other projects that often prioritize the needs of smaller partner organizations. At the same time, there are times when elements of their work that involve giving microgrants to other newsrooms (including, for example, *Kensington Voice*) may yield less funding for those newsrooms than if a funder directly made individual grants to the partners (of course, it is an open question whether small partners would have ever gained the attention of many funders without Resolve). WHYY's NICE project also offers an example of an organization finding a way to pursue its goals for community engagement while also offering support to other local storytelling actors in the system. Its initial efforts highlight the importance of "moving at the speed of trust" with partners but also the value in clearly establishing shared expectations. The example of the NICE project also underlines the need for news organizations to secure investment from across their institutions and find ways to integrate community engagement initiatives with general newsroom operations.

Cases explored here underscore the need to handle collaborations with care and show what can happen when they are not. *Kensington Voices*' experience with the *Inquirer*'s Local Lab illustrated how collaborations with larger partners who may not sustain their investment over time can risk damaging community trust not only in the larger partner but potentially also in the smaller partner who acted as an intermediary to community stakeholders.

FUNDING FOR TRANSFORMATION

Local journalism is of course largely operating without a viable market-based business model for financial sustainability. While innovative revenue efforts are underway, including by many of the journalism organizations discussed in these chapters, larger structural reforms and policy interventions are needed that are beyond the purview of this book.[8] In the meantime, media organizations would do well to look critically at how their aspirations for equitable and antiracist journalism square with their existing business models, which are often enmeshed in highly inequitable racial capitalism and often center imagined white consumers. In addition, in the current moment, philanthropic support from foundations plays a critical role for many news organizations, though as discussed, the degree of their leveraging power is generally greater for smaller news organizations. Funders of journalism may consider lessons in all of the preceding sections related to building both internal and external infrastructure for accountability and to incentivizing equitable collaboration and difficult conversations around organizational governance and opportunities for transitional leadership. In addition, as explored in chapter 6, funders seeking to prioritize a more antiracist and equitable system may do well to recalibrate their budgets so that the bulk of funds go to BIPOC-centered and -led organizations, with some reserved for strategic interventions to support transformational BIPOC leadership within established organizations at key moments.

JOURNALISM EDUCATION

Journalism education in the United States faces both challenges and opportunities, including many that parallel the challenges within the industry. At the same time many J-schools face shrinking enrollments, and elite universities are launching new niche master's programs at eye wateringly high tuition rates. On the other side of the spectrum, concerns over a lack of diversity within the journalism industry have led some to pursue more accessible and inclusive approaches to journalism education. This includes collaborations with community colleges; pay-what-you-wish courses for journalists of color; and initiatives, including City Bureau's Documenters, that challenge the need for journalism school and professionalization more broadly, by training community members directly to commit "acts of journalism."

Of course, many who, like me, are already within the university-based system of journalism education are also invested in reimagining the status quo—and doing repair work within our own institutions.[9] We grapple with many of the same issues as legacy news outlets. We are often disproportionately white faculty, including a sizable number of colleagues who are themselves alumni of harmful legacy outlets. Some left said outlets out of frustration and a desire to repair, but others maintained an allegiance to their former employers' traditions and practices. I have spoken with faculty around the United States who have shared their concerns that while they attempted to teach more equitable iterations of journalism, they also encountered students who had already learned problematic frameworks from other instructors, such as uncritical interpretations of "objectivity" norms.

We have an opportunity in this moment of flux within both the industry and the academy to simultaneously revise and reimagine the canon of journalism education and to create new opportunities for more accessible and inclusive training. When reworking what we explore in classrooms, we can redefine standards of "good journalism" as inherently community-centered, antiracist, and equitable journalism. We can teach competency areas like nonextractive community organizing practices as part of the work of reporting. We can teach strategies for journalists to self-monitor the diversity of their sources and to integrate equitable workflows into their reporting and editing—including monitoring their work for harmful frames. We can train students to be practitioners of what Sue Robinson calls "identity-aware care."[10] We can also teach the development of accountability infrastructure as core practices of newsroom management, and we can explore case studies of newsrooms that have attempted to move in the direction of greater equity and learn from both where they succeed and fall short. The more we can normalize equitable journalism as standard journalism practice, the more students coming out of such journalism education will be prepared to contribute to the reimagining and repair that needs to happen if the larger industry is going to maintain relevance.

PROGRESS OR PERFORMANCE?

Reflecting back on my five years observing Philadelphia media, I am aware that I am offering a very partial snapshot of a moment of flux. But from this slice of observations there are insights to consider. Cumulatively, these cases explore and extend the application of communication infrastructure theory by tracing how interventions attempting equitable and collaborative journalism at multiple levels can affect ties within local storytelling networks. They also illustrate how colorblind ideology, whiteness, and anti-Black racism can be infused into newsroom practices and norms irrespective of the intentions of managers or staff—weakening network ties in turn. But the interventions undertaken by both established and start-up journalism organizations also demonstrated a range of takeaways for newsrooms committed to equitable journalism to consider either adapting or avoiding. Of course, this snapshot is not a comprehensive panorama—for example, none of the interventions involved local broadcast television stations, who are often implicated in circulating problematic narratives like those referenced by frustrated residents in this book's introduction.[11]

Accounting for both the insights and limitations of my observations, what does this snapshot of activity add up to? How should I answer friends who want to know what all the buzz around local journalism in Philly amounts to? Is it real or merely performative? The voices I have introduced in these pages have shown a range of possible answers. Listening to Ernest Owens, even before the Philly JAWN debacle, the conclusion would be pessimistic: "It seems to me that a lot of these groups have gotten better with including more people, but I don't think they've gotten better at advancing more people. . . . Visually the aesthetic is changing, but when we're looking at power, that's not changing. . . . The people who are calling the shots and the serious decision makers still remain largely white."[12]

Independence Public Media Foundation's Molly de Aguiar similarly outlined why she was not optimistic about shifting power:

> There's little perceived incentive for those in power to do the very real, hard work of reimagining the system and sharing or ceding their power in the reimagined system. I say "perceived incentive" because there are real and powerful incentives—like clarity about and liberation from the systems of oppression that trap us—but undertaking this journey requires deep commitment to oftentimes painful self-examination, learning, change, perseverance, and also a vision for what is possible. For most people with power and privilege, it's simply much easier and more comfortable to do nothing, or to do just enough to make them look or feel like they're doing something.[13]

At the same time, none of these people were abandoning efforts to advocate for real shifts of power. Rather, they—and a number of others doing this work—were being more strategic in how and where they invested time and resources. For some this meant investing in change when openings arose and trying to lay foundations for infrastructure that, while unsexy, had potential to be more than performative. Yes, there were elements of performance in how powers within Philadelphia institutions heralded individual DEIB and community engagement initiatives. Critically recognizing this should not take away from the value of these initiatives but rather highlight the need for more advocacy for transformative change that cuts across institutions.

As one DEIB worker noted about the work of becoming a "an antiracist institution": "That is a commitment to a lifestyle, that is a commitment to a culture, that is a commitment to a way of activism that really lasts a lifetime, not just for a quarter." The work of equitable journalism will never be a finished project. For media organizations, the goal should not be a destination to be reached but rather processes to be integrated into institutional frameworks and the day-to-day practice of journalism. There really is not an acceptable alternative to proceeding forward in this work irrespective of the multifaceted challenges facing journalism, as Sachi Kobayashi of Public Media for All notes: "People are like, 'Oh, it's a new pot I have to mind.' And I'm like, 'No, no, no, no. This pot was always here. You've just been ignoring it for multiple decades.' You don't get to treat it like a new one and be like, 'Oh, so novel. I don't know how to juggle this many pots.' You left it on the back burner for decades. Maybe it's time to leave something else on the back burner now, if you really can't handle two things on the burner at once."[14]

It is true that the cooks in the Philly test kitchen of local journalism are still having occasional kitchen fires as they tend to pots and attempt to develop recipes for a more equitable news and information system. But I do think there are chefs to watch here. Some may be more presentation than flavor. But there are also thoughtful kitchen staffers creating infrastructure to slowly simmer multiple pots. Yes, there are things happening here in Philly. Many of these things merit critical skepticism. Many are incomplete, untidy, and uncomfortable. Looking at how existing interventions play out within the system cumulatively, often complicated by complex ties of collaboration and competition, highlights that while there is dysfunction, there is also dynamic movement here. The test kitchen may need a gut rehab, but Philly shows us we can keep stirring pots while the construction work is underway.

APPENDIX

METHODS

I n this book I have explored attempts to push a local news system toward greater equity and antiracism through a series of case studies as well as a long if not linear soak in the waters of Philadelphia's local journalism system. Doing this allowed me to look at overarching research questions including: How do repair efforts at established majority-white media affect practices, norms, and power dynamics within organizations? And how do and don't diversity, equity, inclusion, and belonging (DEIB) efforts connect with work (at these same organizations and at start-up journalism organizations) to encourage more community-centered local news systems? Finally, I looked at how these efforts may affect what communication infrastructure theory, or CIT, calls local "storytelling networks"—where key actors such as local media, community organizations, and networks of residents are each involved in circulating stories about the community.

Grappling with these questions led me to undertake case studies, between 2017 and 2022, where I combined semistructured qualitative interviews, focus groups, and observation of relevant moments (meetings, conferences, etc.), as well as monitoring of media outputs, project documents, and social media. I had previously focused on the information needs and visions of community members for more equitable relationships with local media through a series of interviews, diaries, and focus groups—including with Philadelphia-area residents. These informed my previous book, *Community-Centered Journalism*, and provided a jumping-off point for my exploration in this book. In this book, I also included some qualitative data from additional focus groups with community members, but primarily I centered the perspective of journalists and metaorganizations supporting journalists.

My approach was guided by Burawoy's extended case method of ethnography, where I as a researcher was involved as a participant in activities under study, and I engaged in dialogue with key actors and with theoretical concepts.[1] For the two case studies with established media organizations, WHYY and the *Philadelphia Inquirer*, I initially got involved to offer pro bono help with projects "auditing" the diversity of the people featured in their coverage, with an emphasis on their race/ethnicity.[2] In both cases I reached understandings with managers at the organizations that I would work with them to help with their quantitative "audits" but that I would also conduct and publicly share additional qualitative research to offer context on the work practices and culture behind the numbers.

At WHYY (as explored in chapters 1 and 3) I had two primary periods of observation. The first focused on their "Culturally Competent Newsrooms" project from late 2017 to mid-2019. During this period, in addition to acting as an advisor on their "source audit" project, I also observed five training sessions focused on implicit bias, sourcing practices, radio skills (for primarily BIPOC freelance journalists), and storytelling (for community members). I observed four community outreach events and multiple staff meetings. I conducted interviews about the project and WHYY's efforts to connect with local communities with eighteen staff members (some multiple times), a training consultant, and five outside training participants.[3]

The second phase of my observation was timed over the first year (January 2021–January 2022) of WHYY's News and Information Community Exchange, better known as the NICE project. I interviewed all of the eight founding partners and core project staff and observed several project meetings and events (all online because of the pandemic).[4] I also conducted four

focus groups and interviews with WHYY staff (with twenty-one participants total), which focused on the station's broader DEIB and community engagement efforts, but I also invited participants to share their perceptions of the NICE project and how it connected to their broader work
as a station.[5] In addition, I explored perspectives on NICE and got feedback on audio content partners produced through a series of three focus
groups with residents of communities NICE and WHYY sought to reach
(thirteen residents total). These included one group whose participants
identified as Black residents of a majority-Black area of the city, one Spanish-
language group who identified as Latinx/e residents of the city, and one
group whose participants reflected a range of demographic backgrounds
that roughly reflected the range of existing WHYY listeners.[6] A conve-
nience sample of participants was recruited through a combination of
online postings and snowball sampling. Given the COVID-19 pandemic,
focus groups, interviews, events, and meetings were all held online.

My work with the *Inquirer* (explored in chapters 2 and 3) grew out of a
request in June 2020 to co-lead a team of Temple faculty and staff in conducting a "diversity and inclusion audit," along with my late colleague Bryan
Monroe. I was brought on to this work in part because of my work with
WHYY's source audit. I conducted two waves of qualitative research in
association with the audit process. From August 2020 to November 2020,
as part of the formal audit, my Temple colleague Christopher Malo and I
observed meetings and interviewed forty-six employees[7] about norms and
practices around sourcing, editing, engagement, and workplace culture. Six
months later, I conducted a series of five focus group discussions and additional one-on-one interviews with forty-two staff and managers to follow
up on what progress had and had not been made.[8] I then continued to occasionally check in with *Inquirer* staff through both informal correspon-
dences and occasional recorded interviews and by observing occasional
Inquirer events.

For chapter 4's focus on Resolve Philly and the case of the Germantown
Info Hub (which became a pilot bureau for their community newswire ser-
vice), I drew on a history of participant observation that began in 2018.
With Resolve Philly, from 2018–2019, I sat in on a number of their Broke

in Philly partner meetings, either representing Temple University, the Germantown Info Hub, and/or as an observer. With the Germantown Info Hub, I cofounded the project in association with a community advisory group following a research study I had led. My involvement from 2018–2022 took different forms, first as a co-leader of the project, then as an advisor/ researcher once we had grant-funded project staff (from late 2019 to December 2021), then as an outside observer when it became part of Resolve Philly in January 2022. Early on I was involved with meetings and outreach/ production oversight, later acting more as an observer occasionally assisting with grant applications, etc. I also collaborated with Letrell Crittenden to conduct research on what Germantown community members wanted from local media and other information sources over this time period, though while this data offered background context, I do not discuss it directly in this book.[9] For my exploration in chapter 4, I draw on both semi-structured interviews and informal check- in conversations and emails conducted between February 2022 and September 2022 with the five Resolve Philly staffers (including the two full-time Germantown Info Hub staffers) whose work intersected with the Germantown Info Hub and/or the larger community newswire service (CNS) project. I spoke with key staffers multiple times over this period to get a sense of their perceptions of the process of transitioning the Germantown Info Hub to Resolve and their goals for the Info Hub and the CNS project.

In chapter 5, my discussion of *Kensington Voice*'s place within Philadelphia's news and information built environment similarly drew on observation of the project since its founding in 2018 and particularly from my experience collaborating with *Kensington Voice* beginning in 2019 on a series of grants in conjunction with the Germantown Info Hub. From this time until 2022, I have observed their work and have had intermittent check-ins with their team, watching the evolution of their project. In April 2020, I conducted a series of interviews with staff and focus groups with community members about collaborative efforts to meet the community's information needs in the early stages of the COVID-19 pandemic, though this data only offered background context for this chapter.[10] For this chapter, I drew primarily on a series of interviews with project staff conducted in July and August 2022.

Finally, for my exploration of the role metaorganizations play in influencing local news and information built environments, I drew from interviews conducted between December 2021 and September 2022 with fourteen representatives of philanthropic organizations; journalism support and accountability organizations (national and local); and diversity, equity, inclusion, and belonging (DEIB) trainers.[11] Interviews explored how these organizations developed and deployed strategies to support local journalism efforts to move toward greater equity and antiracism. I also observed and participated in a number of events, trainings, and conferences (online and face to face) where representatives discussed visions for moving Philadelphia and other local news systems toward DEIB and community engagement goals. In addition, I have made an effort to follow and regularly check relevant email listservs and the social media profiles of relevant organizations and individual influencers related to issues around local news, local journalism philanthropy, DEIB work in journalism, and community engagement in Philadelphia and beyond.[12] As noted in the book, there have been a number of instances where issues within the Philadelphia system have been amplified in online spaces, which, while insular, can offer insights into the perspectives of various actors within the local storytelling network and the metaorganizations engaging with them.

For all of these case studies and chapters, I thematically coded and analyzed the transcripts of interview, focus group, and public events, as well as field notes using the NVivo coding platform. Thematic categories were developed in response to research questions, with subthemes added and refined based on initial coding of recurring or theoretically relevant moments. In addition, the cases were associated with four institutional review board protocols at Temple University.[13]

Of course, living and working in Philadelphia, where many of the people and organizations I write about in this book were simultaneously colleagues and even friends, had advantages and disadvantages. On the one hand, building trust with people over time allowed me to be privy to numerous informal conversations and reflections that were key to my thinking about Philadelphia's news and information built environment. These conversations, even if off the record, helped me interpret and make sense of the data I gained as well as the gaps in what people were not able or willing to share on the record. At the same time, my positionality as a white former journalist and as someone immersed in media projects in Philadelphia absolutely colored how I interpreted my findings. I took occasional field notes on my perceptions of how my positionality shaped my interactions with study participants and observations of activities. I tried to be mindful of how white privilege and assumptions of whiteness norms shaped my perceptions, as well as how my interactions were shaped by how others perceived me to be associated with various actors within the local journalism system. Of course, my soak in the waters of local Philly journalism has the mixed blessing of making me aware of how narrow a slice I am able to offer in these pages. There are many important players whose voices are not featured in these pages—from large broadcast television networks to small outlets serving, for example, the local Indonesian community. Nevertheless, my hope is that the dynamics I have explored here through a combination of observation, interviews, focus groups, and monitoring of content and social media have allowed me to offer some insights into both challenges and opportunities for others interested in the normative goal of making local journalism systems more equitable and antiracist.

NOTES

INTRODUCTION: THE CASE FOR REIMAGINING

1. Sample video: https://6abc.com/philadelphia-crime-fighters-father-gunned-down-ger mantown/3584305/.
2. Focus group with Germantown residents, 7/16/18.
3. Focus group with Germantown residents, 7/30/18.
4. Sorin Matei and Sandra Ball-Rokeach, "Watts, the 1965 Los Angeles Riots, and the Communicative Construction of the Fear Epicenter of Los Angeles," *Communication Monographs* 72, no. 3 (2005): 301–23; Teresa Mastin, Shelly Campo, and M. Somjen Frazer, "In Black and White: Coverage of U.S. Slave Reparations by the Mainstream and Black Press," *Howard Journal of Communication* 16, no. 3 (2005): 201–23; Hemant Shah and Michael Thornton, *Newspaper Coverage of Interethnic Conflict* (Thousand Oaks, CA: SAGE, 2003); Catherine Squires, *Dispatches from the Color Line* (Albany: State University of New York Press, 2007); Candis Callison and Mary L. Young, *Reckoning: Journalism's Limits and Possibilities* (Oxford: Oxford University Press, 2019); Joseph Torres et al., *Media 2070: An Invitation to Dream Up Media Reparations*, (Free Press, 2020), https://mediareparations.org/wp-content/uploads/2020/10/media-2070.pdf.
5. Wesley Lowery, "Black City. White Paper," *Philadelphia Inquirer*, February 15, 2022, https://www.inquirer.com/news/inq2/philadelphia-inquirer-racism-equity-diversity -black-journalists-20220215.html; Layla A. Jones, "Lights. Camera. Space," *Philadelphia Inquirer*, March 29, 2022, https://www.inquirer.com/news/inq2/more-perfect-union -action-eyewitness-news-tv-racism-crime-20220329.html.

6. I frequently use the term "BIPOC" throughout this book because I am interested in the possibilities antiracism offers for these communities, and at times I need to use larger identity categories to anonymize research participants. However, I do not mean to conflate the distinct experiences of Black, Indigenous, and people of color communities or to imply that anti-Black racism applies equally to all nonwhite communities.

7. Eduardo Bonilla-Silva, "'New Racism,' Colorblind Racism, and the Future of Whiteness in America," in *White Out: The Continuing Significance of Racism*, ed. Ashley W. Doane and Eduardo Bonilla-Silva (Milton Park, UK: Routledge, 2004), 271–84.

8. George Lipsitz, *How Racism Takes Place* (Philadelphia: Temple University Press, 2011), introduction.

9. Lipsitz, *How Racism Takes Place*, introduction.

10. Lipsitz, *How Racism Takes Place*, introduction.

11. Danielle Kilgo, Tamar Wilner, Gina M. Masullo, and Lance Kyle Bennett, "News Distrust Among Black Americans Is a Fixable Problem," Center for Media Engagement, November 18, 2020, https://mediaengagement.org/research/news-distrust-among-black-americans.

12. These conversations would not have been possible without my research collaborators, especially Letrell Crittenden, Anthony Nadler, Melissa Valle, and Marc Lamont Hill.

13. Interview with Collegeville resident, December 8, 2017.

14. Lipsitz, *How Racism Takes Place*, chap. 1.

15. While this book focuses on efforts to address racism within local journalism, it is with the hope that more reflexive journalism practices will encourage journalists to question how their work is positioned not only in relationship to whiteness but to other intersectional identity categories as well. At the same time, I recognize that additional research and exploration of journalism's history of harm and possibilities for repair for other identity groups is critical, particularly for trans people and people with disabilities.

16. At the time of writing, the term "DEIB" was preferred by a number of organizations, though I recognize preferred terms for these practices are constantly changing.

17. I generally use the term "built environment" rather than "ecosystem" for reasons explained more under the section "Storytelling Networks and Philadelphia's News and Information Built Environment."

18. As I was finalizing my manuscript, a collaboration of metaorganizations (including City Bureau and Free Press) released a "Roadmap for Local News" that advocated shifting focus from the news industry to "civic information" created by "civic media." While throughout this book I refer to journalism and the news and information built environment, there is much that resonates with their conception of civic information. See Elizabeth Green, Darryl Holliday, and Mike Rispoli, "The Roadmap for Local News: An Emergent Approach to Meeting Civic Information Needs," February 2, 2023, https://localnewsroadmap.org/wp-content/uploads/2023/02/The-Roadmap-for-Local-News-Feb-2-23.pdf.

19. Media 2070, *An Invitation to Dream Up Media Reparations*, a project of Free Press, 2020, https://mediareparations.org/wp-content/uploads/2020/10/media-2070.pdf.

20. Chicago Commission on Race Relations, *The Negro in Chicago: A Study of Race Relations and a Race Riot* (Chicago: University of Chicago Press, 1922), 520, http://moses.law.umn .edu/darrow/documents/The_Negro_in_Chicago_1922.pdf.

21. John A. McCone and W. M. Christopher, "Violence in the City: An End or a Beginning?," Report by the Governor's Commission on the Los Angeles Riots, 1965, 84.

22. The National Advisory Commission on Civil Disorders, "The Kerner Commission Report" in *The Essential Kerner Commission Report*, ed. Jelani Cobb and Matthew Guariglia (New York: Liveright, 2021), 241.

23. Media 2070, *An Invitation to Dream Up Media Reparations*; Meredith D. Clark, "The Year Journalism Starts Paying Reparations," NiemanLab Predictions for Journalism 2021, https://www.niemanlab.org/2020/12/the-year-journalism-starts-paying-repara tions/.

24. Keith Lawrence et al., "Structural Racism and Community Building," Aspen Institute Roundtable on Community Change, 2004.

25. See Juan Gonzalez and Joseph Torres, "News for All: The Epic Story of Race and the American Media," in *Will the Last Reporter Please Turn Out the Lights: The Collapse of Journalism and What Can Be Done to Fix It*, ed. Robert McChesney and Victor W. Pickard (New York: New Press, 2011), 185–93; Elizabeth Grieco, "Newsroom Employees Are Less Diverse Than U.S. Workers Overall," Pew Research Center, November 2, 2018, https:// www.pewresearch.org/fact-tank/2018/11/02/newsroom-employees-are-less-diverse -than-u-s-workers-overall/; Lynn C. Owens, "Network News: The Role of Race in Source Selection and Story Topic," *Howard Journal of Communications*, 19, no. 4 (2008): 355–370; Robert M. Entman and Andrew Rojecki, *The Black Image in the White Mind: Media and Race in America* (Chicago: University of Chicago Press, 2000).

26. Nikki Usher, *News for the Rich, White, and Blue: How Place and Power Distort American Journalism* (New York: Columbia University Press, 2021), 60.

27. Lewis Wallace, *The View from Somewhere: Undoing the Myth of Journalistic Objectivity* (Chicago: University of Chicago Press, 2019); Callison and Young, *Reckoning*.

28. Bonilla-Silva, "'New Racism'"; Margaret L. Andersen, "Whitewashing Race: A Critical Perspective on Whiteness," in Doane and Bonilla-Silva, eds., *White Out*.

29. Toni Morrison, *Playing in the Dark: Whiteness and the Literary Imagination* (Cambridge, MA: Harvard University Press, 1992); Andersen, "Whitewashing Race."

30. Eduardo Bonilla-Silva, *Racism Without Racists: Color-Blind Racism and the Persistence of Racial Inequality in America* (Lanham, MD: Rowman and Littlefield, 2006).

31. Michael Omi and Howard Winant, *Racial Formation in the United States: From the 1960s to the 1990s* (New York: Routledge, 1994); Derald Wing Sue et al., "Racial Microaggressions in Everyday Life: Implications for Clinical Practice," *American Psychologist* 62, no. 4 (2007): 271; Michelle Alexander, *The New Jim Crow: Mass Incarceration in the Age of Colorblindness* (New York: New Press, 2012).

32. Michael Omi and Howard Winant, *Racial Formation in the United States*, 3rd ed. (New York: Routledge, 2014), 220; Michael Omi and Howard Winant, "How Colorblindness Co-Evolved with Free-Market Thinking," Political Research Associates, October 8,

2014, https://politicalresearch.org/2014/10/08/how-colorblindness-co-evolved-free-mark
et-thinking.

33. Bill Kovach and Tom Rosenstiel, *Elements of Journalism: What Newspeople Should Know and the Public Should Expect* (New York: Three Rivers, 2007). For a discussion, see American Press Institute, "The Lost Meaning of 'Objectivity,'" API's Journalism Essentials, n.d., https://www.americanpressinstitute.org/journalism-essentials/bias-objectivity/lost -meaning-objectivity/.

34. David T. Mindich, *Just the Facts: How "Objectivity" Came to Define American Journalism* (New York: NYU Press, 2000); Michael Schudson, "The Objectivity Norm in American Journalism," *Journalism* 2, no. 2 (2001): 149–70.

35. Mindich, *Just the Facts*; Wallace, *The View from Somewhere*.

36. Callison and Young, *Reckoning*, 62.

37. Sue Robinson and Kathleen B. Culver "When White Reporters Cover Race: News Media, Objectivity, and Community (Dis)trust," *Journalism: Theory, Practice & Criticism* 20, no. 3 (2019): 375–91.

38. See, for example, the case of the Pittsburgh Post Gazette: Ishena Robinson, "Pittsburgh Post-Gazette Bars Black Reporters from Covering Protests, Citing 'Bias,'" *The Root*, June 7, 2020, https://www.theroot.com/pittsburgh-post-gazette-bars-black-reporters -from-cover-1843944509.

39. Stephen J. Ward, "Inventing Objectivity: New Philosophical Foundations," in *Journalism Ethics: A Philosophical Approach*, ed. Christopher Meyers (New York: Oxford University, 2010), 137–52; Robinson and Culver, "When White Reporters Cover Race"; Meenakshi G. Durham, "On the Relevance of Standpoint Epistemology to the Practice of Journalism: The Case for 'Strong Objectivity,'" *Communication Theory* 8, no. 2 (1998): 117–40; Donna Haraway, "Situated Knowledges: The Science Question in Feminism and the Privileging of Partial Perspectives," *Feminist Studies* 14, no. 3 (1988): 575–99; Callison and Young, *Reckoning*.

40. Gabe Schneider, "What Does Movement Journalism Mean for Journalism as a Whole?," Donald W. Reynolds Journalism Institute, April 15, 2021, https://rjionline.org/reporting /what-does-movement-journalism-mean-for-journalism-as-a-whole/; Anita Varma, "Moral Solidarity as News Value: Rendering Marginalized Communities and Enduring Social Injustice Newsworthy," *Journalism* (2022): 14648849221094669; Clark, "The Year Journalism Starts Paying Reparations."

41. Sue Robinson, *How Journalists Engage: A Theory of Trust Building, Identities, and Care* (Oxford: Oxford University Press, forthcoming), prologue.

42. One of many such industry conversations: Leah Donnella, Cassie Haynes, and Robert Samuels, "What Would Antiracist Journalism Look Like?," panel discussion, National Press Club, August 21, 2020, https://www.press.org/events/what-would-antiracist -journalism-look.

43. Ibram Kendi, *How to Be an Antiracist* (New York: One World, 2019).

44. Eileen O'Brien, "From Antiracism to Antiracisms," *Sociology Compass* 3, no. 3 (2009): 501–12; Mark Patrick George, "Towards a Critical Antiracism: Redefining and

Rethinking the Term 'Antiracism,'" paper presented at the annual meetings of the American Sociological Association, August 2004, San Francisco, California.

45. Adolph Reed Jr., "The Limits of Antiracism," *Left Business Observer* 121, no. 6 (2009).

46. Kimberlé Crenshaw, "Demarginalizing the Intersection of Race and Sex: A Black Feminist Critique of Antidiscrimination Doctrine, Feminist Theory, and Antiracist Politics," in *Feminist Legal Theories*, ed. Karen Maschke (New York: Routledge, 2013), 23–51. For a discussion of the link between the Combahee River Collective and Black Lives Matter, see Keeanga-Yamahtta Taylor, ed., *How We Get Free: Black Feminism and the Combahee River Collective* (Chicago: Haymarket, 2017).

47. Combahee River Collective, "The Combahee River Collective Statement," in *How We Get Free*, ed. Taylor, 25.

48. Omi and Winant, *Racial Formation in the United States*; Reed, "The Limits of Antiracism."

49. Emily M. Drew, "'Coming to Terms with Our Own Racism': Journalists Grapple with the Racialization of Their News," *Critical Studies in Media Communication* 28, no. 4 (2011): 370.

50. Gwyneth Mellinger, *Chasing Newsroom Diversity: From Jim Crow to Affirmative Action* (Champaign: University of Illinois Press, 2013), 11.

51. See Sarah Scire, "'Crushing Resistance': Yet Again, Newsrooms Aren't Showing Up to the Industry's Largest Diversity Survey," *NiemanLab*, April 12, 2022, https://www.niemanlab.org/2022/04/crushing-resistance-yet-again-newsrooms-arent-showing-up-to-the-industrys-largest-diversity-survey/.

52. Sandra J. Ball-Rokeach, Yong-Chan Kim, and Sorin Matei, "Storytelling Neighborhood: Paths to Belonging in Diverse Urban Environments," *Communication Research* 28, no. 4 (2001): 392–428; Yong-Chan Kim and Sandra J. Ball-Rokeach, "Civic Engagement from a Communication Infrastructure Perspective," *Communication Theory* 16, no. 2 (2006): 173–97.

53. Kim and Ball-Rokeach, "Civic Engagement from a Communication Infrastructure Perspective."

54. Garrett Broad, Carmen Gonzalez, and Sandra Ball-Rokeach, "Intergroup Relations in South Los Angeles—Combining Communication Infrastructure and Contact Hypothesis Approaches," *International Journal of Intercultural Relations* 38 (2014): 47–59; Nien-Tsu (Nancy) Chen, Katherine Ognyanova, and Nan Zhao, "Communication and Sociodemographic Forces Shaping Civic Engagement Patterns in a Multiethnic City," in *Communication and Community*, ed. Patricia Moy (New York: Hampton, 2013), 207–32.

55. Bonilla-Silva, *Racism Without Racists*; Omi and Winant, *Racial Formation*; Lipsitz, *How Racism Takes Place*.

56. Anthony Nadler, "Natures Economy and News Ecology: Scrutinizing the News Ecosystem Metaphor," *Journalism Studies* 20, no. 6 (2019): 823–39.

57. For a related discussion of "built environment," not in a geographic place-based context but as a way to explore efforts to transform journalism and its relationship to trust and engagement, see Robinson, *How Journalists Engage*.

58. According to Nielsen's 2021 "Designated Market Area" rankings, https://mediatracks
.com/resources/nielsen-dma-rankings-2021/. A 2020 Impact Architect study identified
fifty-three outlets but acknowledged the list was incomplete (and indeed it did not include
a number of hyperlocal and other outlets). Hannah Stonebraker and Lindsay Green-
Barber, *Healthy Local News and Information Ecosystems: A Diagnostic Framework* (Impact
Architects, March 2021), https://s3.us-east-2.amazonaws.com/files.theimpactarchitects
.com/ecosystems/full_report.pdf.

59. The 2020 Impact Architect study noted that Philadelphia was one of the most heavily
funded of the U.S. regions it examined, with philanthropic investment in journalism at
more than $50 per capita. Stonebraker and Green-Barber, *Healthy Local News and Infor-
mation Ecosystems*, 10.

60. Jan Schaffer, "Exploring a Networked Journalism Collaborative in Philadelphia," J-Lab,
April 19, 2010, 17, http://www.j-lab.org/wp-content/pdfs/exploring-net-j-philly-report
.pdf.

61. For additional context, see Chris W. Anderson, *Rebuilding the News: Metropolitan Journalism in the Digital Age* (Philadelphia: Temple University Press, 2013), chap. 6.

62. Joshua Breitbart, "Toward a Healthy Media Ecosystem for Philadelphia," Prometheus
Radio Project, May 25, 2010, https://www.prometheusradio.org/node/2319.

63. Recognizing that language is always changing, I use the gender-neutral term "Latinx/e."
At the time of writing some within these communities preferred "Latine," but "Latinx"
was still widely circulating. While it is ideal to follow how individuals self-identify, this
can be challenging when speaking about a community in general, or anonymizing study
participants.

64. Michael X Delli Carpini, Mariela Morales Suárez, and Burt Herman, "Being Informed:
A Study of the Information Needs and Habits of Philadelphia Residents," Lenfest Institute, October 2018, https://live-lenfest-institute.pantheonsite.io/wp-content/uploads/2019
/09/Being-Informed.-Information-Needs-of-Philadelphia-Residents.-Delli-Carpini
-Morales-Sua%CC%81rez-and-Herman-final.pdf.

65. Stonebraker and Green-Barber, *Healthy Local News and Information Ecosystems*.

66. Timothy Neff, Pawel Popiel, and Victor Pickard, "Philadelphia's News Media System:
Which Audiences Are Underserved?," *Journal of Communication* 72, no. 4 (2022): 476–87.

67. Preliminary data shared September 13, 2022, at the Lenfest Institute's Reimagining Philadelphia Journalism Summit; survey data was still undergoing analysis at the time of
writing.

68. Phyllis Kaniss, *Making Local News* (Chicago: University of Chicago Press, 1991).

69. Anderson, *Rebuilding the News*.

70. Magda Konieczna, "The Collaboration Stepladder: How One Organization Built a Solid
Foundation for a Community-Focused Cross-Newsroom Collaboration," *Journalism
Studies* 21, no. 6 (2020): 802–19.

71. Anderson, *Rebuilding the News*.

72. Garrett Broad "Communication Infrastructure Theory and Community-Based Program
Evaluation: The Case of Media Mobilizing Project and the CAP Comcast Campaign,"

in *The Communication Ecology of 21st Century Urban Communities*, ed. Yong-Chan Kim, Matthew Matsaganis, Holley Wilkin, and Joo-Young Jung (New York: Peter Lang, 2018), 220–36.

73. Todd Wolfson and Peter N. Funke, "Communication, Class, and Concentric Media Practices: Developing a Contemporary Rubric," *New Media & Society* 16, no. 3 (2014): 363–80.

74. Letrell Crittenden and Antoine Haywood "Revising Legacy Media Practices to Serve Hyperlocal Information Needs of Marginalized Populations," *Journalism Practice* 14, no. 5, (2020): 608–25. For a valuable ethnographic look at the workings of PhillyCam, see also Clemencia Rodriguez, "PhillyCAM: A Hub for Media Makers on Ranstead Street," unpublished manuscript, 2020.

75. Crittenden and Haywood, "Revising Legacy Media Practices."

76. "The Local News Dynamics in: Philadelphia-Camden-Wilmington, PA-NJ-DE-MD," Pew Research Center, Database, March 26, 2019, https://www.pewresearch.org/journ alism/interactives/local-news-habits/37980/.

77. Mike Shields, "The Changing Distribution of Poverty in Philadelphia," Economy League, December 16, 2020, https://economyleague.org/providing-insight/leadingindi cators/2020/12/16/phlpov19; Stonebraker and Green-Barber, *Healthy Local News and Information Ecosystems*, 10.

78. To disclose fully, I have struggled with whether and how it is possible to ethically write about racism as a white person without centering whiteness and benefiting from it. Such an effort is perhaps inherently fraught. I have not come up with a "solution" to this reality. While the writing of an academic book may accrue little in the way of financial revenue, such books can generate professional capital. I am mindful that I have a responsibility to find ways to leverage and share this capital. Recognizing this, I hope to work to facilitate opportunities to highlight the perspectives of BIPOC colleagues doing critical work in this field and find ways to share power whenever possible.

79. My work on both projects was pro bono.

80. IndependenceMedia, "Independence Public Media Foundation Announces $2.6 Million in Media-Making and Digital Equity Grants to 33 Projects and Organizations," December 15, 2021, https://independencemedia.org/news/independence-public-media-founda tion-announces-26-million-media-making-and-digital-equity.

1. REPAIRING AND REIMAGINING A MORE PUBLIC MEDIA

1. Names and gender identifiers of WHYY staffers are withheld and by default are referred to by the pronoun "they." When relevant, I sometimes note identity categories for participants such as race/ethnicity, gender identity, and/or sexual orientation. However, I often omit these categories to avoid jeopardizing participants' anonymity.

2. U.S. Census Bureau, Quickfacts, Philadelphia city, Pennsylvania, https://www.census .gov/quickfacts/philadelphiacitypennsylvania.

3. Eduardo Bonilla-Silva, *Racism Without Racists: Color-Blind Racism and the Persistence of Racial Inequality in America* (Lanham, MD: Rowman and Littlefield, 2006); Michael Omi and Howard Winant, *Racial Formation in the United States: From the 1960s to the 1990s* (New York: Routledge, 1994).

4. The initiative was funded by the Lenfest Institute: https://www.lenfestinstitute.org /profile/whyy-creating-culturally-competent-newsrooms/.

5. This chapter adapts research that informed Andrea Wenzel, "Sourcing Diversity, Shifting Culture: Building 'Cultural Competence' in Public Radio," *Digital Journalism* 9, no. 4 (2021): 461–80.

6. See Sandra J. Ball-Rokeach, Yong-Chan Kim, and Sorin Matei, "Storytelling Neighborhood: Paths to Belonging in Diverse Urban Environments," *Communication Research* 28, no. 4 (2001): 392–428; Yong-Chan Kim and Sandra J. Ball-Rokeach, "Civic Engagement from a Communication Infrastructure Perspective," *Communication Theory* 16, no. 2 (2006): 173–97; and the discussion of CIT in the introduction.

7. *A Formula for Change: The Report of the Task Force on Minorities in Public Broadcasting*, Corporation for Public Broadcasting, Washington, DC., November 1978, xiv, https:// files.eric.ed.gov/fulltext/ED172269.pdf.

8. See, for example, the 2010 Knight Foundation white paper: https://knightfoundation.org /reports/rethinking-public-media-more-local-more-inclusive/.

9. Elizabeth Jensen, "New On-Air Source Diversity Data for NPR Show Much Work Ahead," NPR Public Editor, December 17, 2019, https://www.npr.org/sections/public editor/2019/12/17/787959805/new-on-air-source-diversity-data-for-npr-shows-much -work-ahead. NPR's website includes a running list of their DEIB initiatives: https:// www.npr.org/about-npr/970764791/our-ongoing-work.

10. See for example: Celeste Headlee, "An Anti-Racist Future: A Vision and Plan for the Transformation of Public Media," Medium, January 18, 2021, https://celesteheadlee .medium.com/an-anti-racist-future-a-vision-and-plan-for-the-transformation-of -public-media-224149ab37e6; Julie Drizen, "Why Is Public Media So White," *Current*, June 24, 2020, https://current.org/2020/06/why-is-public-media-so-white/; We Make NPR/SAG-AFTRA, "It's Time for Action," We Make NPR, https://wemakenpr .squarespace.com/dei-demands.

11. Christopher A. Chávez, "Whose Is the Voice of the American Public? Latinx/e Speech and the Standard Language Ideology of Public Radio," *Communication and Critical/Cultural Studies* 16, no. 4 (2019): 308–25.

12. Laura Garbes, "'Their Accent Is Just Too Much': Racialized Evaluation of Voice in Public Radio Production," *SocArXiv*, preprint, August 7, 2021, https://osf.io/preprints/socar xiv/vzjhb/.

13. Jennifer Lynn Stoever, "Fine-Tuning the Sonic Color-Line: Radio and the Acousmatic Du Bois," *Modernist Cultures* 10, no. 1 (2015): 99–118.

14. Public Media for All, "Mission & Vision," https://www.publicmediaforall.com /missionandvision.

15. Caroline Lester, "A Confrontation in Public Media," *Columbia Journalism Review*, November 9, 2020, https://www.cjr.org/analysis/public-radio-for-all-diversity-equity .php.

16. Interview with Sachi Kobayashi, 2/2/22.

17. Interview with Sachi Kobayashi, 2/2/22.

18. Public Media for All 2020–2021 Annual Report, https://static1.squarespace.com/static /5f4d4833c92f28725b7a4b3f/t/619306d950b3f56cfc485592/1637025517914/PMFA+2020– 2021+Annual+Report.pdf.

19. Celeste Headlee, "An Anti-Racist Future: A Vision and Plan for the Transformation of Public Media," Medium (blog), https://celesteheadlee.medium.com/an-antiracist-future -a-vision-and-plan-for-the-transformation-of-public-media-224149ab37e6.

20. Interview with Celeste Headlee, 2/2/22.

21. According to WHYY market research (Scarborough), 78 percent of WHYY listeners are white, compared with 67 percent of their regional coverage area (which includes the suburbs surrounding Philadelphia).

22. As of July 2018: April Simpson, "WHYY Efforts Focus on Increasing Racial Diversity of Staff, Audiences," *Current: News for People in Public Media*, July 20, 2018, https://current .org/2018/07/whyy-efforts-focus-on-increasing-racial-diversity-of-staff-audiences/.

23. Correspondence with the VP for news and civic dialogue, 9/7/19.

24. Lenfest Institute, "WHYY Creating Culturally Competent Newsrooms," https://www .lenfestinstitute.org/profile/whyy-creating-culturally-competent-newsrooms/.

25. In the sections that follow in this chapter, I draw from research that informed Wenzel, "Sourcing Diversity, Shifting Culture." This study included interviews with eighteen staffers in addition to participant observation of an initial source diversity audit process and follow up trainings.

26. Bonilla-Silva, *Racism Without Racists.*

27. WHYY's source diversity newsroom experiments list. Shared October 1, 2018.

28. Follow-up cultural competency training, 9/20/18.

29. Hannah Haynes, "Q&A: Wisconsin Public Radio's Source Demographic Project," Donald W. Reynolds Journalism Institute, University of Missouri, November 10, 2020, https://rjionline.org/technology/qa-wisconsin-public-radios-source-demographic -project/.

30. See API's Source Tracker: https://www.americanpressinstitute.org/publications/api -updates/track-the-diversity-of-your-sources-with-source-matters-an-easy-automated -tool-from-api/.

31. See Caroline Bauman, "Here's Everything We Learned About Source Diversity Auditing," *Chalkbeat*, June 21, 2021, https://www.chalkbeat.org/2021/6/21/22543675/source -diversity-auditing-tracking-chalkbeat-rji-equity-work.

32. WHYY data shared via email in May 2022. Year 3 data (gathered 11/19–10/20) was compiled in January 2021. The compilation of Year 4 data was on hold because of the vacancy of the VP for news and civic dialogue position. Note that it is important to caution that

the comparison between the two times is not perfect. The first drew from a random composite of dates, and the second draws from a cumulative running total.

33. Interview, 5/22/18.

34. Interview, 6/20/18.

35. WHYY News Staff by Race/Ethnicity according to Staff Diversity Tracker, 5/20/22 (shared by email).

36. For some perspective on journalists of color who leave journalism, see Murphy's "Leavers" survey: https://opennews.org/projects/2020-leavers-survey/.

37. Interview, 7/3/19.

38. Interview, 5/17/18.

39. Interview, 5/20/18.

40. Interview, 5/14/19.

41. Interview, 5/17/18.

42. Interview, 7/5/18.

43. I document one such "accountability conversation" hosted by the Germantown Info Hub in Andrea D. Wenzel, *Community-Centered Journalism: Engaging People, Exploring Solutions, and Building Trust* (Bloomington: University of Illinois Press, 2020), 120.

44. See Stoever, "Fine-Tuning the Sonic Color-Line"; Garbes, "'Their Accent Is Just Too Much.'"

45. This section adapts research that informed this Tow Center white paper: Andrea Wenzel, "Mutual Aid and the 'Messy Middle': Pushing Public Radio Toward Antiracism," Tow Center for Digital Journalism, September 29, 2021, https://www.cjr.org/tow_center_reports/mutual-aid-and-the-messy-middle-pushing-public-radio-toward-antiracism.php.

46. The NICE project was funded by the Knight-Lenfest Local News Transformation Fund.

47. "What's N.I.C.E.?," WHYY.org, https://whyy.org/nice/.

48. Dean Spade, *Mutual Aid: Building Solidarity During This Crisis (and the Next)* (New York: Verso, 2020).

49. Darryl Holliday, "What Journalism Can Learn from Mutual Aid," *CJR*, Winter 2020, https://www.cjr.org/special_report/the-power-of-community-journalism.php.

50. George Lipsitz, *How Racism Takes Place* (Philadelphia: Temple University Press, 2011).

2. REPAIRING AND REIMAGINING AN "ANTIRACIST" LEGACY NEWSPAPER

1. Journalists of Color of the *Philadelphia Inquirer* to the leadership of the *Philadelphia Inquirer*, June 3, 2020, https://docs.google.com/document/u/1/d/e/2PACX-1vRSXh3A TPo_bjl5iUfrFnTuC-_Z-CQKt8DGtzoLgTzURnRwiPR-SEfNcaWlMMl9PNXX MhQ_nVFGvacK/pub. I recognize that referring to staff members as BIPOC or "journalists of color" can flatten the differences experienced by different groups within those categories. However, in order to preserve anonymity, I often use these larger

groupings rather than referencing people's specific identities (e.g., Black, Asian American, etc.).

2. For an overview, see Paul Farhi and Sarah Ellison, "Ignited by Public Protests, American Newsrooms Are Having Their Own Racial Reckoning," *Washington Post*, June 12, 2020, https://www.washingtonpost.com/lifestyle/media/ignited-by-public-protests-american-newsrooms-are-having-their-own-racial-reckoning/2020/06/12/be622bce-a995-11ea-94d2-d7bc43b26bf9_story.html.

3. The veteran journalist and DEIB advocate Bryan Monroe tragically passed away in January 2021, just before the completion of the audit. In addition to Bryan and me, our Temple audit team included Jillian Bauer-Reese, Marnice Davis Charles, Christopher Malo, Arlene Notoro Morgan, Aron Pilhofer, and Linn Washington Jr. We also had support from staff members of the *Philadelphia Inquirer*, the Lenfest Local Lab, and the Brown Institute for Media Innovation.

4. While this project was supported by funding from the Lenfest Institute for Journalism, I did not accept a fee for this work.

5. The *Philadelphia Inquirer* Diversity and Inclusion Audit, https://drive.google.com/file/d/1MJB8IaP4MC_kpP47ZGsVo5y1cAR3VByR/view. Every person mentioned in stories from forty-two randomly selected days (six weeks) between the period of August 2019 and July 2020 was coded for race/ethnicity and gender—generating 14,416 individual identifiable people. Professor Bryan Monroe led the quantitative side of the audit.

6. In addition to me, my colleague Christopher Malo conducted interviews in this initial portion of the study. The forty-six interview participants included a range of newsroom teams and levels of seniority (twenty-three reporters/columnists/photographers and twenty-three editors/managers). BIPOC staff members and women were oversampled to ensure their perspective and concerns were included—with six identifying as Asian, ten as Black, four as Latinx/e, and twenty-six as white. Twenty-eight identified as women and eighteen as men.

7. When relevant, I sometimes note identity categories for participants such as race/ethnicity, gender identity, and/or sexual orientation. However, I often omit these categories to avoid jeopardizing participants' anonymity.

8. The forty-two participants in five focus groups and interviews included nineteen editors/managers and twenty-three nonmanagers. Of these, eighteen identified as men, twenty-four as women, twenty-eight identified as non-Hispanic white, eight as Black, three as Asian, and three as Hispanic/Latinx/e.

9. Here referring to "storytelling networks" in the context of communication infrastructure theory. See Sandra J. Ball-Rokeach, Yong-Chan Kim, and Sorin Matei, "Storytelling Neighborhood: Paths to Belonging in Diverse Urban Environments," *Communication Research* 28, no. 4 (2001): 392–428; Yong-Chan Kim and Sandra J. Ball-Rokeach, "Civic Engagement from a Communication Infrastructure Perspective," *Communication Theory* 16, no. 2 (2006): 173–97.

10. For context on its recent history, see Kristen Hare, "In Philadelphia, 3 Newsrooms Had to Become 1. Now They're Beginning a Whole New Kind of Change," *Poynter*, May 18,

2017, https://www.poynter.org/tech-tools/2017/in-philadelphia-3-newsrooms-had-to-transform-into-one-now-theyre-beginning-a-whole-new-kind-of-change/.

11. Wesley Lowrey, "Black City, White Paper," *Philadelphia Inquirer*, February 15, 2022, https://www.inquirer.com/news/inq2/philadelphia-inquirer-racism-equity-diversity-black-journalists-20220215.html.

12. Arlene Morgan, "I Spent 31 Years at *The Inquirer*, and I'm Proud of Our Diversity Efforts," *Philadelphia Inquirer*, March 7, 2022, https://www.inquirer.com/opinion/commentary/inquirer-diversity-efforts-arlene-morgan-20220307.html.

13. Lowrey, "Black City, White Paper."

14. Interview, 8/24/22.

15. Given the COVID-19 pandemic, *Inquirer* staff members were working remotely over the course of my observation.

16. See this volume's introduction and David T. Mindich, *Just the Facts: How "Objectivity" Came to Define American Journalism* (New York: NYU Press, 2000); Michael Schudson, "The Objectivity Norm in American Journalism," *Journalism* 2, no. 2 (2001): 149–70.

17. Eduardo Bonilla-Silva, *Racism Without Racists: Color-Blind Racism and the Persistence of Racial Inequality in America* (Lanham, MD: Rowman and Littlefield, 2006).

18. George Lipsitz, *How Racism Takes Place* (Philadelphia: Temple University Press, 2011).

19. Jacob L. Nelson, *Imagined Audiences: How Journalists Perceive and Pursue the Public* (Oxford: Oxford University Press, 2021).

20. For more information on this, see Corinne Chin and Lauren Frohne, "How a *Seattle Times* Slack Channel Lets People Speak Up About Insensitive Coverage," *Better News*, November 2017, https://betternews.org/sharable-win-seattle-times-slack-channel-sensitive-subjects/.

21. Interview, 6/17/21.

22. See *Philadelphia Inquirer* Anti-Racist Workflow Guide, https://drive.google.com/file/d/1q7lT1iN-K7wnGJGFgJfhpSI3dc_zNqeq/view.

23. Interview, 5/11/22.

24. Interview, 5/20/22.

25. Interview, 5/11/22.

26. Sue Robinson, *How Journalists Engage: A Theory of Trust Building, Identities, and Care* (Oxford: Oxford University Press, forthcoming).

27. Andrea Wenzel, *Community-Centered Journalism: Engaging People, Exploring Solutions, and Building Trust* (Champaign: University of Illinois Press, 2020).

28. Free Press, "Coalition Sign On Letter to *Philadelphia Inquirer*," Free Press, June 22, 2020, https://www.freepress.net/sites/default/files/2020-06/coalition_sign_on_letter_to_philly_inquirer_final.pdf. The signing organizations included the Germantown Info Hub project that I cofounded and is discussed more in chapter 4.

29. One of the points of controversy and confusion around the desk has been where in the newsroom it would be positioned and the extent to which it would focus on news versus engagement—variation in what name people used for it over the course of its development reflected that.

30. "The Lenfest Institute Announces $1.3 Million in Grants to Support the *Philadelphia Inquirer*'s Community-Focused Journalism," Lenfest Institute, May 20, 2021, https://www.lenfestinstitute.org/local-journalism/lenfest-institute-announces-1-3-million-in-grants-to-support-the-philadelphia-inquirers-community-focused-journalism/.

31. Inquirer for All DEI Update, shared 1/15/21.

32. Joseph Lichterman, "The *Philadelphia Inquirer* Hires Sabrina Vourvoulias as First Senior Editor, Communities and Engagement," Lenfest Institute, October 27, 2021, https://www.lenfestinstitute.org/diverse-growing-audiences/the-philadelphia-inquirer-hires-sabrina-vourvoulias-as-first-senior-editor-communities-and-engagement/.

33. Email responses to questions, 10/6/22.

34. "Jawn" is slang term local to Philadelphia that acts as a substitute noun for a thing, place, person, or event.

35. Philly JAWN proposal document, accessed 5/13/22.

36. Philly JAWN was developed out of synergies from both Free Press' involvement in the Shift the Narrative Project as well as the Lenfest Institute's Visioning Table, which will be discussed more in chapter 6. The latter involved many leaders of BIPOC journalist affinity groups and contributed to leaders informally discussing strategies to work toward greater accountability for the *Inquirer* and other newsrooms.

37. This larger project had a multipronged approach that included not only Free Press' work with the *Inquirer* and with Philly JAWN but also included work with the Movement Alliance Project on community narratives and the Media, Inequality, and Change Center's work researching Philadelphia media coverage of crime.

38. Email correspondence with Free Press, 7/2/21.

39. Ernest Owens, "The Inquirer Needs a Racism Intervention," *Philadelphia Inquirer*, February 17, 2021, https://www.inquirer.com/opinion/commentary/inquirer-diversity-inclusion-race-audit-newsroom-20210217.html.

40. Interview with Ernest Owens, 12/21/21.

41. Interview, 5/11/22.

42. Indeed, the lack of Black reporters would lead to a social media controversy involving Philly JAWN in August 2022, as discussed further in chapter 6.

43. Email responses to questions, 10/6/22.

44. Lenfest Institute, "Constellation News Leadership Initiative," https://www.lenfestinstitute.org/philadelphia-news-ecosystem/lenfest-constellation-news-leadership-initaitive/.

45. Interview, 5/11/22.

46. For more background on how the *Philadelphia Inquirer*'s current structure evolved, see Hare, "In Philadelphia, 3 Newsrooms Had to Become 1."

47. "Discrimination Grievance Filed," NewsGuild of Greater Philadelphia, Local 38010 Communications Workers of America, February 17, 2022, https://www.local-10.com/2022/02/discrimination-grievance-filed/.

48. Interview, 5/11/22.

49. Anna Orso and Jesenia De Moya Correa, "Editor Gabriel Escobar promoted to Philadelphia Inquirer's top newsroom job," *Philadelphia Inquirer*, November 11, 2020,

https://www.inquirer.com/news/philadelphia-inquirer-promotes-gabriel-escobar-to-newsroom-editor-senior-vice-president-20201111.html.

50. For more on microaggressions, see D. W. Sue et al., "Racial Microaggressions in Everyday Life: Implications for Clinical Practice," *American Psychologist* 62, no. 4 (2007): 271–86.

51. Interview, 5/11/22.

52. Interview, 6/24/21. For more discussion on this phenomena within legacy outlets, see Nikki Usher, *News for the Rich, White, and Blue: How Place and Power Distort American Journalism* (New York: Columbia University Press, 2021).

53. Interview, 5/20/22.

54. This survey was qualitative and exploratory, so I make no claims to representativeness or statistical significance.

3. INSTITUTIONALIZING ACCOUNTABILITY INFRASTRUCTURE

1. Wesley Lowery, "Black City. White Paper," *Philadelphia Inquirer*, February 15, 2022, https://www.inquirer.com/news/inq2/philadelphia-inquirer-racism-equity-diversity-black-journalists-20220215.html.

2. Elizabeth H. Hughes, "From the Publisher of the *Inquirer*: An Apology to Black Philadelphians and Journalists," *Philadelphia Inquirer*, February 16, 2022, https://www.inquirer.com/opinion/commentary/inquirer-publisher-more-perfect-union-apology-20220216.html.

3. Harold Brubaker, "WHYY Has Lost at Least Half Its Journalists. Many Complain About Pay, Morale, and Lack of Innovation," *Philadelphia Inquirer*, February 17, 2022, https://www.inquirer.com/business/whyy-departures-leave-npr-philadelphia-public-radio-20220217.html.

4. Ernest Owens (@MrErnestOwens), "So let me get this straight," Twitter, February 17, 2022, 2:05 PM, https://twitter.com/MrErnestOwens/status/1494387606431444993.

5. Newsguild of Greater Philadelphia, "Discrimination Grievance Filed," press release, February 17, 2022, https://www.local-10.com/2022/02/discrimination-grievance-filed/.

6. NewsGuild of Greater Philadelphia (@PhillyNewsGuild), "We wish publisher Lisa Hughes' actions spoke louder than her carefully penned apology Wednesday to Philadelphia's Black residents and communities and to The Inquirer's Black journalists, past and present," Twitter, February 17, 2022, 1:14 PM, https://twitter.com/PhillyNewsGuild/status/1494374782263046145.

7. Ernest Owens, "The *Inquirer*'s Attempt at a Buzzy Anti-Racist Apology Failed. It Didn't Have To," *Philadelphia*, February 23, 2022, https://www.phillymag.com/news/2022/02/23/inquirer-more-perfect-union/.

8. Darryl C. Murphy (@darrylcmurphy), "To whom it may concern, your skill set is valuable and greatly appreciated. If not where you are, definitely somewhere else. Get yours," Twitter, February 17, 2022, 2:33 PM, https://twitter.com/darrylcmurphy/status/149439 4586931863557.

9. x (@xalopez), "Almost 50% of NPR member station WHYY's Journalists have left in the last year due to the negligence from upper management." Twitter, February 17, 2022, 4:07 PM, https://twitter.com/xalopez/status/1494418203115667459.

10. Molly de Aguiar (@MollydeAguiar), "'But fortunately for us,' he said, 'even in a super tight labor market, we've been able to replace those people in kind and in some instances with people with a higher skill set' is a truly terrible and unacceptable thing for Marrazzo to say," Twitter, February 18, 2022, 11:04 AM, https://twitter.com/MollydeAguiar/status/1494704456402935813.

11. Brubaker, "WHYY Has Lost at Least Half Its Journalists."

12. Interview, 11/06/18.

13. Interview, 5/17/18.

14. Interview, 5/21/19.

15. Interview, 5/21/19.

16. Interview, 12/30/21.

17. Interview, 12/30/21.

18. Interview, 6/13/22.

19. Interview, 6/3/22.

20. Interview, 5/13/22.

21. As of 2019, as detailed in Brubaker, "WHYY Has Lost at Least Half Its Journalists."

22. For a related discussion of executive pay disparities, see Gabe Schneider, "Well-Funded Journalism Leaders Stop Making Disparate Pay," *NiemanLab*, December 2022, https://www.niemanlab.org/2022/12/well-funded-journalism-leaders-stop-making-disparate-pay/.

23. Since 1997.

24. Interview, 5/13/22.

25. Interview, 6/13/22.

26. Harold Brubaker, "WHYY Names New VP for News and Civic Engagement," *Philadelphia Inquirer*, June 1, 2022, https://www.inquirer.com/business/whyy-vp-news-civic-engagement-sarah-glover-20220601.html.

27. Interview, 1/5/2022.

28. As I discuss in chapter 6, it seems the work may have been interrupted by this leadership vacuum, or at least the gap may have contributed to the less-than-constructive back and forth with Philly JAWN.

4. IMAGINING A COMMUNITY-CENTERED WIRE SERVICE

1. At the time of writing, Resolve was considering changing the name of the project to the Community Information Network.

2. See Sandra J. Ball-Rokeach, Yong-Chan Kim, and Sorin Matei, "Storytelling Neighborhood: Paths to Belonging in Diverse Urban Environments," *Communication Research* 28, no. 4 (2001): 392–428; Yong-Chan Kim and Sandra J. Ball-Rokeach, "Civic

Engagement from a Communication Infrastructure Perspective," *Communication Theory* 16, no. 2 (2006): 173–97; and the discussion of CIT in the introduction.

3. Interview, 3/17/22.

4. Lily Medosch, Gabriela Rivera, and Kristine Villanueva, "How *Resolve Philly*'s Equally Informed Bridges the City's Digital Divide," *Resolve Philly*, May 7, 2021, https://resolvephilly.org/news/how-resolve-phillys-equally-informed-bridges-citys-digital-divide.

5. Interview, 3/17/22.

6. Ball-Rokeach, Kim, and Matei, "Storytelling Neighborhood"; Kim and Ball-Rokeach, "Civic Engagement."

7. For a discussion on shifts in the field's competition norms, see Lucas Graves and Magda Konieczna, "Sharing the News: Journalistic Collaboration as Field Repair," *International Journal of Communication Studies* 9 (2015): 1966–84.

8. Interview, 3/17/22.

9. For more information on City Bureau's documenters network, see https://www.citybureau.org/documenters. At the time of writing, Resolve Philly was in the process of working with City Bureau to launch a new Philadelphia Documenters program.

10. Interview, 7/7/22.

11. Interview, 7/7/22.

12. Interview, 7/8/22.

13. Friedman-Rudovsky interview, 3/17/22.

14. Friedman-Rudovsky interview, 3/17/22.

15. Interview, 3/17/22.

16. Interview, 7/12/22.

17. Interview, 7/8/22.

18. From 2018–2019, I sat in on a number of Broke in Philly meetings, either representing Temple University, the Germantown Info Hub, and/or as an observer.

19. Meeting fieldnotes, 10/18/18. Before Resolve had its own dedicated office, they used to host collaborative meetings in a rotation of partners' offices.

20. The Reentry Project, https://thereentryproject.org/.

21. Magda Konieczna, "The Collaboration Stepladder: How One Organization Built a Solid Foundation for a Community-Focused Cross-Newsroom Collaboration," *Journalism Studies* 21, no. 6 (2020): 802–19.

22. Chris W. Anderson, *Rebuilding the News: Metropolitan Journalism in the Digital Age* (Philadelphia: Temple University Press, 2013).

23. Interview, 3/17/22.

24. Interview, 7/7/22.

25. Interview, 3/17/22.

26. Interview, 7/8/22.

27. Interview, 7/12/22.

28. Interview, 7/7/22

29. I am currently collaborating with Resolve to research and pilot possible models for community accountability groups going forward. Alternative models for community advisory and accountability groups and boards will be discussed further in chapters 5 and 6.

30. Interview, 7/7/22.

31. Interview, 7/12/22.

32. Interview, 7/12/22.

33. Shared via email correspondence, 9/20/22.

34. Jean Friedman-Rudovsky and Cassie Haynes, "A Shift from Conversation to Action," *NiemanLab*, 2021, https://www.niemanlab.org/2020/12/a-shift-from-conversation-to-action/.

35. Interview, 7/12/22.

36. Interview, 7/8/22.

37. In 2022, I received funding from the Knight-Lenfest Local News Transformation fund for a collaborative research project to work with local media partners including Resolve and Philadelphia Neighborhoods (and possibly others). To date, we have organized focus groups and participatory workshops to get input from community members in North and Northeast Philadelphia on what accountability infrastructure they would find valuable. We plan to pilot interventions throughout 2023.

38. Interview, 7/12/22.

39. Interview, 7/7/22.

5. IMAGINING COMMUNITY-GOVERNED SERVICE JOURNALISM

1. Initial funds include a small collaborative grant from the Lenfest Institute, followed by a substantial multiyear grant from the Independence Public Media Foundation.

2. Interview, 7/19/22.

3. Interview, 7/19/22.

4. "VOTE TODAY in Kensington Voice's Summer 2022 Free, All-Ages Community Art Contest!," *Kensington Voice*, 2022, https://docs.google.com/forms/u/1/d/e/1FAIpQLSc DruxlLdWHq_K6qosxJmFc-kKwv6pCaTcqeYNlmB2JTzoRjA/viewform.

5. Interview, 7/19/22.

6. Sandra J. Ball-Rokeach, Yong-Chan Kim, and Sorin Matei, "Storytelling Neighborhood: Paths to Belonging in Diverse Urban Environments," *Communication Research* 28, no. 4 (2001): 392–428; Yong-Chan Kim and Sandra J. Ball-Rokeach, "Civic Engagement from a Communication Infrastructure Perspective," *Communication Theory* 16, no. 2 (2006): 173–97.

7. Interview, 7/19/22.

8. Interview, 7/19/22.

9. Interview, 7/19/22.

10. Interview, 7/19/22.

11. Interview, 7/19/22.

12. Interview, 7/19/22.

13. Interview, 7/19/22.

14. Interview, 7/19/22.

15. Interview, 7/19/22.

16. Bauer-Reese is sometimes paid for her work in the summer, and at the time of writing received one course release each semester from Temple to work on the project.

17. Interview, 7/19/22.

18. Interview, 7/19/22.

19. Khysir Carter and Siani Colón, "Keeping Cool in Kensington: What to Expect from the Heat and How to Stay Safe as Temperatures Rise," *Kensington Voice*, July 21, 2022, https://kensingtonvoice.com/en/keeping-cool-in-kensington-what-to-expect-from-the -heat-and-how-to-stay-safe-as-temperatures-rise/.

20. Interview, 8/23/22.

21. Interview, 8/23/22.

22. Interview, 8/23/22.

23. Email correspondence, 9/6/22.

24. The experience of *Juniata News* highlights the often overlooked challenges facing small community newspapers, which are rarely included in "future of local news" conversations. *Kensington Voice* had a relationship with *Juniata News* until they closed.

25. Sarah Schmalbach and Matt Boggie, "The Lenfest Local Lab Joins the *Philadelphia Inquirer* Product Team," Lenfest Institute, March 9, 2021, https://www.lenfestinstitute.org /lenfest-local-lab/the-lenfest-local-lab-joins-the-philadelphia-inquirer-product-team/.

26. A former staffer explained that they were working to pay *Kensington Voice*, but that never happened because the newsletter never launched. They said they had been able to pay two community organizations who offered consultation for some related work.

27. Interview, 7/19/22.

28. Interview, 7/19/22.

29. Interview, 8/18/22.

30. Interview, 8/23/22.

31. Referencing their strategic plan in an interview, 8/18/22.

32. Outlier Media, "About Us," n.d., https://outliermedia.org/about-outlier/.

33. Interview, 8/18/22.

34. Interview, 8/18/22.

35. I myself have been involved in fundraising and project management for such projects. For example, when I was with BBC Media Action in Afghanistan, an NGO or aid agency might offer funds for media to be produced focusing on maternal and child health, and media producers would work with their own in-house researchers to explore needs and the most effective ways to tell and distribute stories addressing audiences' information needs.

36. Interview, 8/18/22.

37. See Victor Pickard, *Democracy Without Journalism? Confronting the Misinformation Society* (New York: Oxford University Press, 2019); and Timothy Neff and Victor Pickard, "Funding Democracy: Public Media and Democratic Health in 33 Countries," *International Journal of Press/Politics* (2021): 19401612211060255.

38. See Wilson Lowrey, Danielle Deavours, and William Singleton, "Agents of Meta: Institutional Actors in the Journalism Space and the Innovation of Local News," *Journalism* (2022): 14648849221095898.

6. EXTERNAL SUPPORT FOR EQUITABLE LOCAL JOURNALISM

1. WURD, "WURD Radio's Founder's Day Commemorates the Vision of Walter P. Lomax Jr., M.D.," press release, August 22, 2022, https://wurdradio.com/2022/08/22/wurd-radios-annual-founders-day-celebrates-community-and-commemorates-the-vision-of-walter-p-lomax-jr-m-d/.

2. WURD hosts Charles Ellison and Envy McKee on Founders Day panel, 8/31/22.

3. WURD host Brother Shomari on Founders Day panel, 8/31/22.

4. Jim Friedlich (@JimFriedlich) "@onwurd #foundersday panel: 'What is the role of Black media?'" Twitter, August 31, 2022, 3:38 PM, https://twitter.com/jimfriedlich/status/1565061407917342720?s=21. Lenfest's CEO Jim Friedlich and program director Shawn Mooring were in attendance.

5. URL's cofounder Sarah Lomax-Reese is also the CEO of WURD. See https://url-media.com/. I have worked with projects that have received support from the Lenfest Institute and currently have a project that is supported by the Knight-Lenfest Local News Transformation Fund.

6. Patrick Ferrucci, "Conclusion: Understanding the Institutions Influencing Journalism: Ideas for Future Work," in *The Institutions Changing Journalism: Barbarians Inside the Gate*, ed. Patrick Ferrucci and Scott A. Eldridge II (New York: Routledge, 2022); Wilson Lowrey, Danielle Deavours, and William Singleton, "Agents of Meta: Institutional Actors in the Journalism Space and the Innovation of Local News," *Journalism* (2022); Sue Robinson, *How Journalists Engage: A Theory of Trust Building, Identities, and Care* (Oxford: Oxford University Press, forthcoming).

7. Magda Konieczna, "Foundations and Journalism: A New Business Model, a New Set of Logics," in *The Institutions Changing Journalism: Barbarians Inside the Gate*, ed. Patrick Ferrucci and Scott A. Eldridge II (New York: Routledge, 2022), 92.

8. Lowrey, Deaverson, and Singleton, "Agents of Meta."

9. Here referring to "storytelling networks" in the context of communication infrastructure theory. Sandra J. Ball-Rokeach, Yong-Chan Kim, and Sorin Matei, "Storytelling Neighborhood: Paths to Belonging in Diverse Urban Environments," *Communication Research* 28, no. 4 (2001): 392–428; Yong-Chan Kim and Sandra J. Ball-Rokeach, "Civic Engagement from a Communication Infrastructure Perspective," *Communication Theory* 16, no. 2 (2006): 173–97. Interview, 7/19/22.

10. For details on the "Reimagining Philadelphia Journalism Summit," see https://www.lenfestinstitute.org/2022-reimagining-philadelphia-journalism-summit/.

11. From a panel at Lenfest's Reimagining Philadelphia Journalism Summit, 9/12/22.

12. Patrick Ferrucci and Jacob L. Nelson, "The New Advertisers: How Foundation Funding Impacts Journalism," *Media and Communication* 7, no. 4 (2019): 52.

13. Editor Sabrina Vourvoulias responded to an email query (10/6/22) about her absence by saying: "I realized I was very overcommitted, so I opted not to participate. I knew the Inquirer would be represented at the summit by other members of the staff and board, so I felt I could bow out without leaving anyone in the lurch." However, only one sports editor was represented as a panelist over the course of the summit.

14. Interview 9/30/22; Rodney Benson, "Can Foundations Solve the Journalism Crisis?," *Journalism* 19, no. 8 (2018): 1060.

15. Brian Creech and Anthony Nadler, "Post-Industrial Fog: Reconsidering Innovation in Visions of Journalism's Future," *Journalism* 19, no. 2 (2017): 182. One of the biggest funders, the Knight Foundation, has been criticized for ties to far-right organizations in a February 2023 study by the Community Info Co-op.

16. Konieczna, "Foundations and Journalism," 100.

17. Interview, 8/30/22.

18. Interview, 8/30/22.

19. I spoke with seven people currently or formerly connected with local journalism philanthropy. Other local media-centered foundations include Independence Public Media Foundation (IPMF) and the Knight-Lenfest Local News Transformation Fund (a collaboration between Lenfest and the Knight Foundation), with local funders such as Comcast and the William Penn Foundation playing a role, as well as national media funders.

20. Hannah Stonebraker and Lindsay Green-Barber, *Healthy Local News and Information Ecosystems: A Diagnostic Framework* (Impact Architects, March 2021), https://s3.us-east-2.amazonaws.com/files.theimpactarchitects.com/ecosystems/full_report.pdf, 10.

21. Philanthropic worker interview, 9/1/22.

22. How contributions are reported is complicated by Lenfest's participation in Knight-Lenfest, to which Lenfest contributes half of the funds. Also funds are reported when contracted, meaning multiyear grants made in prior years were not included in this $1.2 million. Of the $1.2 million in "ecosystem" grants reported in 2021, Lenfest contributed $1 million and Knight-Lenfest contributed $0.2 million. In addition, Lenfest invested $567.5K via its contribution to Knight-Lenfest grants that were multiyear grants in 2021 (these totaled $1.135 million). Funds were often directed by donors to Lenfest who specifically wanted to support the *Inquirer*. Email correspondence with Jim Friedlich, 9/30/22.

23. Email correspondence with Jim Friedlich, 9/30/22.

24. Philanthropic worker interview, 9/12/22.

25. Philanthropic worker interview, 8/26/22.

26. Via email correspondence with Molly de Aguiar, 9/6/22.

27. Borealis Philanthropy, "Racial Equity in Journalism Fund: Overview," n.d., https://borealisphilanthropy.org/wp-content/uploads/2021/06/REJ_Overview.pdf; philanthropic worker interview, 9/1/22.

28. Philanthropic worker interview, 9/6/22.

29. Benson, "Can Foundations Solve the Journalism Crisis?," 1060.

30. Lenfest Summit, 9/13/22.

31. There is promise of movement on the U.S. journalism philanthropy horizon with the announcement of Democracy Fund's new Equitable Journalism Strategy. See https://democracyfund.org/idea/democracy-funds-new-equitable-journalism-strategy/.

32. Via email correspondence with Molly de Aguiar, 9/6/22.

33. Interview, 8/26/22.

34. See, for example, Andrea Wenzel and Letrell Crittenden, "Reimagining Local Journalism: A Community-Centered Intervention," *Journalism Studies* (2021); and Andrea Wenzel and Letrell Crittenden, "Collaborating in a Pandemic: Adapting Local News Infrastructure to Meet Information Needs," *Journalism Practice* (2021).

35. American Press Institute, "API Launches Diversity Initiative in Pittsburgh to Improve How News Organizations Serve Communities of Color," press release, June 28, 2022, https://www.americanpressinstitute.org/news-releases/api-launches-journalism-inclusion-index/.

36. Interview, 8/26/22.

37. Interview, 1/27/22.

38. I would like to acknowledge that I as a white journalist and as a researcher have made the mistake of asking BIPOC colleagues for input on my own work prematurely when I could have done more of my own homework first. (And in general I have a bad habit of sharing premature "word vomit.") I have tried to be more mindful of this and also to seek ways to acknowledge contributions or approach work as more equitable collaborations when possible.

39. Interview, 1/27/22.

40. Interview, 8/26/22.

41. These included: the *Pittsburgh Post-Gazette*, the *Pittsburgh Tribune-Review*, the *Pittsburgh City Paper*, *Public Source*, and *Pitt News*.

42. Interview, 8/26/22.

43. And at the time of writing, they were engaged in preliminary conversations about potentially doing a cohort program in Philadelphia.

44. Ernest Owens (@MrErnestOwens), "THREAD: Philly, we have a problem," Twitter, August 28, 2022, 9:57 AM, https://twitter.com/MrErnestOwens/status/1563888444207730690.

45. The letter was signed by Ernest Owens (PABJ), Jingyao Yu (AAJA), Vanessa Maria Graber (NAHJ), and Tauhid Chappell (Free Press-News Voices).

46. Philadelphia Association of Black Journalists, "Open Letter to *Philadelphia Inquirer* Calling for Immediate Action on DEI Failures," August 31, 2022, https://www.thepabj.org

/in-the-news/open-letter-to-philadelphia-inquirer-calling-for-immediate-action-on
-dei-failures.

47. Interview, 9/13/22.

48. She did reply to questions about accountability and communication of DEIB work by sharing publicly available information about the *Inquirer*'s DE&I team working on community engagement and communications, among other things.

49. At the time of writing, I am working on the early phases of a research study to explore a variety of models for community accountability groups. In addition to following the work of Philly JAWN and community-led boards like *Kensington Voice*, I will be collaborating with Resolve Philly and Temple's Philadelphia Neighborhoods to pilot models for community accountability groups.

50. Movement Alliance Project, "Shift the Narrative Project," 2022, https://movementalliance .org/blog/project/police-and-violence-narrative-project/.

51. At the time of writing, the *Inquirer* had not responded to Philly JAWN or the leadership of PABJ, NAHJ, or AAJA—but they had circulated an internal email inviting to staffers who belonged to these groups to "lunch and learn" sessions and had hired one Black male reporter on the communities and engagement desk.

52. Interview with Celeste Headlee, 2/2/22.

53. Interview with Sachi Kobayashi, 2/2/22.

54. Celeste Headlee, "An Anti-Racist Future: A Vision and Plan for the Transformation of Public Media," *Medium*, January 18, 2021, https://celesteheadlee.medium.com/an -antiracist-future-a-vision-and-plan-for-the-transformation-of-public-media-224149 ab37e6.

55. From a panel at Lenfest's Reimagining Philadelphia Journalism Summit, 9/12/22.

56. Alvarez also noted separately that she sees "creating value along the way" (as opposed to only waiting for "big wins" from investigative work) as a key part of Outlier's work: "We need to prioritize creating value for people on a daily basis if we want to be certain we're having impact and earning our keep." Email communication, 10/10/22.

57. City Bureau, "The Documenters Network," n.d., https://www.citybureau.org/documenters.

58. Documenters had an earlier iteration as part of the Chicago civic tech funder collaborative Smart Chicago Collaborative: Andrea Faye Hart, "How Did City Bureau's Documenters Program Get Started?," City Bureau, March 21, 2018, https://www.citybureau .org/notebook/2019/7/16/how-did-city-bureaus-documenters-program-get-started.

59. Laura Hazard Owen, "City Bureau Gets $10 Million to Make Public Meetings More Public," *NiemanLab*, July 7, 2022, https://www.niemanlab.org/2022/07/city-bureau-gets -10-million-to-make-public-meetings-more-public/.

60. See, for example, the Center for Media Engagement's study of how Chicagoans viewed their news coverage: Center for Media Engagement, "Chicago News Landscape," January 10, 2018, https://mediaengagement.org/research/chicago-news-landscape/.

61. See Wenzel, "Community-Centered Journalism," for more discussion of this process model.

62. See Lowrey, Deaverson, and Singleton, "Agents of Meta."

63. At the time of writing, several national initiatives were being released that had grown from these invitation-only convenings, including a "Local News Roadmap" (https://localnewsroadmap.org/) and a Future of Local News Network (FLN) "Care Collaboratory," though it was too early to understand how these national efforts would affect local initiatives.

CONCLUSION: TRANSFORMING THROUGH PROCESS AND INFRASTRUCTURE, NOT PROJECTS AND DESTINATIONS

1. Hannah Stonebraker and Lindsay Green-Barber, *Healthy Local News and Information Ecosystems: A Diagnostic Framework* (Impact Architects, March 2021), https://s3.us-east-2.amazonaws.com/files.theimpactarchitects.com/ecosystems/full_report.pdf, 10.
2. Sandra J. Ball-Rokeach, Yong-Chan Kim, and Sorin Matei, "Storytelling Neighborhood: Paths to Belonging in Diverse Urban Environments," *Communication Research* 28, no. 4 (2001): 392–428; Yong-Chan Kim and Sandra J. Ball-Rokeach, "Civic Engagement from a Communication Infrastructure Perspective," *Communication Theory* 16, no. 2 (2006): 173–97.
3. Kim and Ball-Rokeach, "Civic Engagement."
4. See discussion in this volume's introduction and in George Lipsitz, *How Racism Takes Place* (Philadelphia: Temple University Press, 2011).
5. See Timothy Neff, Pawel Popiel, and Victor Pickard, "Philadelphia's News Media System: Which Audiences Are Underserved?," *Journal of Communication* 72, no. 4 (2022): 476–87.
6. See chapter 6 for additional discussion of liminal or transitional leadership, including a case for it by a member of the Public Media for All coalition.
7. I've received support from the Knight-Lenfest Local News Transformation fund for this research.
8. See Victor Pickard, *Democracy Without Journalism? Confronting the Misinformation Society* (New York: Oxford University Press, 2019); and Timothy Neff and Victor Pickard, "Funding Democracy: Public Media and Democratic Health in 33 Countries," *International Journal of Press/Politics* (2021): 19401612211060255.
9. For a valuable and more thorough discussion regarding the future of journalism education, see Brian Creech *Journalism Education for the Digital Age: Promise, Perils, and Possibilities* (New York: Routledge, 2021).
10. Sue Robinson, *How Journalists Engage: A Theory of Trust Building, Identities, and Care* (Oxford: Oxford University Press, forthcoming), chap. 1.
11. The one exception being NBC10/Telemundo, which was a partner in Resolve Philly's Broke in Philly collaboration.
12. Interview, 12/21/21.
13. Via email correspondence with Molly de Aguiar, 9/6/22.
14. Interview with Sachi Kobayashi, 2/2/22.

APPENDIX: METHODS

1. Michael Burawoy, "The Extended Case Method," *Sociological Theory* 1, no. 1 (1998): 4–33.
2. I don't go into detail about the quantitative methods used for these audits as I don't focus on that data in this book.
3. Staff members' demographics included ten white, six Black, one Asian, one more than one race, and fourteen women and four men. The trainer identified as Black, and I spoke with four Black and one Latinx/e training participant.
4. Project partners included four women and four men, who identified as Black (four), white (two), Latinx/e (one), and Asian (one).
5. Of the station staff, twelve identified as white, eight as Black, one as Latinx/e, one as Latinx/e and white, and one as Black and Asian, with thirteen identifying as women, nine as men, and one as nonbinary.
6. Community members participating in focus groups included five who identified as Black, four as Latinx/e, three as white, and one as Native American. Women were over-represented, with eleven identifying as women and two as men. The average age was forty-seven.
7. This included twenty-three reporters/columnists/photographers and twenty-three editors/managers. Of these, six identified as Asian, ten as Black, four as Latinx/e, and twenty-six as white. Twenty-eight identified as women and eighteen as men.
8. Nineteen of whom were editors/managers and twenty-three who were not. Of these, eighteen identified as men, twenty-four as women. In terms of race and ethnicity, twenty-eight identified as non-Hispanic white, eight as Black, three as Asian, and three as Hispanic/Latinx/e.
9. Crittenden was a professor at Jefferson University at the time. I've written elsewhere on research with Germantown residents and the methods it involved, including Andrea Wenzel and Letrell Crittenden, "Reimagining Local Journalism: A Community-Centered Intervention," *Journalism Studies* (2021).
10. This study, done in collaboration with Letrell Crittenden, offered context on how *Kensington Voice* collaborated with other actors in the built environment, including Resolve Philly: Andrea Wenzel and Letrell Crittenden, "Collaborating in a Pandemic: Adapting Local News Infrastructure to Meet Information Needs," *Journalism Practice* (2021).
11. Of these, twelve identified as BIPOC, two as white, and nine as women and five as men.
12. For example, I subscribe to e-newsletters and announcements listservs produced by metaorganizations including American Press Institute, *Columbia Journalism Review*, Democracy Fund's Local News Lab, Free Press's Media Power Collaborative, Independence Public Media Foundation, Lenfest Institute, Nieman Journalism Lab, and the Tow Center for Digital Journalism (and I followed these and many more key influencers and organizations on Twitter).
13. One focused on WHYY and cultural competency/DEIB in public media; one focused on the *Inquirer*; one on community engagement interventions that included *Kensington Voice*, the Germantown Info Hub, and Resolve Philly; and one that focused on efforts to make local journalism more inclusive.

BIBLIOGRAPHY

Alexander, Michelle. *The New Jim Crow: Mass Incarceration in the Age of Colorblindness*. New York: New Press, 2012.

Andersen, Margaret L. "Whitewashing Race: A Critical Perspective on Whiteness." In *White Out: The Continuing Significance of Racism*, ed. by Ashley "Woody" Doane and Eduardo Bonilla-Silva. Jackson: University Press of Mississippi, 2003.

Anderson, C. W. *Rebuilding the News: Metropolitan Journalism in the Digital Age*. Philadelphia: Temple University Press, 2013.

Ball-Rokeach, Sandra J., Yong-Chan Kim, and Sorin Matei. "Storytelling Neighborhood: Paths to Belonging in Diverse Urban Environments." *Communication Research* 28, no. 4 (2001): 392–428.

Benson, Rodney. "Can Foundations Solve the Journalism Crisis?" *Journalism* 19, no. 8 (2018): 1060.

Bonilla-Silva, Eduardo. *Racism Without Racists: Color-Blind Racism and the Persistence of Racial Inequality in America*. Lanham, MD: Rowman and Littlefield, 2006.

Broad, Garrett. "Communication Infrastructure Theory and Community-Based Program Evaluation: The Case of Media Mobilizing Project and the CAP Comcast Campaign." In *The Communication Ecology of 21st Century Urban Communities*, ed. Yong-Chan Kim, Matthew Matsaganis, Holley Wilkin, and Joo-Young Jung, 220–36. New York: Peter Lang, 2018.

Broad, Garrett, Carmen Gonzalez, and Sandra Ball-Rokeach. "Intergroup Relations in South Los Angeles—Combining Communication Infrastructure and Contact Hypothesis Approaches." *International Journal of Intercultural Relations* 38 (2014): 47–59.

Burawoy, Michael. "The Extended Case Method." *Sociological Theory* 16, no. 1 (1998): 4–33.

Callison, Candis, and Mary L. Young. *Reckoning: Journalism's Limits and Possibilities*. Oxford: Oxford University Press, 2019.

Chávez, Christopher A. "Whose Is the Voice of the American Public? Latinx/e Speech and the Standard Language Ideology of Public Radio." *Communication and Critical/Cultural Studies* 16, no. 4 (2019): 308–25.

Chen, Nien-Tsu (Nancy), Katherine Ognyanova, and Nan Zhao. "Communication and Sociodemographic Forces Shaping Civic Engagement Patterns in a Multiethnic City." In *Communication and Community*, ed. Patricia Moy, 207–32. New York: Hampton, 2013.

Chicago Commission on Race Relations. *The Negro in Chicago: A Study of Race Relations and a Race Riot*. Chicago: University of Chicago Press, 1923.

Cobb, Jelani, and Matthew Guariglia, eds. *The Essential Kerner Commission Report*. New York: Liveright, 2021.

Creech, Brian, and Anthony Nadler, "Post-Industrial Fog: Reconsidering Innovation in Visions of Journalism's Future." *Journalism* 19, no. 2 (2018): 182.

Crenshaw, Kimberlé. "Demarginalizing the Intersection of Race and Sex: A Black Feminist Critique of Antidiscrimination Doctrine, Feminist Theory, and Antiracist Politics." In *Feminist Legal Theories*, 23–51. New York: Routledge, 2013.

Crittenden, Letrell, and Haywood, Antoine. "Revising Legacy Media Practices to Serve Hyperlocal Information Needs of Marginalized Populations." *Journalism Practice* 14, no. 5, (2020): 608–25.

Drew, Emily M. " 'Coming to Terms with our Own Racism': Journalists Grapple with the Racialization of their News." *Critical Studies in Media Communication* 28, no. 4 (2011): 353–73.

Durham, Meenakshi G. "On the Relevance of Standpoint Epistemology to the Practice of Journalism: The Case for 'Strong Objectivity.' " *Communication Theory* 8, no. 2 (1998): 117–40.

Entman, Robert M., and Andrew Rojecki. *The Black Image in the White Mind: Media and Race in America*. Chicago: University of Chicago Press, 2000.

Ferrucci, Patrick, and Scott A. Eldridge II. *The Institutions Changing Journalism: Barbarians Inside the Gate*. New York: Routledge, 2022.

Ferrucci, Patrick, and Jacob L. Nelson. "The New Advertisers: How Foundation Funding Impacts Journalism." *Media and Communication* 7, no. 4 (2019): 52.

Garbes, L. " 'Their Accent Is Just Too Much': Racialized Evaluation of Voice in Public Radio Production." https://doi.org/10.31235/osf.io/vzjhb.

George, Mark Patrick. "Towards a Critical Antiracism: Redefining and Rethinking the Term 'Antiracism.' " Paper presented at the annual meetings of the American Sociological Association, San Francisco, California, August 2004.

Giddens, Anthony. *The Constitution of Society: Outline of the Theory of Structuration*. Berkeley: University of California Press, 1984.

Gonzalez, Juan, and Joseph Torres. "News for All: The Epic Story of Race and the American Media." In *Will the Last Reporter Please Turn Out the Lights: The Collapse of Journalism and*

What Can Be Done to Fix It, ed. Robert McChesney and Victor W. Pickard, 185–93. New York: New Press, 2011.

Graves, Lucas, and Magda Konieczna. "Sharing the News: Journalistic Collaboration as Field Repair." *International Journal of Communication Studies* 9 (2015): 1966–84.

Haraway, Donna. "Situated Knowledges: The Science Question in Feminism and the Privileging of Partial Perspectives." *Feminist Studies* 14, no. 3 (1988): 575–99.

Kaniss, Phyllis. *Making Local News*. Chicago: University of Chicago Press, 1991.

Kendi, Ibram, X. *How to Be an Antiracist*. New York: One World, 2019.

Kilgo, Danielle K., Tamar Wilner, Gina M. Masullo, and Lance Kyle Bennett. "News Distrust Among Black Americans Is a Fixable Problem." Center for Media Engagement, November 2020. https://mediaengagement.org/research/news-distrust-among-black-americans.

Kim, Yong-Chan, and Sandra J. Ball-Rokeach. "Civic Engagement from a Communication Infrastructure Perspective." *Communication Theory* 16, no. 2 (2006): 173–97.

Konieczna, Magda. "The Collaboration Stepladder: How One Organization Built a Solid Foundation for a Community-Focused Cross-Newsroom Collaboration." *Journalism Studies* 21, no. 6 (2020): 802–19.

Kovach, Bill, and Tom Rosenstiel. *Elements of Journalism: What Newspeople Should Know and the Public Should Expect*. New York: Three Rivers, 2007.

Lawrence, Keith, Stacey Sutton, Anne Kubisch, Gretchen Susi, and Karen Fulbright-Anderson. "Structural Racism and Community Building." Aspen Institute Roundtable on Community Change, Aspen Institute, 2004.

Lipsitz, George. *How Racism Takes Place*. Philadelphia: Temple University Press, 2011.

Lowrey, Wilson, Danielle Deavours, and William Singleton. "Agents of Meta: Institutional Actors in the Journalism Space and the Innovation of Local News." *Journalism* (2022): 14648849221095898.

Mastin, Teresa, Shelly Campo, and M. Somjen Frazer. "In Black and White: Coverage of U.S. Slave Reparations by the Mainstream and Black Press." *Howard Journal of Communications* 16, no. 3: (2005): 201–23.

Matei, Sorin Adam, and Sandra Ball-Rokeach. "Watts, the 1965 Los Angeles Riots, and the Communicative Construction of the Fear Epicenter of Los Angeles" *Communication Monographs* 72, no. 3 (September 1, 2005): 301–23. https://doi.org/10.1080/0363775050020655.7.

McCone, John A., and W. M. Christopher. "Violence in the City: An End or a Beginning?" Report by the Governor's Commission on the Los Angeles Riots, 1965.

Mellinger, Gwyneth. *Chasing Newsroom Diversity: From Jim Crow to Affirmative Action*. Urbana: University of Illinois Press, 2013.

Mindich, David T. *Just the Facts: How "Objectivity" Came to Define American Journalism*. New York: New York University Press, 2000.

Morrison, Toni. *Playing in the Dark: Whiteness and the Literary Imagination*. Cambridge, MA: Harvard University Press, 1992.

Nadler, Anthony. "Nature's Economy and News Ecology: Scrutinizing the News Ecosystem Metaphor." *Journalism Studies* 20, no. 6 (2019): 823–39.

Neff, Timothy, Pawel Popiel, and Victor Pickard. "Philadelphia's News Media System: Which Audiences Are Underserved?" *Journal of Communication* 72, no. 4 (2022): 476–87.

Neff, Timothy, and Victor Pickard. "Funding Democracy: Public Media and Democratic Health in 33 Countries." *International Journal of Press/Politics* (2021): 19401612211060255.

Nelson, Jacob L. *Imagined Audiences: How Journalists Perceive and Pursue the Public.* Oxford: Oxford University Press, 2021.

O'Brien, Eileen. "From Antiracism to Antiracisms." *Sociology Compass* 3, no. 3 (2009): 501–12.

Omi, Michael, and Howard Winant. *Racial Formation in the United States: From the 1960s to the 1990s.* New York: Routledge, 1994.

Owens, Lynn C. 2008. "Network News: The Role of Race in Source Selection and Story Topic." *Howard Journal of Communications* 19, no. 4 (2008): 355–70.

Pickard, Victor. *Democracy Without Journalism? Confronting the Misinformation Society.* Oxford: Oxford University Press, 2019.

Reed, Adolph, Jr. "The Limits of Antiracism." *Left Business Observer* 121, no. 6 (2009).

Robinson, Sue, and Kathleen B. Culver. "When White Reporters Cover Race: News Media, Objectivity, and Community (Dis)trust," *Journalism: Theory, Practice & Criticism* 20, no. 3 (2019): 375–91.

Robinson, Sue. 2023. *How Journalists Engage: A Theory of Trust Building, Identities, and Care.* Oxford: Oxford University Press, forthcoming.

Rodriguez, Clemencia. 2020. "PhillyCAM: A Hub for Media Makers on Ranstead Street." Unpublished manuscript.

Schudson, Michael. 2001. "The Objectivity Norm in American Journalism." *Journalism* 2, no. 2: 149–70.

Shah, Hemant, and Michael Thornton. 2004. *Newspaper Coverage of Interethnic Conflict: Competing Visions of America.* Thousand Oaks, CA: Sage, 2001.

Spade, Dean. *Mutual Aid: Building Solidarity During This Crisis (and the Next).* London: Verso, 2020.

Stoever, Jennifer Lynn. "Fine-Tuning the Sonic Color-Line: Radio and the Acousmatic Du Bois." *Modernist Cultures* 10, no. 1: (2015): 99–118.

Sue, Derald Wing, Christina M. Capodilupo, Gina C. Torino, Jennifer M. Bucceri, Aisha Holder, Kevin L. Nadal, and Marta Esquilin. "Racial Microaggressions in Everyday Life: Implications for Clinical Practice." *American Psychologist* 62, no. 4 (2007): 271.

Squires, Catherine R. *Dispatches from the Color Line: The Press and Multiracial America.* Albany: State University of New York Press, 2007.

Taylor, Keeanga-Yamahtta, ed. *How We Get Free: Black Feminism and the Combahee River Collective.* Chicago: Haymarket, 2017.

Torres, Joseph, Alicia Bell, Colette Watson, Tauhid Chappell, Diamond Hardiman, and Christina Pierce. "Media 2070: An Invitation to Dream Up Media Reparations." Free Press, 2020. https://mediareparations.org/wp-content/uploads/2020/10/media-2070.pdf.

Usher, Nikki. *News for the Rich, White, and Blue: How Place and Power Distort American Journalism.* New York: Columbia University Press, 2021.

Varma, Anita. "Moral Solidarity as a News Value: Rendering Marginalized Communities and Enduring Social Injustice Newsworthy." *Journalism* (2022): 14648849221094669.

Wallace, Lewis. R. *The View from Somewhere: Undoing the Myth of Journalistic Objectivity*. Chicago: University of Chicago Press, 2019.

Ward, Stephen J. "Inventing Objectivity: New Philosophical Foundations." In *Journalism Ethics: A Philosophical Approach*, ed. Christopher Meyers, 137–52. New York: Oxford University, 2010.

Wenzel, Andrea D. *Community-Centered Journalism: Engaging People, Exploring Solutions, and Building Trust*. Urbana: University of Illinois Press, 2020.

———. "Sourcing Diversity, Shifting Culture: Building 'Cultural Competence' in Public Media." *Digital Journalism* 9, no. 4 (2021): 461–80.

Wenzel, Andrea D., and Letrell Crittenden. "Reimagining Local Journalism: A Community-centered Intervention." *Journalism Studies* 22, no. 15 (2021): 2023–2041.

Wenzel, Andrea D., and Letrell Crittenden. "Collaborating in a Pandemic: Adapting Local News Infrastructure to Meet Information Needs." *Journalism Practice* (2021): 1–19.

Wolfson, Todd, and Peter N. Funke. "Communication, Class, and Concentric Media Practices: Developing a Contemporary Rubric." *New Media & Society* 16, no. 3 (2014): 363–80.

INDEX

GPSR Authorized Representative: Easy Access System Europe, Mustamäe tee
50, 10621 Tallinn, Estonia, gpsr.requests@easproject.com